Different Latitudes

Different Latitudes

My Life in the Peace Corps and Beyond

MARK D. WALKER

A PEACE CORPS WRITERS BOOK

DIFFERENT LATITUDES: MY LIFE IN THE PEACE CORPS AND BEYOND
A Peace Corps Writers Book
An imprint of Peace Corps Worldwide
Copyright © 2017 Mark D. Walker
All rights reserved.
Printed in the United States of America
by Peace Corps Writers of Oakland, California.
No part of this book may be used or reproduced in any manner
whatsoever without written permission except in the case of
brief quotations contained in critical articles or reviews.
For more information, contact peacecorpsworldwide@gmail.com.
Peace Corps Writers and the Peace Corps Writers colophon
are trademarks of PeaceCorpsWorldwide.org.

ISBN-13: 9781935925811
ISBN-10: 1935925814
Library of Congress Control Number: 2017936072
Peace Corps Writers

First Peace Corps Writers Edition, April 2017

Edited by First Person Editing Services

The author is grateful for permission to reproduce excerpts from the following work:
"If You Forget Me", by Pablo Neruda, translated by Donald D. Walsh, from *The Captain's Verses*, copyright, 1972 by Pablo Neruda and Donald D. Walsh. Reprinted by permission of New Directions Publishing Corp.

This is a work of nonfiction about events spanning over forty years. I've reconstructed conversations and events using my memory, journals, extensive notes, reports, and innumerable photo albums. I have cited sources when describing a historic period or facts but have not included footnotes as this is not a thesis or academic paper but a memoir. In some cases, I've changed people's names because my intention is to tell a story, not to embarrass anyone—although presenting an honest account means a certain level of embarrassment for everyone involved, especially me. I have changed the names of some of the philanthropists I've worked with out of respect for their privacy. These are my memories and opinions: although I've made every effort to check and double-check them for accuracy, I have been wrong more than once in my lifetime, which will become clear as you read this book.
You can contact the author at: mark@millionmilewalker.com or millionmilewalker.com

WHAT OTHERS ARE SAYING

Mark's vivid reflection of his time as a Peace Corps Volunteer in Guatemala reminded me of my own enthusiasm and eagerness to make a difference in the world, and a career launched by serving in the Peace Corps. Returned Peace Corps Volunteers will surely see themselves in his experiences, but all will benefit from his perceptive recollections and astute observations of living and working in Guatemala. It's one of the best RPCV memoirs I've read (and I have gone through quite a few).

Glenn Blumhorst, Returned Peace Corps Volunteer (RPCV) Guatemala 1989 to 1991. President of the National Peace Corps Association

Mark Walker's valuable and pragmatic "lessons-learned" are delightfully described and taught in this well-written book! Professionals in international affairs and development will profit by reading it; and persons interested in foreign relations and foreign cultures will enjoy the author's insights. Mark, whom I have known for a quarter century, has "been there and done that." He draws on five decades of working, living and traveling, not only in developing countries on three continents, but also in Western Europe. Rare are the Americans who have immersed themselves into both Latin American and African cultures; who have truly lived, worked with, and known as friends and relatives foreigners in their own environments; and have contributed successfully to foreign poor communities' development by working with private organizations and government entities at all social/economic levels. Mark has done all this. If you read this book you will not only gain knowledge and understanding, you will enjoy it.

Furthermore Mark's book is a "must-read" for fund-raisers for civic and religiously inspired non-governmental organizations (NGOs) that help the "needy" in developing countries. Mark's success during a half-century of work with poor communities, his immersion in Latin American and African cultures, and his remarkable success with fund-raising in North America and among wealthy elites of developing countries make his "lessons-learned" valuable and effective. Enjoy learning, and have a good read!

Ambassador (ret.) Edwin G. Corr, Career Foreign Service Officer. US Ambassador to Peru, Bolivia and El Salvador

"He is searching day and night for truth, learning and meaning," wrote Hubert Smith, chancellor of the Law-Science Academy about 20-year old Mark Walker. And through this book it is obvious that he never stopped. Walker finds the humanity in all of us, from ranchers in rural Colorado, and farmers in the throes of civil war in Guatemala, to peoples around the world where the ripple effects of Walker's work continue to be felt. An inspiring read for those of us who want to work in the world community.

Alana DeJoseph, RPCV Mali 1992 to 1994. Award winning producer and director of the Peace Corps documentary *A Towering Task*, www. peacecorpsdocumentary.com

Mark's socio-political overview of the multi-decade cultural and civil war in Guatemala is both insightful and accurate, and a timely primer on human rights injustices and their insidious perpetration by authoritarian rulers the world over. It is a lesson we should all be studying as we prepare to address the possibility of such changes in our own countries and communities.

Ellen Urbani Hiltebrand, RPCV Guatemala 1991 to 1993. Author of *When I Was Elena: A Memoir.*

Mark Walker recounts a delightful life journey filled with adventures, fascinating people, and remarkable achievements to help build a better world. Like many of us, the Peace Corps was a life-changing experience that shaped his values and launched a search for life's larger truths. Along the way, he discovered multiple truths and he shares them with us in this marvelous book.

Charles F. "Chic" Dambach, RPCV Colombia 1967 to 1969. Past President, National Peace Corps Association, President of the Alliance for Peacebuilding.

As I've read through the various chapters you sent, I've experienced a virtual rollercoaster of emotions. At times your vivid descriptions provoke a sense of deep

warmth, smiles, and laughter as your narrative brings to mind my own fond memories of living and working among the amazing people of Guatemala. But reading the chapter "GUATEMALA, GUATEPEOR" (There's a Spanish saying, "Salir de Guatemala y entrar en Guatepeor"—a play on words that means to go from bad (*mala*) to worse (*peor*) — *your reflections on the inequities, injustice, the corruption, the violence, and the role of the US government in the midst of all that — brings back tears and long suppressed feelings of anger and outrage towards the evil of it all. It surprises me at times how strongly those memories still affect me after all these years.*

Buck Deines, RPCV Guatemala, 1975-1978. Held executive roles with Medical Teams International, World Concern and Food for the Hungry.

I have known Mark and counted him as a friend and mentor for more years than I care to admit. He writes with the same passion that he lives; and like him, his memoir is full of life and the joy of service. Reading Mark's memoir not only inspires one to get involved, it provides a framework for making a difference in a hungry and hurting world. Writing with clarity and insight, Mark has distilled his decades of service into a valuable resource for all of us.

Ray Buchanan, Founder & International President, "Stop Hunger Now" and Co-Director of the Society of St. Andrews.

You are a strong fundraiser as the examples in your book attest. Mark, the book does you justice. It describes who you are and what you believe in; your remarkable abilities to move things forward with great sensitivity and gentle persistence, and your way with all people — but especially those with large discretionary funding. They truly wanted to change the world and you led them to the fulfilment of their dreams. And, you are also an expert in international community-based development. Your leadership and experience in Latin America, particularly Guatemala, have been without equal. I really enjoyed the last chapter that describes where you ended up spiritually. I think I liked it so much because it describes where I have landed too, in terms of soul winning and long-term sustainable development.

Jeff Cotter, Executive Director SG Foundation and MEG Family Foundations, Executive Director, Allan Hancock College Foundation, National Pastorates, United Presbyterian Church, USA.

I love the personal warmth that I feel as I read each chapter... Well, Mark, I learned so much as I walked with you thru your 40+ years. Thank you for the opportunity. Peace Bill

Bill Brackett, Former CEO World Neighbors.

If you use Mark's book as an inspiration and a guide, as I did, there is nothing that can stop you, if you put your mind to serving the needs of those less fortunate than yourself. It's what the world needs, so volunteer yourself and see what you can accomplish!

John Harbison, Engineer, Past President of Grand Island Rotary Club and Past Chairman of Rotary District 7090's International World Service Committee.

To Ligia Liliana Rodriguez de Walker, my wife and editor in chief of more than forty years. This book, and the little I've accomplished, wouldn't have been possible without her.

IN MEMORY OF
Dr. Hubert Winston Smith,
Chancellor of the Law-Science Academy of America

Table of Contents

List of Graphics

Map of Guatemala: End of chapter two. Perry-Castañeda Library Map Collection, University of Texas at Austin

24 photographs throughout the book: go to the author's web site under "Gallery" at millionmilewalker.com to see them in color as well as other photos of the author's travels around the world

Map of travels and residence end of book. You can find a Google Interactive map on the author's website .millionmilewalker.com

Timeline at the end of the book (you can also find the complete version at the author's website under "About Us" and then "My Journey" millionmilewalker.com)

Preface

I began writing this book in 1971, when I joined the Peace Corps. The major reason was to tell the whole truth. I went on to say in my journal, "I shall do this not because I am noble or unselfish, but because life slips away and I need a star that will not be false to me, a compass that will not lie for the rest of my journey."

At the end of my two-year stint in Guatemala as a Peace Corps volunteer, I realized I'd learned far more from the communities I worked with than I was able to teach them. I also realized there was no one "truth" to reach for, but many different truths, as well as a variety of opportunities to make a difference in the lives of the people I served and who came into and enriched, my life. I'd need to find an alternate way to measure success than what I'd been taught in U.S. society.

The years and experiences that followed my time with the Peace Corps were like grains of sand. Each success and failure, each new program and new friend, each new educational course and conference, each trip far and near—not to mention the experiences I shared with my wife and children—all these grains of sand would form the pearl of my very being, the person I became after years of travel and learning.

During my global sojourn, I'd see more than my share of suffering, poverty, injustice, and violence against the most vulnerable of people: the disenfranchised, women and children. And as I wrote in my journal all those years ago, "There are some of us who will no longer accept poverty, corruption, inequality—we will do everything in our power to end it, study, travel, learn, write, protest, and change our way of life."

I should have asked my parents not to be disturbed by the unconventional path I followed in my life, for they provided the financial support and made possible the education that allowed me to study and travel as well as certain Christian values, to contemplate the state of our world and what we could do to make a difference. I was part of a new generation, with the time and resources (and, in my case, the Peace Corps) to focus on the needs of the poorest of the poor without worrying about where their own next meal would come from.

That our country's tradition of freedom and equality often wasn't applied to many of our own people in the U.S. frustrated my generation and kept us fighting for the have-nots. That's how I felt at the beginning of my journey in the early '70s, and it's taken a lifetime of travel and learning, and a career trying to impact the lives of the poor, to write a story worth sharing, one that might help others determine what direction their lives and careers can take and how they, too, can make a difference in the world.

My story might be sung to Neil Young's "Old Man," except I took a very different road than did my father, a WWII vet who worked for a multinational corporation yet never traveled outside the U.S., but who did pass on the solid Christian values I've tried to follow.

Old man look at my life,
Twenty-four
and there's so much more
Live alone in a paradise
That makes me think of two.

In my case, Guatemala would be my paradise, and my new wife, Ligia, and I would become the two, and what followed would be a career of travel and revelation. And if I haven't found as many answers as I've sought, I have found some elucidation on what makes life worthwhile and how we can impact those around us and make a difference for those who are in need of our help and support. Hopefully, my story will help the boomers reflect on their lives and why we did what we did, and also motivate a new generation of travelers and cultural changers. This is my story . . .

One

The Formative Years

Life is complex. Each one of us must make his own path through life. There are no self-help manuals, no formulas, no easy answers. The right road for one is the wrong road for another.

— M. Scott Peck, *The Road Less Traveled*

I was born twice, the first time in Plainfield, New Jersey, in 1948. I was reborn in 1971, when I left college for the Peace Corps and embarked on a forty-year career and journey throughout the world.

When I was sixteen, my father, who worked for Johnson & Johnson, decided to move our family of five from New Jersey to Colorado, where he'd gone to the University of Denver. I went to high school (1964–1967), in Evergreen, nestled in the foothills of the Rockies, less than forty-five minutes from Denver. Evergreen was a cut below a large resort like Aspen but many steps above some of the small cabins and trailer parks you can find in other communities. During the summer I worked at Hiwan Golf Club, cutting greens that were set back into the hills and surrounded by ponderosa pines, with an occasional small lake in the distance. I considered many of the homes I passed on the way to work mini-mansions. I also worked in the clubhouse kitchen, preparing the prime rib buffets and the many small sandwiches and healthy salads the members craved. During several summers I also did yardwork for some of these giant homes. Always working, making a buck in order to get into college. On any given morning, I could look up toward our home on Pine Drive to see a family of elk traipsing through the backyard. I was a successful student, part of Boys State—an event hosted by Kiwanis for future civic leaders—and honorable mention all-state on the high school football team. Life was good.

I received a wake-up call to the real world as part of a twenty-member youth group of the Church of the Hills in the summer of 1969. I'd been brought up in the Presbyterian Church in Plainfield, where I sang in the boys' choir, and Church of the Hills would become my new church home after we moved to Colorado. My mom sang in the choir, and my dad was an elder. My buddy Dave and I needed to raise the funds to participate in an outreach project with the youth group. Luckily, Dave was a very entrepreneurial guy, with his own truck and several lawn mowers, so we headed up Bear Creek and cut the lawns of some of the massive mansions on the riverside. Several of the mansions had an indoor pool and purebred horses in the back. We figured these places would go for a million dollars easily but were content with twenty-five dollars cutting their majestic lawns.

By July we had raised the funds we needed to participate in the youth group project. The group's collective goal was to fix a church in Ignacio, a small farming community in the southeastern part of Colorado. On a warm morning, our group piled into several vans and headed south on 285 through South Park, down past the monumental Great Sand Dunes National Park, across the San Juan Mountains, and over the Continental Divide and Wolf Creek Pass, which, at almost 11,000 feet, is the most dangerous pass in the state during the winter. As we headed down the mountain, into Pagosa Springs, the land began to take on a flatter, more arid look until we finally reached Ignacio, near the New Mexico border. It was also on the border of the Southern Ute Indian Reservation, so a good portion of the residents were cattle ranchers or supported the cattle industry. This was pre-casino days, so things were slow in this rural community of 1,000 or so inhabitants.

The church pastor and several of the local church members met us with a fantastic home-cooked meal in the local Grange, a few blocks down from the church, with some of the tastiest warm biscuits I'd ever had the pleasure of scarfing down. Dave and I walked around town with a few of our group and were surprised that it was strangely devoid of megastores and malls. Life was a lot simpler than what we were used to even in Evergreen, which had a few pubs and small shopping strips to check out.

Our youth leaders, Merv and Emily, explained that our task was twofold: Paint the church inside and out, and replace the leaky roof with a new metal one. For the next few days we painted up a storm. When several of us got out of hand, slinging the paint places other than the intended walls, Merv patiently reminded us where we were—in a church in someone else's community. We were just teenagers and needed to let off some steam. At night we slept in the church and, bright and early the next morning, went over to the Grange for eggs, bacon, and more biscuits. They also served pinto beans at both dinner and breakfast, which I thought was strange.

When the painting was finished, we began tearing down the old roof and replacing it with the new metal version. We needed several pairs of sunglasses due to the bright sun. The church and community members were always friendly and willing to share whatever they had, including some additional sunglasses.

On the long drive back to Evergreen, I was able to reflect on what a different world I'd been introduced to—one where isolation and poverty didn't seem to keep people down or affect their willingness to invite strangers into their homes to help build a better community. I didn't know it at the time, but this experience would impact my worldview and stimulate the desire to help others who had less than I was accustomed to in Evergreen. I began to think more about what was beyond my little community and what new experiences and needs might exist outside our country.

• • •

After graduating from high school, I chose to study at a small liberal arts school in Gunnison called Western State College of Colorado (before it became Western State Colorado University). On the western slope of Colorado, Western State offered a smaller setting than I would have experienced had I gone to the University of Colorado Boulder as well as provided an opportunity for more personalized interaction with my professors. I received a scholastic scholarship and the opportunity to work as a dorm counselor in Mears Hall. I was one of five counselors responsible for one floor, and one night the new students showed their appreciation of my leadership by filling my doorframe with empty soda pop cans, which made quite a racket the next morning when I opened the door. On my last night as an adviser, I unlocked my door, only to find that my room was filled with shaving cream. My fellow students had filled paper bags with the cream, pushed the open end of the bags under my door, and stamped on the bags, propelling the white, fluffy cream into my room. I couldn't imagine how many shaving cream cans it took to accomplish this feat.

I was an ideal authority figure target from the students on my floor, as many were having a good time and just being young, fun-loving college students. I, on the other hand, was way too serious. Up each morning doing exercises, I knew which classes I had that day and which ones I wanted to take the next semester. I always looked for the toughest professors, which just seemed out of place in the eyes of many of the other students. And I could take a joke and could respond in kind with an occasional blast of shaving cream under the doors of the perceived perpetrators.

• • •

Different Latitudes

O ne afternoon, while getting a haircut, I was telling the barber that I'd just appeared on the *Voices of Youth* TV program in Denver to discuss the important qualities of a successful young leader. A large, stately customer at the other end of the shop—prominent nose, eyeglasses, white hair—asked, "So what did you tell them?"

"Well," I said, "that one must define one's core values, make a plan, stay focused, and ask lots of questions in order to get ahead."

"Are you a student at Western State?" he asked.

"Yes. This is my second year, and I'm a counselor at one of the dorms."

"Excellent," the man said. "I'm Hubert Smith, the chancellor of the Law-Science Academy, which is made up of distinguished lawyers, physicians, and scholars from all the other main intellectual disciplines. We have a unique teaching program in Crested Butte, where I'm looking for someone to help develop our youth program."

"Interesting," I said. "Let me show you around our campus."

After showing Dr. Smith around, we stopped by Mears Hall, where I introduced him to the dorm director, Mrs. Hampton. She told him what an effective counselor I'd been (well, there'd been no fatalities on my watch). Fortunately, no pop cans blocked my door, nor was my room inundated with shaving cream when Dr. Smith visited my room. He immediately checked out my bookshelf, which included many Western classics as well as *The Annals of America*, published by Encyclopedia Britannica.

"Fabulous," he said. "I've never seen such a variety of masterpieces in literature, social and psychological sciences, and the humanities on the bookshelves of an undergraduate student before."

Wow, I thought, *my investment in the great books sure did pay off quickly.* I'd bought them just two weeks before this chance encounter.

We sat down to get better acquainted, and I learned that Dr. Smith was also the director of Interprofessional studies at the College of Law at the University of Oklahoma and had an MBA from the University of Texas. He was also one of the only people to have graduated from both Harvard Law School *and* Harvard Medical School, making him uniquely qualified to bring lawyers and doctors together to clarify terminology and issues that came up during cases that involved medical material. In 1954 he incorporated the Law-Science Academy of America.

During our time together, I realized that the man was a genius. And I came to appreciate his more integrated and synthesized approach to knowledge and learning rather than the more traditional fragmenting of information into disciplinary specializations.

"So, Dr. Smith, how do you think I can help you and the Law-Science Academy?" I asked.

"Our summer courses start in July," he said. "Why don't you come up to see me in Crested Butte next week? We'll discuss your role heading up the youth section of the four- week lecture series, which will include top physicians, lawyers, and politicians from all over the country. I'll also need your help organizing our 'Great Ideas' sessions, where we bring in top speakers on contemporary issues of interest to the local public. And finally we'll want you to design some programs for the youth. How does that sound?"

"I can't wait" was the only thing I could think of saying. Thinking about what an incredible opportunity this was, I was ecstatic. I'd make additional money during the summer, and I'd get to meet some of the speakers and interesting lawyers and doctors attending the courses. Also, as I'd always done in the past, I would be able to prove my worth to an entrepreneur, and that might lead to other things. Indeed, all of this came to pass. I ended up managing Dr. Smith's twelve Victorian houses for the rest of the year, which covered all my school fees, provided free housing and a truck, and paid for a season pass and an opportunity to learn how to parallel ski on the pristine slopes of Crested Butte.

• • •

Dr. Smith took me in and mentored me on the classics and humanities. His comments to the director of the Peace Corps, Joseph Blatchford, in a handwritten reference letter for my application, reflected his confidence in my potential, making him one of my greatest advocates:

> *It has been the prime satisfaction of my life to discover persons seeking to find and understand reality. For that reason I gain a special pleasure when such a unique piece of "raw material" as Mark D. Walker shows up. He is searching day and night for truth, learning and meaning—ready to fight for a better world rather than reject it because there are still un-addressed injustices . . . At heart, Mark Walker longs to travel—to see other lands and people—to identify with an international view of human problems—to be a world citizen. He is very loyal to his country—he is not a drop-out, a constant critic, but sees always the tremendous surge of progress one can make through the ballot box. He abhors violence . . . I have predicted to some of Mark Walker's friends that Mark is destined to be one of the dynamic great leaders of our times; I feel his multiple quali-ties will make him unique and innovative, fearless and inspiring, as a follower or leader, in the Peace Corps and in whatever career he chooses.*

I don't know what went into the process of selecting volunteers at the Peace Corps headquarters in Washington, D.C., but I can't help but think that Dr. Smith's words of praise enhanced the odds that I'd be one of them.

Dr. Smith rented his old, Victorian houses to students and ski bums during the school year, and in the summer used them to house speakers visiting the Law-Science Academy. The rent for a room in one of these homes was about a third of that of similar student housing in Gunnison, where Western State College was located. Dr. Smith hired a local miner, Rudy Sedmalk, to repair his homes. Rudy had been a ski lift operator for over twenty years, but he wasn't comfortable dealing with the students and skiers, so the rent was often overdue. Some of the homes needed to be repainted and refurbished, so I spent the last part of the summer overseeing the home improvement work and getting the rent payments up-to-date.

A number of the renters were Western State students in name only: while their parents footed the bill, they weren't taking many classes, and some were simply skiers. One afternoon Dr. Smith told me, "Mark, I really appreciate how you're able to connect with these kids despite their hang-ups." He said that, although they were "emotionally disturbed", they all seemed "reasonably happy and cooperative" once I'd worked with them. "And I've noticed as of late they've all been paying the rent!"

When I started managing the properties, I'd be able to pick up the rent for all the homes in one evening. Later it took two, and finally three, evenings, due to the growing hospitality offered. When I walked into a home, I'd often find a giant hookah in the middle of the room, and the young renters would invite me to stay for a while and, of course, take a hit or two. Undoubtedly, I got to know my renters in Crested Butte far better than I did the students at Mears Hall on campus.

Among the books on many homes' shelves were Hermann Hesse's *Siddhartha, Steppenwolf,* and *The Glass Bead Game*—all literary rites of passage. The other title nearly every household had was the *Whole Earth Catalog,* a cultural phenomenon and the "unofficial handbook of the counterculture." The book was an efficient way to spread powerful ideas that altered the interests and lifestyles of millions. Its expressed philosophy was:

> *We are as gods and might as well get good at it. So far, remotely done power and glory—as via government, big business, formal education, church—has succeeded to the point where gross defects obscure actual gains. In response to this dilemma and to these gains a realm of intimate, personal power is developing—power of the individual to conduct his own education, find his own inspiration, shape his own environment, and share his adventure with whoever is interested. Tools that aid this process are sought and promoted by the* WHOLE EARTH CATALOG.

Each edition of the *Catalog* was organized into broad subjects such as "Understanding Whole Systems" to "Nomadics" and "Learning." You could buy Indian desert moccasins or read a review of *Atlas Shrugged*

by Ayn Rand: "This preposterous novel has some unusual gold in it."
The *Catalog* unexpectedly became a best seller and in 1972 won the first
National Book Award in the Contemporary Affairs category. It contained
a lot of useful information for millions in the counterculture.

• • •

I've seen the needle and the damage done
A little part of it in everyone
But every junkie's like a settin' sun.

NEIL YOUNG, "THE NEEDLE AND THE DAMAGE DONE"

At that time, the sheriff of Crested Butte reportedly said the community had the most drugs of any community west of the Mississippi.
I didn't buy it, unless he was thinking most drugs per capita. Hashish
could be found in the bowl of any respectable hookah, or a hand-rolled
joint would be offered, or, occasionally, that great Native American product, peyote, could be found. You would have to inquire as to what other
than walnuts were in the brownies, or you might not make it home until
the next day. Of course I could claim that "I never inhaled," but that
really wasn't a viable option when you walked into one of those smoke-filled abodes.

Although most of the students and skiers I worked with weren't really interested in the Law-Science Academy and its Great Ideas series,
many of them did attend the lecture by the criminologist and psychiatrist
Walter Bromberg. Their enthusiasm was enhanced when Dr. Bromberg
soundly supported the decriminalization of marijuana and, according
to the article by George Sibly in the Winter 1993 edition of the Crested
Butte Magazine, recommended that its use be "left up to the conscience
of the individual." Obviously he was ahead of his time, but his opinion
was consistent with that of many of the young people in town. The article

tells of a second expert whose lecture I either don't remember or didn't attend. But Dr. Arthur Grollman's presentation, "The Physical Effects of Drug Abuse," was given a less-than-enthusiastic reception by the youth of Crested Butte.

• • •

Despite these many distractions in the last two years of college, my studies always took priority, and I pushed to get top grades in the history courses of Duane Vandenbusche, who had started teaching at Western State in 1962 and, after more than fifty years of teaching, is an icon there. A compact guy with blond hair, dark blue eyes, and a steady grin, Dr. Vandenbusche loved details and trivia of all sorts. Among his books is the classic *The Gunnison Country*. He was notorious for his quizzes and detailed tests, which covered a myriad of facts about life in the mining camps. I was always competing for the highest scores with a Hawaiian Japanese American named Kelly Lee. She was really smart and studied even harder than I did.

Dr. Vandenbusche was an avid athlete and skier. He coached the cross-country team when he wasn't teaching history. He skied at Monarch Mountain and Crested Butte and encouraged me to learn, so I got a season pass and began careening down the slopes of Crested Butte until I was able to parallel ski. I took a night ski class and was having so much fun, I forgot that the temperature could drop to twenty or more below zero and had to soak my fingers in cool water after they'd turned black and blue. One afternoon I was heading down one of the steeper slopes, and I heard Dr. Vandenbusche, from far up on the lift, shout, "Way to go, Mark!"

During my last year at Western State, I wrote my thesis for Dr. Vandenbusche on the small mining town of Gothic, just north of Crested Butte. Gothic grew out of the discovery of rich silver ore in the West Elk Mountains during the late 1870s, and by 1881 the town was larger and more prosperous than Crested Butte, as it supplied all the mining camps in the area. However, it would all but disappear within a few years due to the high cost of transporting the ore and the decreasing value of silver. I spent many hours in library at the Colorado Historical Society in Denver, studying the microfilm issues of the *Elk Mountain Bonanza.* Dr. Vandenbusche appreciated my hard work, and I believe he was able to use some of my research in his some of his books.

Dr. Vandenbusche would become my lifelong teacher. My wife and I took his class on mining towns in the San Juan range more than forty-five years after my graduation as part of Western State's extension program.

While Dr. Vandenbusche focused on the history of the Western United States, most of my professors specialized in international literature, politics, and economics, which stimulated my interest in seeing some of the fascinating places they talked about.

Professor Abbott Fay's courses on Asian history opened another, wider window to the world. He told our class that in Calcutta a million people lived on the streets in cardboard boxes. A family of five might depend on a small cook stove for their simple meal, and if someone took their stove, they might starve. I don't know if I accepted that premise, but I was amazed that so many people could live in such precarious circumstances and wanted to know more.

Fay was an unorthodox teacher in many ways, and much of his most impactful teaching occurred outside the classroom. He was a relatively small man with a buzz cut—I don't think he actually combed his hair—and he often wore a red tie with baggy cashmere sweaters and smoked a pipe. He led a group of young male students—I was one—called the Quigley Club, named after one of the college's presidents, the purpose of which was to help students discover self-discipline by learning and doing various tasks. He told us about the Trappist monastery hermitage in Snowmass, Colorado, and, impressed by its contemplative lifestyle, I asked him why someone would join such a group.

"Read Thomas Merton's *Seven Story Mountain,*" Fay said, "as he describes his growing restlessness in search of peace and faith, which would lead him at twenty-six to take vows of one of the most demanding Catholic orders."

I went on to read many of Merton's books, some of which describe his attempts to find a balance between his contemplative lifestyle and the desire and need to express himself as an author—a balance I would often struggle with myself, although I was never really cut out for that level of isolation.

I came across an essay written by Fay called "What Is a Student?" in which he reflected on much that we did in the Quigley Club and confirmed my own view that studying is a lifelong process:

> The student, however, is one of dignified calling. When he has earned the honor of society in bestowing upon him the baccalaureate degree, he knows his days of permission as a novice are ended and he must now be at the commencement of a lifetime of being a recognized student. May he never be less.

• • •

Several weeks after taking on my new role with the Law-Science Academy Dr. Smith asked me to haul a trailer of his belongings back to their permanent home in Norman, where he was a professor at the University of Oklahoma. So I loaded up a trailer and hooked it to the old faded green Chevy, filled it up on a crisp fall day, and headed out for Oklahoma. The truck climbed over Monarch Pass at over 10,000 feet, with the Red Mountains to the right, past Cripple Creek, under Pikes Peak, and came out of Colorado Springs shooting east over the plains of Kansas—mile after mile of empty fields. Fortunately, I had my tape player going full blast with some *Easy Rider* music from Steppenwolf:

Get your motor runnin'
Head out on the highway

Different Latitudes

Lookin' for adventure
In whatever comes our way.

Almost ten hours and 800 miles later, I was heading out of Kansas, into the north central part of Oklahoma, the infamous Tornado Alley. Fortunately, it wasn't tornado season, although the winds never seemed to die down. After the Dust Bowl, Oklahomans dammed up most of their rivers in order to avoid such disasters in the future, which explained the many lakes I saw along the way—over 200, the most per square mile of any other state.

Norman, Oklahoma, was done up all in red in preparation for their beloved Sooners taking the football field. I dropped off the furniture with Dr. Smith's wife, Catherine, before heading back to Colorado. Catherine, with her drawl, reminded me of a Southern belle. She was a gifted Dallas art teacher now in Norman since her husband was teaching. She also had done portrait painting at the Edinburgh College of Art while Dr. Smith dissected cadavers as a first-year medical student at the University of Edinburgh Medical School. She was very business-oriented and made all the decisions on which improvements to make on the rental properties in Crested Butte. I just made sure that the changes were completed.

This was harvest season in Oklahoma and Kansas, so the combines were bringing in the corn, sorghum, and soybeans from the endless dry brown fields, but fall was in the air and the roads never seemed to end. The drive north was broken up with such controversial Motown classics as Marvin Gaye's "What's Going On":

Mother, mother
There's too many of you crying
Brother, brother, brother
There's far too many of you dying
You know we've got to find a way

What should have been a grueling nine-hour drive back was made easier listening to "Many a Mile to Freedom" by Traffic and a few of my other favorites by Dave Mason, Led Zeppelin, Pink Floyd, The Who, Jethro Tull, Steely Dan, and Blind Faith. As much as I enjoyed this music's incredible mix of blues and jazz, the lyrics reflected the anxieties and issues of the decade: the Vietnam War, racial tensions, inflation and unemployment, and environmental calamity, as well as the battle over women's equality.

As I pulled up to my house in Crested Butte, Steppenwolf's "Magic Carpet Ride" was blaring:

> *I like to dream yes, yes, right between my sound machine*
> *On a cloud of sound I drift in the night*
> *Any place it goes is right*
> *Goes far, flies near, to the stars away from here*

I turned off the car and sat in silence, exhausted, then I dozed off and had an epiphany. I realized that I'd turned around in Oklahoma and taken the exact route back to where I'd come from. What was that about? I realized that I had become complacent and had opted for what seemed most comfortable, and by so doing had missed all the twists and turns that can come from a new route back home. This would be a lesson I'd never forget.

• • •

During my last year at Western State, I, like many young American men, was searching for alternatives to the draft. I don't remember many protests in Gunnison, but we'd all seen the Kent State students killed by the National Guard, heard the music at Woodstock, and took note of the daily statistics on the increasing number of dead soldiers and the hundreds of thousands of wounded, not to mention the 500,000 hooked on drugs for no good reason.

Several of my high school classmates had already been sent back in body bags. Based on this reality and my Christian upbringing, I registered as a conscientious objector. One of my professors, whose religious studies class I'd attended and who happened to be a pastor, submitted a reference letter. But the Lakewood draft board was evidently unimpressed and rejected my request.

When I explored possible career options, the Peace Corps seemed a perfect vehicle for me to pursue my interests in international history and literature, my two key subjects on the undergraduate level. When I conducted information interviews with history graduate students who were at the top of their class, I learned that most of the students were recruited by the CIA or became teachers. I knew enough about U.S. politics and the role the CIA played in toppling popularly elected governments in Latin America to know that it wasn't for me.

Also, my experience with the community in Ignacio and the epiphany on my return from Oklahoma led me to realize that one way to overcome the fear of the unknown was to jump in with both feet, so I joined the Peace Corps and probably would have, even if there hadn't been a war going on. Dr. Smith submitted a handwritten reference letter, as did a few of my professors, and within six months I received the much-awaited letter informing me that I'd been accepted. And although the Peace Corps was not a legitimate deferment at that time, the draft board never went after me. So it was *adiós* to my family, my friends, Colorado, and everything I was familiar and comfortable with.

¡Hasta luego!

Two

Innocents Abroad

The Road Not Taken

Two roads diverged in a yellow wood,
And sorry I could not travel both
And be one traveler, long I stood
And looked down one as far as I could
To where it bent in the undergrowth...

I shall be telling this with a sigh
Somewhere ages and ages hence:

Two roads diverged in a wood, and I—
I took the one less traveled by,
And that has made all the difference.

— Robert Frost

Initially, the Peace Corps deemed me "unacceptable" based on psychological tests which were given to all candidates because I "couldn't adapt to the rigors of intercultural exchange," but after constant calls on my part, the Peace Corps staff gave in and made an offer. And yet, once I was finally accepted, I found that some of the volunteers I met, from prestigious schools, afterward dropped out because of vague "political" values or because they weren't willing to deal with the challenges of living in rudimentary circumstances and sometimes in isolated locations. Several of the volunteers from New York City insisted on comparing everything they saw with the Big Apple and became disenchanted because wherever they were or were to be sent couldn't compare with the town they adored. But in the end, motivation and perseverance would become my greatest allies.

• • •

The first program the Peace Corps offered me was a rice-growing project on one of two Malayan states on the island of Borneo in Southeast Asia called Sarawak, which surrounds the independent state of Brunei. But, alas, all the slots were filled before my application could be processed. How my life would have been changed if that had been my site. I would have been in the middle of a tropical rain forest where the major mode of transportation was canoe. I don't do that well with mold and fungi, and I wasn't sure if I would ever dry off. And I would have learned several languages that would have been limited to the islands around Malaysia.

Once again I incessantly called the Peace Corps offices in Washington to inquire about other openings, and finally an agricultural fertilizer experimentation position opened in Guatemala. This would prove to be the beginning of my career and render the results of the psychological profiling less than accurate.

My first stop was Puerto Rico, for the initial language and cross-cultural training. Fortunately, the Peace Corps no longer focused on survival training in order to deal with difficult physical circumstances, as it had initially. About twenty of us began basic language training in Ponce, then went on to Liberia, in Costa Rica, for the agricultural training, and then made an initial site visit to Guatemala.

Initially, I was placed in a relatively nice, middle-class home in Ponce with David Thompson, who had taken enough Spanish in high school to understand most of the telenovelas we watched in the afternoon. David was a lanky guy with black hair, a mustache, and brown eyes. He had a boyish smile and kept everyone in good spirits. He would be one of several lifelong friends I'd make during this journey. Our host family had a nice clean house with tile floors. This wasn't what I'd signed up for, so I complained to Zapata, one of our trainers, and requested to be relocated to an area that might reflect the types of people we could expect to work with after the training was completed.

Zapata was a no-fuss-save-the-complaints-for-your-mama type of guy, so he sent me to live in one of the worst slums in the city, called Punto Bravo. Nobody spoke a word of English, and the locals taught all the dirty words first. It was still dark each morning when I walked toward the outhouse, and I was very careful when returning, as the lady of the house often threw the "night water" out of the open bedroom window with not even a heads-up. Breakfast often included a fish head and some bread with an egg. In the afternoons, all the children in the neighborhood sat around the television laughing at the antics of the Three Stooges. No linguistic skills were necessary to enjoy these guys.

• • •

We were given jobs as part of our cross-cultural training, and mine was to load trucks from warehouses and deliver the items to the local stores. This allowed me to see a good part of the city and to learn the words for most of their merchandise.

At Christmas I turned down an invitation from the host family of one of the other volunteers to join them on their yacht destined for Saint Thomas. What was I thinking? Most reasonable people would jump at an opportunity to chill out on the beaches of an exotic Caribbean island, but I found it difficult to relax and enjoy life when I was determined to learn something new and challenging like a new language and culture, so Saint Thomas is still on my bucket list.

Instead, that Christmas I joined the processions which are part of the *posada*, the celebration recreating the Holy Pilgrimage to Bethlehem in Punto Bravo (and much of Latin America), walking from house to small house, singing traditional songs, in this case with a guitar. Naturally I didn't understand the lyrics, but I knew what Christmas was, so I caught on quickly. Traditional food included *lechon,* pork stuffed with rice, among other things, and cooked underground until the meat literally falls off the bones. Together with red beans, this would become my favorite local dish. The families of the houses we visited also offered local liquor, so we had quite a time. I've never forgotten the great music and have become a fan of all salsa and Caribbean music.

Early one morning, as I was walking through the muddy streets of Punto Bravo, I had the eerie feeling that people were watching me from their windows. It was as if I were from another planet, or just that I didn't belong there. I didn't know the language, many of the traditions, or the names of most of the people in that community. I wasn't from there, wasn't accepted by the locals, and just felt out of step with my surroundings.

When I reached my host family's place, I realized that this sensation was something I'd have to deal with for most of my life if I continued to move to new places, whether it be a poor community to help, or a new organization with its own culture and way of doing things. In the end, I'd never stay in one place long enough to really feel at home—at least not in my overseas career. I would always be moving on to the next challenge or work opportunity with people in different lands, with different languages and different expectations. On the other hand, part of the fun is getting to know and appreciate how others live, getting to know them and their families, appreciating their skills and idiosyncrasies, and feeling that what I'm doing is making a difference and is appreciated by those I'm working with.

• • •

I n Liberia, Costa Rica (in the state of Guanacaste, in the northwestern part of the country), I received agricultural and language training during the day and returned to our host home in the evening. The man of the house, Carlos, worked at the local slaughterhouse. He was in his forties, with brown hair and brown eyes. He usually wore a white long-sleeved shirt and Levi's and always talked to me when he got home from work, although I understood less than half of what he said. He was obviously proud of his community, his job, and his family, and wanted to share it all with me. One day he greeted me at the door.

"Mark, welcome! I've brought you something very special from my office—you'll love it!"

He threw open the refrigerator door, and I was confronted by a large tongue hanging off a plate with two massive Rocky Mountain oysters (bull testicles).

"Carlos," I tried to say enthusiastically, "what a surprise! Yes, these look very special indeed."

Of course I was thinking, *Was that a tongue, or what?*

That evening I learned that Rocky Mountain oysters and tongue are actually quite tasty when properly prepared. The tongue is simmered for a long time in a tomato sauce with lots of garlic, making the meat tender and tasty. Normally, I wouldn't eat the local salad because of a strange taste I disliked, but that evening it was excellent so I asked what wasn't in it.

"Cilantro," Carlos said, referring to an herb I'd learn is utilized in all the soups and other recipes throughout Latin America. So I'd always tell folks to hold the cilantro on my tacos.

The highlights of my time in Costa Rica were the weekend trips to the spectacular beaches on the Pacific. One evening Carlos took me out to harvest turtle eggs. I tried two of them by breaking a hole in the shells and putting in some chili sauce and slurping the contents down—a bit salty for my taste, but, hey, we were on the beach, after all. When I finished, Carlos asked, "Mark, would you like another one?"

I said, "Thank you, Carlos, but I had two *huevos*, and that's more than enough."

Different Latitudes

Everyone had a good laugh, since *huevos* also means "testicles." This system of double meanings for many words, or the same words having different meanings in each country, became a source of much laughter, usually at my expense. I'd run into a similar problem in Guatemala, where I'd often mix up the meaning of *miércoles*, which can either mean "Wednesday" or "shit."

• • •

After a month of training, we were sent to Guatemala for several weeks of site surveys in order to be sure we had a place to stay and to successfully implement our program. I had no idea that Guatemala was such a spectacular place and that over time it would become my second country. The rich colonial history, interwoven with the indigenous Maya culture, had produced twenty-three different languages and a lifetime of things to learn about.

But my initial introduction to Guatemala was a cold one. I had been informed that it was a warm, tropical country, so I brought a lot of short-sleeved cotton shirts. The scenery during my drive through the highlands from Guatemala City included large herds of sheep, broad sweeping wheat fields, and many colorfully dressed Maya, and it was downright cold. Arriving at Quetzaltenango, at 7,600 feet the Maya capital of the highlands, I realized this part of the country was anything but tropical, and *National Geographic* had lied to me—or a more likely scenario was that I hadn't been paying attention during orientation. Fortunately, I was able to purchase a few sweaters while changing buses in Quetzaltenango, or Xela, as the locals refer to it.

I purposely chose the most isolated site in our program, a place called Ixchiguán, in order to avoid anyone who spoke English. Ixchiguán is located close to the border with Mexico, on a high plateau at almost 10,000 feet, making it the highest town in Central America. Ixchiguán is surrounded by strangely shaped mountains and hills, with a dozen streams that meander through the alpine forests and tundra-like "quasi-páramo" grasslands. The surrounding area looks like a moonscape—barren, rocky, and inhospitable to any form of life. The mountains in the area are part of the Cuchumatanes, which in turn are part of the Sierra Madre volcanic mountain range, and include some of the isthmus's highest volcanoes, Tacaná and Tajumulco, at 13,320 feet and 13,845 feet, respectively. So much for the tropical wonderland I'd been expecting.

Twelve hours from Guatemala City, our bus finally arrived in Ixchiguán. I disembarked and headed over to the municipal building to meet a few low-level officials, who didn't seem to expect me at all—or maybe they couldn't understand what I was trying to tell them. They showed me a room down the hall, where I spent the next five nights freezing. The room had no windows, no electricity, and no source of heat other than a few candles. The frame around the entry door was filled with holes, which provided an effective air-conditioning system, thanks to the freezing night air. Most of the locals spoke Mam, the local Mayan language, and their Spanish was almost as basic as mine. After talking to a number of municipal officials in the following days, I learned that nobody had been informed of my arrival or the nature of my fertilizer experiments.

As I was exploring the town late one afternoon and the cold mist that hugged the ground engulfed me, I came across a few local farmers hauling a heavy rack of pottery on their backs in order to sell their wares. I tried to ask them where they were going, but they didn't understand Spanish and I didn't know Mam, but eventually I figured out they were heading down to the South Coast. How arduous and long that trip must have been for these two relatively small local Maya farmers. I felt totally out of my element. I couldn't even call home since the landlines in town did not work that well, and the mail service could take months to and from the States. Everything seemed so strange, so lunar. During the next few weeks, I never did meet anyone I was able to connect with to learn more about how things worked in Ixchiguán. By the end of my site visit, I realized that this wouldn't make a viable site for the next two years.

I later learned that Joe, the Peace Corps volunteer who supposedly had done the site survey, hadn't even visited Ixchiguán. He just found a place on the map and chose it. This place was so cold, I had to break the ice off the water basin, or *pila*, in the morning. Thanks, Joe—way to go! The best known local product in Ixchiguán was *ixchbach*, a hard liquor that, according to the locals, utilized human feces in the fermentation process. I avoided this concoction when offered and eventually developed a taste for Guatemalan beer, Gallo or, my personal favorite, Cabro, which came in liter bottles. I quickly learned that drinking with the boys—in this case, the local development officers—entailed long storytelling sessions at the local bars.

After a week, I hiked several hours south of Ixchiguán to a village known as Calapté, a community at a lower altitude, so it was warmer, and where they dress in European-style clothes and speak Spanish, which was helpful since I didn't speak Mam. It had a beautiful flat valley below. I met with the local teachers, and they put me up in a windowless room attached to the schoolhouse. Each afternoon, when I opened my door in hopes of getting some sun—a thick mist engulfed the community in the mornings most of the year—my room would immediately be filled with some twenty-five children looking at the maps on my wall. But I had no real alternative, as the door was the only source of natural light. I felt like a fish in an aquarium.

• • •

After returning from Guatemala, I completed my agricultural training in Costa Rica, and then our group of twenty volunteers flew back to Guatemala City and the Peace Corps offices for an initial orientation. Guatemalan Jose Alvizuras would be our program director, and, like Zapata in Ponce, he was a large guy with a big cowboy hat, although he was a lot more fun than Zapata. My other key staffer would be Frances Asturias, the head administrator, who spoke fluent English and could resolve problems of every imaginable type, whether financial, cultural, or linguistic—whatever it was, she was the go-to person. Frances was large for a Guatemalan woman, with blondish tinted hair and brown eyes, and she always wore colorful local dresses. Later, I learned that she'd been made the office executive officer, a position she'd hold for over thirty years.

One of Frances's many responsibilities was to share options on how volunteers could put their monthly readjustment allowance to work. Each volunteer received a certain amount, which we couldn't touch until our term finished so we'd have resources for the transition process. On this occasion, Frances recommended we consider government bonds, at which point Greg, a fellow volunteer, asked, "Do you know what that money will be used for?"

Another volunteer responded with, "Rifles and bullets."

Greg came back with, "I'd rather spend my money on a more worthy investment."

This was in the early '70s and would be the last time I heard anything about government bonds. It became abundantly clear that I wasn't the only antiwar volunteer in our group.

• • •

After our initial administrative orientation, I needed to transport some furniture and other basic items to my site with the help of Alex Newton, a volunteer and regional supervisor who had a pickup truck. Once I'd delivered my bags and a few pieces of furniture to Calapté, I headed up the mountain and out of the village, onto the main road, where I marveled at the massive volcano, Tajumulco, which loomed in front of us. When I reached the summit, it was snowcapped and surrounded by low-hanging clouds. The high, dry area could support only some scruffy grasses and sheep, and once again I felt small and especially insignificant amid the wide, open spaces and majestic scenery.

Different Latitudes

On the way down to the South Coast, where I needed to return the truck, I passed through several spectacular ecosystems. Within a few hours of Calapté, I was passing by lush, green coffee plantations and then the banana plantations and sugar cane farms of the South Coast. The large orange globe setting over the Pacific Ocean convinced me that this was a place to spend some time in. And I would—over six years in all.

• • •

Our Peace Corps program was a soil fertilization project under the auspices of the Guatemalan Ministry of Agriculture (*Ministerio de Agricultura, Departamento de Edafología*) in cooperation with the University of North Carolina through a contract with USAID. Dr. Jim Walker (no relation) was the program director and a professor at the university.

The intent of our group of some twenty volunteers was to inventory the soil productivity in our site by taking soil samples and sending them to UNC for analysis. UNC produced an experimental design for each of the plots sampled based on the nutrient composition, or lack of nutrients, in the soils. We also tested new seed varieties (corn, wheat, beans, and potatoes, in our area of the country) treated with several different types of fertilizers. The volunteers in the East and South Coast areas tested other types of crops in addition to corn, such as *ajonjolí* (sesame).

The potato varieties we planted in the highlands area produced much larger potatoes than the ones typically planted by the local farmers, or *campesinos*. The indigenous potatoes in Ixchiguán were so small, the farmers called them *maizillos*, or "large corn kernels." The farmers were thrilled by our new varieties of large potatoes, which would feed a lot more people.

• • •

E ach morning at dawn, the small village of Calapté would be engulfed in low-hanging fog mixed with the smoke from hundreds of small houses preparing their breakfasts. I often speculated about what was going on in those small adobe dwellings. After an ice-cold shower, I'd stroll over to a nearby family whom I'd pay twenty-five cents per meal. My monthly rent was a whopping twelve dollars which I paid to the head school teacher. One day I was about to complain because I was receiving only one egg a day along with my black beans and tortillas, until it dawned on me that I was the only one in the family of six who ever ate an egg. This was one time where my lack of language skills kept me out of trouble. Staying in the background, keeping one's mouth shut, and simply observing can have its advantages in cross-cultural settings.

Doña Martha who lived in two adobe buildings was the real head of the family. One building was where all six children and their parents lived, while the smaller building included the kitchen, where we had our meals. Most of the day Doña Martha could be found in this relatively small space beneath a thatched roof, where chickens darted in and out and an occasional rat would run across the ceiling slats. The chimneyless room was always smoke-filled as the smoke simply filtered through the thatched roof. I can't imagine what my lungs would have looked like after several years of breathing in this smoke.

The cooking fire was set on a box, some four to five feet in diameter, filled with earth. Doña Martha, in a yellow dress and apron, would sit in a small chair next to the fire, making corn tortillas she'd then throw on a large round clay dish, or *comal*. Meanwhile, the black beans would be boiling in a black clay pitcher and the coffee brewing in a small pot. When the beans were placed on one of the handmade tortillas, I was definitely a happy camper, as that nutty beanlike taste would stay with me all morning.

My other local favorite was *tamales de chipilín. Chipilín* is a bush, and the leaves make you sleepy. I always asked Martha to cut the tamales in slices to toast (burn them, really) on the *comal*, which would enhance their rather bland taste, and I'd eat them with honey.

Different Latitudes

As I hiked a half a mile or so over the mountain and then down to my experimental fields, I passed by the cemetery and often wondered why so many of the graves were so small, which seemed to be the case in all the cemeteries I saw in that area. Initially, I thought they might have buried their dogs there, but one weekend the villagers organized a major celebration, with lots of drinking and dancing to their national instrument, the marimba. I didn't notice any national or religious holidays on my calendar, so I asked the head teacher, Don Hector, "What's the reason for the big celebration?"

Don Hector said, "The villagers are celebrating the deaths of the *angelitos,* children who died before their first birthday. They go directly to heaven because they haven't committed any sins, so this is a happy time."

It dawned on me how such traditions masked the tragically high rate of child mortality so common in the highlands (the closest health clinic was an hour's hike to Ixchiguán), but I guess it helped them persevere under very difficult circumstances. I also realized how this fatalistic world-view would make real change difficult at best. When climbing down the steep hill toward my experimental fields, I often came across an old guy known as Pancho. I really couldn't say how old he was, but then it was hard to guess how old any of the other adults in the community were. A thirty-year-old woman with eight children might look like she was sixty. Life was hard out in the *campo* rural areas. Pancho obviously didn't know what to think of this large, blond gringo careening down the mountain and never talked to me, but he always waved and smiled before walking on. Pancho's smile revealed just a few yellow teeth. He had a thick brown and white beard and wore a dilapidated broad-brimmed hat. He was usually carrying several limbs for firewood placed in an itchy thatch bag thrown over his shoulder and tied with a piece of rope. He wore a long sleeved blue shirt and some old, brownish pants held up by another piece of rope and sandals made out of old tires. I never figured out where he actually lived, and nobody in Calapté seemed to know either. These encounters helped me appreciate how little I really understood about those around me. The gap between my reality and that of the villagers I worked with would never be totally bridged.

Several villagers helped me take soil samples in the field where we'd eventually grow wheat. After four hours under the sun, we headed back up the mountain, to Doña Martha's round thatched kitchen for lunch. Earlier that morning, I'd seen her cleaning some nasty-looking cow intestines. She was cleaning the tripe with a stick and would eventually prepare a horrid-tasting clear soup, and I could only pray, *Please, God, don't let that be our lunch today.* But it was, so I tried to improve it by adding a few of the most powerful chilies, *chiltepes*. Unfortunately, I wiped my eye with my chili-covered fingers and immediately felt an intense burning, as if someone had pierced my eye with a hot poker. All of this, plus the thick smoke emanating from the cooking fire, was a challenge for my contact lenses, and I was obviously in real pain. Doña Martha noticed my dilemma and with a straight face handed me a towel and a small bowl of water to rinse my eyes with.

After a few more hours in the field, I headed back up the mountain yet again, but before reaching my room, I stopped to visit Don Refugio and his family. He was a *ladino*, which meant *mestizo*, the Hispanicized people in Central America commonly referred to as nonindigenous peoples who speak Spanish and have adopted European dress and customs. *Ladinos* were more willing to deal with outsiders and were more open to new technologies than some of the more traditional, conservative Maya groups in the area. Refugio and his wife, Maria, had eight children. They lived in two small adobe dwellings painted white, with wood-shingled roofs. I asked to take a photo of him and his family, so he brought out six of their children, each carrying one of their many farm animals or crops.

Refugio lined up on the right side, holding a large white and black spotted rabbit. He wore a broad brimmed hat, a shirt, brown pants with a real belt, a light blue coat, and beat-up leather shoes. His older son was next in line, with a massive squash almost as big as he was, and the next son had a giant cabbage that covered his face and most of the rest of his body. Then a daughter, about ten years old, held up a large bunch of carrots, a smaller daughter hung on to a small puppy, and an even smaller daughter held a kitten. An older girl held a small orange and black spotted piglet in her arms. Maria, who was even shorter than her husband, wore an old dress and a blue sweater and wore her black hair down. Despite living in relative isolation and poverty, they all had an air of confidence. They were probably one of the most progressive, well-to-do families in the community, and the first to try out the new seeds we were introducing.

Refugio and his family represented the many small farmers in the highlands, who made up eighty-nine percent of the farmers in Guatemala although they were located on a mere fourteen percent of the land in the country, while two percent of the large farmers owned more than seventy-two percent of the arable land. This system of land tenure went back to the sixteenth century, when the Spanish crown granted *encomiendas,* or large tracts of land, to a small group of colonists. Not only would they get the land but also the rights to the native population, who would pay the colonist in produce or personal service. Naturally, the rural population resisted this process by refusing to work in the field or refusing to pay tributes. Consequently, the Spaniards created *reducciónes,* small villages set up to concentrate the rural population more effectively, as their labor was crucial to the plantations. Other small farmers pushed back into the highlands to avoid this exploitative system, thus forming the small farms that dominate the rural economy even today. Well into the nineteenth century, the central government devised several forms of forced labor, including laws that obligated all residents to work on roads three days of each month. This situation has been exacerbated over the centuries as farmers further divided their small parcels among their sons, with the oldest getting the land rights. (Sources of this information include Thomas Melville's *Guatemala: The Politics of Land Ownership.*) Even though I appreciated the improvements Refugio had made in his home, I also appreciated the impact of a centuries-old tenure system that worked against the interests of the small landowner, especially the indigenous Maya communities.

After taking a few photos and saying good-bye, I headed over to my room. The children had all left the school for home so I was the only one in the area. It began to get dark, and a cold, damp mist engulfed the little rural community. No local pub or recreation center existed, so I closed the door to my room and put on the oil lantern with a few candles for heat. My battery-run shortwave radio provided the only source of entertainment at night: the BBC, the Dutch stations, and Radio Moscow. On Fridays I'd look forward to the *Voice of America Jazz Hour.* VOA's news programs were hopeless, as it was generic and favored our government's interpretation of reality, but the station did have some great jazz. Still, this proved to be a lonely, rather depressing existence.

The next morning, I awoke with a horrendous pain in my stomach, and I was sweating profusely and only semiconscious. I must have had a nasty intestinal infection, which is a rite of passage among Peace Corps volunteers. I didn't even have the strength to get out of bed, let alone walk the forty-five minutes uphill to the only daily bus that passed. I vaguely remembered the Peace Corps staff assuring me that if I ever got ill or had an accident, I'd be medevacked in a helicopter, an impressive option until I learned that the telegraph system was down and the one phone in the community didn't work. In effect, I was stuck up the proverbial creek, and nobody from the outside world knew my situation. Fortunately, when I didn't appear at Martha's for breakfast, she gathered two of her friends and found me in bed in a daze. They immediately began applying, and had me drink, a series of local herbs and remedies.

"*No tenga pena, Don Marcos. Le vamos a ayudar y ya mero vas estar bien,*" said Doña Martha. *Don't worry, Mr. Mark. We'll take care of you, and you'll be okay in no time.* And with that, I already felt better.

One often forgets the incredible amount of health and medical knowledge found within these small communities. They know all the right herbs to deal with almost any ailment. Many of our "modern" medications have their origins in some herb or plant in the Amazon Basin. Those three women from this small village probably saved my life using centuries-old medicinal remedies.

Their words of encouragement and kindness caused me to reflect on the words of Christoph Friedrich Blumhardt, in his book *The Gospel of God's Reign*: "People from humble circumstances are sometimes our angels. The despised of this earth are actually here to help us. Those who usually don't have much to say sometimes speak the most important word." I have personally experienced this. Several times God has sent my way a very humble, rejected person who said something that I needed to hear. When this happens, my first reaction is usually, "Why should he have something to say to me?" But later on, I'd realize that I am ignoring the very voice of God. Often God puts someone in our path to prevent an accident or to sharpen our character. I learned time and time again that I must always be ready to listen and welcome even the humblest in our midst.

I was lucky to learn early on to focus on the needs of the poor and humble and to try to make a difference, but to always listen to their pleas, supplications, and, most of all, their wisdom, based on a lifetime of living and suffering. Doña Martha and her two friends, Don Refugio and even Pancho, shared part of themselves with me and helped ground me in reality and an appreciation of who they were and what they represented in their community.

• • •

A fter three days, I was able to walk up to the road, where the bus would stop so I could start my twelve-hour journey on several chicken buses (so called because the number of chickens outnumbers that of passengers) and return to the Peace Corps office in Guatemala City for additional medical treatment. But evidently the Peace Corps staff didn't like the precarious situation in Calapté, so they changed my site to the more accessible San Jerónimo, far to the east, in Baja Verapaz, where I continued my fertilizer experiments with several varieties of vegetables. I lived in town and worked out of the local agricultural experimental station. The climate was warm, and the land was rich and unusually flat for Guatemala.

My Guatemalan counterpart and friend, Adolfo Gutierrez, who worked at the experimental station, was the funniest of all the *peritos agrónomos* (people with degrees in agricultural sciences) and liked hauling his gringo buddy around town. He was a relatively small guy, even for a Guatemalan, with a devilish smile and a wink whenever he told a small lie or exaggeration, which was often. His one flaw, which would be fatal, was his consumption of alcohol, including a hard liquor called *guaro* and Venado, the most popular brand. Adolfo would remain a close friend for many years until, tragically, five years later, I'd find him filthy and disheveled, begging in front of a McDonald's, and he died after his kidneys gave out, a few months later.

In San Jerónimo we lived together in a small room, and I'd start each day with coffee and oatmeal with peanuts and honey, all of which were easily available. For dinner I'd often make eggs with tomatoes and vegetables from our garden behind our room, using some of my newly acquired agricultural skills. It took a while to get used to the giant rats that scampered over the ceiling beams as we entered the kitchen area, but they never bothered us.

• • •

We must be willing to fail and to appreciate the truth that often
"Life is not a problem to be solved, but a mystery to be lived."

— *"THE ROAD LESS TRAVELED," M. SCOTT PECK*

After six months in San Jerónimo, I realized that my experiments would benefit only the wealthier farmers with flat land and irrigation, so I returned to the area of greatest need, the Ixchiguán/Calapté area, and joined the Guatemalan President's Community Development Department. There, I was integrated into a multidisciplinary team that included the agronomist and leader Rodrigo Ruiz as well as a nurse, a social worker, and a community organizer. This turned out to be a controversial move on my part. A letter I sent to my parents in June 1972 explains why I was in hot water with my program sponsor USAID (US Agency for International Development):

Different Latitudes

I've been under a lot of real pressure from all sides as of late and can't explain it all by mail, but when I return I'll lay it on you. For one thing, I left my old site in San Jerónimo to begin work with Desarrollo de la Comunidad with reforestation projects (we'll plant over 200,000 pine trees through various organizations), the 3 associations (all have 40 members and projects in vegetables, reforestation, alfalfa, different varieties of corn and wheat, etc.), and 5 school gardens. I also completed two thorough site surveys and made many personal contacts for the incoming school garden program and got information to be used for the training program.

But while I was away from my vegetable experiments (I only had 2 left), I lost part of the harvest because the farmer harvested a day early. So my host agency was threatening to do away with me, and the Peace Corps leadership was perturbed since I was working with an agency that is politically "hot." (Anything relating to the presidency is considered political, and oftentimes "development" programs are designed to gain votes.) So all through this "policy" hassle, they forgot to look at how successful my programs have been and how many people we are assisting. My next step is to consolidate the projects and phase myself out—making sure that Guatemalans can handle all aspects of it. And eventually begin working on the training program for an income-generating school garden program.

Obviously, I was struggling to fit into a highly structured situation. My Peace Corps program was well thought out and planned, but I was determined to focus on meeting the needs of, and helping, those with the greatest need, and these small, poor farmers didn't own a nice flat piece of land appropriate for doing the fertilizer experiments. I also preferred working with Guatemalans through local agencies that could establish and then leave behind the leadership and programs that would mobilize local resources to meet local needs.

• • •

Returning to Calapté, I felt disconnected from the community and wasn't sure where to start. Also, the moistness and cold of Calapté bothered me, not to mention the vestiges of culture shock. This initial feeling of despair passed quickly, though, after running into friends around the community and eating and relaxing around the fire at Doña Martha's thatched kitchen. Soon I felt I was back "home" and ready to get to work.

Several days after my arrival, the head teacher, Orlando, asked me to drive the Land Rover to a community close by Serchil for an animal husbandry course organized by the President's Community Development group. I'd help facilitate the course, although this wasn't my specialty. He'd been drinking for several weeks with fellow teacher Chente (it gets lonely in them thar hills), and their eyes were bloodshot and their heads shaking, and I could almost see the *guaro* killing their brain cells.

The Land Rover was leaking oil since none of the teachers knew how to maintain it, and the roads were horrendous. The engine would always stall when I came to a stop so the idea was to keep moving no matter what, which I accomplished by staying in first or second gear. As we crawled along, I felt a thump in the back and a scraping sound, so I stopped and found that the right rear tire had fallen off. What amazed me wasn't so much that a tire simply fell off but the Guatemalans' nonchalant response and their joking around as they looked for the missing lug nuts, jacked up the vehicle, and forced on a few bolts (which weren't even for a Land Rover). I guess they were lucky I knew nothing about vehicle maintenance, or I might have gotten upset.

Over fifty local farmers attended the three-day animal husbandry course, which started by showing off some of the massive local sheep raised using the crossbreeding techniques the President's Community Development group had promoted. We were shown a series of pictures and posters to illustrate how to feed, groom, and take care of the sheep. Naturally, the section on castration generated an unlimited number of sexually oriented jokes for our all-male audience. Rodrigo and several of the other group members also taught how to graft fruit trees, which would provide an additional income source. Our one mistake was passing out notebooks and pencils, which was a waste, as many couldn't see the chalkboard due to poor eyesight and didn't know how to write.

At the celebration that followed, several participants shared poems, and three of the men sang songs, all using the loud microphones favored by local leaders for broadcasting speeches throughout the community. Refugio from Calapté impressed me in this nonagricultural setting by presenting a mini play of local life, which generated lots of laughs. Finally, we presented the certificates of participation. During the entire ceremony, innumerable children continually came onstage, crying, laughing, and playing.

The local school was filled with pine needles in anticipation of a celebration dance, which followed the certificate presentations. The women spread the pine needles everywhere so that the fragrance covered the smell of sweat, puke, and urine, among other things. The dance was to start at 5:30, although nobody was there until 7:30 since most of the women were feeding their families. As part of the festivities, several of the local leaders passed around shot glasses with Ixchiguán's especially nasty local brew, *ixchbach*, and during the confusion I dumped mine on the ground in order to save a few more brain cells. The music and dancing would go into the wee hours, and while I was never game enough to make it to the end, I recognized that these festivities were important to small communities where the social interaction and entertainment options were limited.

• • •

The team of the President's Community Development Department worked in one of the most isolated areas of the highlands, on the Mexican border, far beyond Ixchiguán and Tacaná. We often drove for hours on horrid roads to reach places like San José Ojetenam and then rode horses for several more hours to reach the communities we served. We stayed with families in places that didn't have running water or electricity. We'd usually eat our meals in a smoke-filled kitchen with chickens or pigs running around. Sometimes over a hundred peasants would come out of the woodwork to attend one of our training sessions on animal husbandry and tree grafting, among other things (partially because we had slides and videos, a novelty in these far-flung locations), but we'd notice that many actually utilized the new techniques on their own land. As I hiked back through these areas, the local priests were often the only source of "civilization" as I knew it. Several priests had lived in these isolated places for fifteen or twenty years. They were real heroes from my perspective, as they were often the only advocates for the local indigenous population.

After a month of reading in my windowless room and listening to the BBC on my shortwave, I'd be ready to get out of Dodge—or Calapté, in my case—to meet up with other Peace Corps volunteers, or PCVs, in Chimaltenango for the monthly "Gringo Night" sponsored by Dr. Carroll Behrhorst, known as the Schweitzer of Central America. Dr. Behrhorst had founded his clinic and hospital in 1962 to serve the rural Kaqchikel people of the highlands. His approach, combining health and community development, was selected in 1975 by the World Health Organization as a model for effective community development programs.

Gringo Night was a great opportunity to kick back with a cold beer and catch up with some of the other Peace Corps Volunteers (PCVs) who were in the highlands. After one such event, twenty-six of us converged on my fellow fertilizer experiment specialist Dave Thompson's place in Tecpán for a home-cooked Thanksgiving dinner. The turkey was tender and tasty, as were the yams, and tortillas provided a Latin touch to our celebration. All of this was topped off with magic brownies. On the whole, alcohol was far more prevalent than drugs, although occasionally a friend of a Guatemalan friend would hand me a joint.

• • •

M any of the volunteers I met at Gringo Night had some of the same
books I saw in Crested Butte, from Hermann Hesse's to the *Whole
Earth Catalog*. By and large, the PCVs hated Nixon and Agnew, the hypoc-
risy of big business, and materialism in general. Bob and Joyce Jackson,
who lived in Uspantán, an isolated part of the department, or province,
of El Quiché, seemed to live out the self-sufficient and natural, organic
approach emphasized in the *Catalog*. They grew all their own vegetables
and raised rabbits, among other edible animals, as well as pet deer for
their small son. They harvested biogas from their latrine and had water
from their well hooked up to their small but very functional kitchen.
Bob and Joyce were a handsome couple and practiced their philosophy
of life each and every day.

After Dave's Thanksgiving feast, my supervisor, Alex Newton, invited me to see one of his sites, Todos Santos, which is perched on top
of the Cuchumatanes mountains, at over 9,500 feet. The Maya men
in this region still wore their traditional colorful pants, although most

indigenous men had changed them for the slacks worn by the more Westernized *ladinos*. Their pants, like almost everything else, were made of white cotton, with wide red stripes running down the legs. They wore flat-brimmed hats, which were also worn by the women, and the older men wore bandannas around their heads. Their shirts were also white, with pinstripes and one thick red strip in the middle, up to the collar, which included a small pocket where they kept their change.

The locals were distrustful and were rumored to have killed outsiders they suspected of stealing their children or harvesting vital organs like kidneys. This had happened a few years earlier to a tourist couple from Japan. I never felt threatened when I was in Todos Santos as most of the locals knew Alex and the agricultural work he was doing with them. Alex and a few other PCVs were introducing contoured terraces. The agricultural land was so steep, I saw several local farmers tied to a tree or rock so they wouldn't tumble down the mountain.

On the way back to my site, Alex took a photo of me on the top of the Cuchumatanes. At almost 10,000 feet, overlooking the dry, expansive mountains below, I was well tanned, my hair totally bleached out. What I didn't have was a hat, nor did I know what sunscreen was. Little did I know that, for the majority of my adult life, I'd be paying dearly for this fond memory as dermatologists would cut, slice, and dice to their hearts' content in order to keep various varieties of skin cancer at bay.

• • •

Not long after I had introduced my first fertilizer experiments, Dr. Jim Walker invited me and fellow PCV Paul Hickey to introduce this program to the Atlantic coast of Honduras. One night, at a rudimentary but clean hotel in the town of Tela, I headed into the bathroom and felt something crunch under my boot. It sounded like a piece of glass, but when I looked down, I found I'd inadvertently stepped on a massive cockroach, which prosper and grow to amazing sizes in the tropics.

Different Latitudes

In Honduras we installed several fertilizer experiments with agriculture ministry officials who were responsible for increasing agricultural production among small farmers. One of the most memorable parts of the trip was drinking from a cold coconut on one of the incredible white sand beaches on the coast and drinking a few local cold beers at the Maya ruins of Copán with Paul, Jim Walker, and Jim's assistant, Luis. This would be the first of many trips for me to the ancient ruins that can be found throughout Latin America and attest to an impressive precolonial civilization.

Copán was known for its well-preserved stelae, the stone banners raised to glorify the king and record his deeds. The imagery created during the Classic Period of the Maya (c. 250–600) is among the earliest examples of mythological scenes. Over the years, I'd return with friends to these and other incredible Maya monuments, including the nearby ruins of Quiriguá and the largest Maya city of Tikal, deep in the Petén jungle in the northern part of Guatemala.

• • •

The culmination of my Peace Corps work in Calapté was the inauguration of the new, five-room schoolhouse. It replaced a dark and dingy hundred-year-old structure, with no windows, chalkboards, or books. The students' desks could barely stand up on their own. After two and a half hours of flowery rhetoric about the benefits of democracy that the locals loved to hear, I received five diplomas from all the institutions that had given me funding, including the Peace Corps, USAID, CARE, the Ministry of Agriculture and the Ministry of Education. The community was out in full force for the formal presentations.

The partnering agencies also brought in 300 pounds of food for undernourished children, hundreds of books for the new library, and 6,000 seedlings for erosion control, as well as 20 films on health and agriculture for the Crusader projector. Even Peace Corps program director Jose Alvizuras made it to my site for this event, although it was no small feat, considering how isolated the place was. The new schoolhouse, which was designed to withstand earthquakes, had cement floors and metal sheeting for the roof, and we even managed to bring in sturdy desks for the kids.

• • •

W hile still in San Jerónimo, just before I returned to my highlands site of Calapté, I was walking down the middle of the only street in town with my friend Adolfo and saw a strawberry blonde girl riding a white horse just ahead of us. I asked Adolfo, "Who is she? Do you know her?"

"Her name is Ligia, and she was the queen for the local festival a few months ago. I've never met her, but I know her cousin."

"Can you set something up?" I said.

"I'll try, but she's too hot for you, my *gringito* friend."

True to his word, the next afternoon, Adolfo and I stopped by one of the tiny local stores to have a beer, and there was Ligia and her cousin *La Perlita*. My Spanish was just good enough to ask her name, where she lived, and whether we could meet up the next time I was in Guatemala City.

With her long strawberry blonde hair and green eyes, Ligia was definitely not like any of the women I saw up-country, or anywhere else in Guatemala, for that matter. Little did I know that she would be the love of my life and would affect what I did and where I went for the next forty-some years.

Ligia began making inquiries of her cousin and friends about the hippie in the blue bandana, with his long hair hanging out, who could be seen running alongside the irrigation canals early each morning. I was even seen carrying manure through my room, for the vegetable garden out in the back, but I'm sure it generated some gossip among the local residents. Satisfied that I was okay, Ligia agreed to see me.

Our courtship moved along at a brisk pace. In 1973 my journal read, "I went to Lake Amatitlán with my strawberry-blonde-haired, green-eyed Guatemalan girlfriend, and my roommate, Adolfo, by train. We went row boating, on the lake and I could really get to like her."

Different Latitudes

During that memorable train ride, I learned that Ligia had just broken up with her boyfriend so her father had suggested she get out of town and accompany him to his small horse ranch, which was the only reason she was in San Jerónimo in the first place. (Years later, I'd find out that the rejected boyfriend was an heir to the Novella cement company.)

As the train made its way to Lake Amatitlán, I asked, "So, where did you go to school?" I wanted to find out if she'd gotten through basic level, equivalent to U.S. high school.

She responded in Spanish. "Well, actually, I have several degrees. One is a teaching certificate, and the other is a degree in agricultural engineering from the University of San Carlos." I learned later that she had the teaching degree in biology and chemistry and was pursuing two degrees in civil and chemical engineering.

Wow! A degree in agriculture. She might even appreciate these fertilizer experiments I've been doing!

"So, do you work at all?" I asked, thinking she probably just hung around her house.

"Yes, I'm teaching third-graders at Juana de Arco. When I was a child, I studied in the Colegio Belga, which was run by Belgian nuns." She went on to tell me some interesting stories about how she and her friends avoided the innumerable restrictions the nuns imposed and learned how to smoke at a school retreat. Evidently, Ligia and her friend Maria Rene were considered renegades.

"What do you do when you're not teaching?" I asked, thinking she was probably partying with her friends.

"Oh, I love drama and have been involved in the university theater. *Carmina Burana* is by far my favorite play."

Carmina who?

Ligia and I spent many enjoyable weekends and Easter holidays on her family's coffee plantation, San Francisco Miramar, on the South Coast side of the volcano Atitlán, above the community of Patulul. This was one of several plantations in Ligia's family. At the turn of the century, the "big house" had two stories (as opposed to the one story I saw), and mules would haul the coffee to the port on the South Coast. It was an imposing place, with lots of bedrooms, but the house was neglected, because there were no matrons in the house since Ligia's grandmother Mimi had died. Ligia's grandfather and uncle Coco managed the house; although it needed a woman's touch, it was a great place.

Ligia's father, who also stood out, with his blond hair and blue eyes due to his Swiss heritage, held the record for the javelin and shot put for Central America. Ricardo was one solid block of a man and someone not to mess with. He had been the coffee plantation administrator for many years, so we'd discuss some of the agricultural issues such as soil conditions, production, and the growth cycle.

Ironically, many of the farmers from the highlands villages I'd worked with would work on plantations like this one for three or four months each year to supplement their meager incomes. They made the equivalent of one dollar a day for arduous work under the hot tropical sun, wearing their traditional cotton clothing, which was far more comfortable in the cool highlands than in the heat of the coast. An entire family would often harvest coffee for over twelve hours a day. They lived communally on a simple concrete platform with a metal roof and no walls to separate families. They slept on straw mats called *petates* and often didn't even have latrines, although they did at San Francisco Miramar.

With these visits to the coffee plantation, I had a foot in two worlds. On one hand, I would get to know Ligia's family, and they were all friendly. Her grandfather, Mariano, would often joke about my supposed affiliation with the CIA. The workers, on the other hand, would tell me where they're from and how long they'd work on the plantation, what they did and whether they planned to return the next year. Since I worked with farmers in similar circumstances in the highlands, I appreciated how limited their economic options were and how important it was to finish out the year, for the small amount of income they made.

Different Latitudes

Ligia and I often rode horses up through the coffee plantation *cafetal* (the location of the coffee plants) in the afternoons, with Atitlán in the background. She wore white boots, brown pants, an embroidered smock, and a broad-brimmed hat. It was cool as we rode up into the *cafetal*, as shade trees protected the lush, dark green coffee plants. During the spring, when the plants were flowering, the *cafetal* would be filled with the heavy perfume of white coffee blooms. Occasionally, we'd come across entire families of workers who were tending the plants or cutting the grass between the coffee trees, but we usually found a nice quiet place to chat and get better acquainted.

Back at the big house, I amused the maids when I entered the kitchen (foreign territory to most males) and tried to learn how to make my favorite dessert, *rellenitos de plátano,* fried plantains stuffed with black beans. I was proud of my accomplishments in the kitchen, and the *muchachas,* or female servants, got a great laugh out of my culinary antics. I realized that such interaction with the kitchen help was not acceptable socially, but chose to act out of gringo ignorance.

Sometimes Ligia and I drove down to the beach on the South Coast, although the beaches tend to be steep and black because of the volcanic ash, and dangerous because of the strong undertow. But beach time together was always a good time. I was impressed by how well Ligia protected herself from the sun, with long-sleeved shirts and broad-brimmed hats, but never realized why until it was too late.

Although it would have been easy for me to just carry on at her father's horse farm in San Jerónimo, I realized I still had a calling to finish up what I'd started, so I told Ligia I needed to return to work in Calapté and focus my remaining months as a Peace Corps volunteer where the needs were the greatest. When she agreed that I should finish up my work, I knew that my Guatemalan girlfriend would turn out to be an important part of my life. She would, in fact, change me in many unforeseen ways. Our fun times together would lead to a long-term partnership that would span the globe.

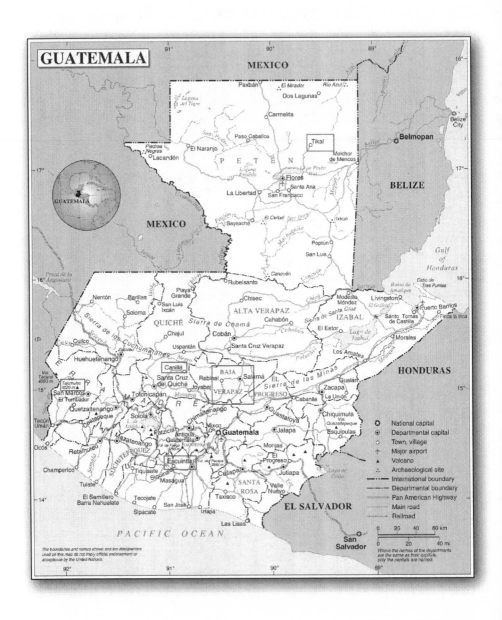

Three

LIFE WITH LIGIA: BECOMING PART OF
AN EXTENDED LATINO FAMILY

With time we appreciate that someone who is capable
of loving you with all your defects without trying
to change you is able to bring you happiness.

--JORGE LUIS BORGES

Share our similarities, celebrate our differences.

--M. SCOTT PECK

After I'd returned to Calapté, to work with the President's Community Development group, I regularly endured the twelve-hour trek on chicken buses—refurbished Blue Bird school buses from the U.S. that are the key form of transportation of the rural population around the country—to spend a few days with Ligia in Guatemala City. As soon as I arrived in the big city, I'd stock up on all the chocolate-covered caramel candies I could find at the street stalls (they weren't available in Calapté) and then head to a designated coffee shop or restaurant to chat with Ligia. I had cut my hair in case we ran into any of her many family members around town. We'd often head over to the Capri, a hamburger joint, for a fresh melon and *piña* smoothie (melon and pineapple mixed with ice and water) and then over to the Lux to see a movie. I never had much money, but that didn't stop us from getting together.

We met in the center of town, a few blocks from the Cathedral and the National Palace. The *Sexta Avenida* was still the center of commerce but would soon be abandoned as more businesses moved to malls to meet the needs of the growing middle class. Eventually the *Sexta* would be closed to traffic and totally remodeled in the hope of capturing some of the tourist business. Over the years, I'd stay at the Hotel Pan American on the Sexta which was one of the first hotels in the country run by an Evangelical Christian family. The staff wore *traje*, traditional Maya-designed clothing. The rooms were small and quaint, and the food represented the best of Guatemalan cuisine.

Parents in Latin America tended to be highly protective, especially when it came to their daughters, to a point I thought bordered on the obsessive. Ligia would usually be accompanied by one of her two brothers or one of her innumerable male cousins on a date. Fortunately, she knew how to circumvent the system, so we were able to get together when she was in San Jerónimo or I was in Guatemala City. Neither of us cared much about what other people thought, which would explain a lot about our future together. And I think Ligia realized that this "crazy gringo" would be taking her out of her traditional setting, with all the restrictions that came with it, and that, for her, was a good thing.

Her mother, Neta—short for Antonieta— or *La Negra* (referring to her dark hair), as her husband called her was one of three sisters who produced most of the children I'd get to know over the years. Her aunt Rosa had two sons and a daughter, and Aunt Regi had four daughters, and eventually most of *them* would have children, so the family would continue to grow over the years.

• • •

Different Latitudes

After a number of months of serious courting, I realized that Ligia could be my better half, as she had that rare combination of brains and natural beauty, and so I asked her to marry me June 23d 1973, kicking off a lifelong partnership. One of her mother's cousins, Enriqueta "Queta" Sartoris Ruiz, opened her home for the ceremony and celebration. My best man was my closest friend, Grant Gerrish. I'd followed Grant around for months helping with a myriad of projects he'd designed to help young peasant families. I borrowed a brown suit coat and a black, brown and beige striped tie from my fellow Peace Corps volunteer Bill Freeman. The coat was a tad small, but it worked, and this would be the first and last time I'd wear a tie. My blond hair was long again, curled up in the back with dark, massive sideburns. Ligia's long hair hung over her flowing white dress printed with beige flowers. An angel, a vision of innocence and beauty, and soon to be mine!

We were married in a civil ceremony by a friend of Ligia's father, Villagrán "Paco" Kramer. Kramer would become the Vice President of the country under General Romeo Lucas García and the Guatemalan ambassador to the United Nations. As it turned out, Paco was also a Presbyterian pastor, and so he married us by the church as well. After the ceremony, we toasted with champagne around a small table covered with a Guatemalan flag, on which we'd sign our marriage certificate.

Although I didn't realize it at the time, many of those in the room would become lifelong friends and acquaintances, as I'd now become part of a much-extended Latino family. We're talking hundreds of individuals, including family and some university friends, although Ligia had assured me that just the "immediate family" would attend. Along with everyone else, I was drinking Johnnie Walker whiskey and champagne, accompanied by traditional music from the marimba, the country's national and revered instrument and we drank and schmoozed until the wee hours.

Obviously, this event was all about Ligia's family, and I was so focused on figuring out who was who, not to mention how to deal with married life that I didn't even inform my own family in Colorado of the ceremony until after the fact. My parents never actually saw our first child until Michelle was ten months old and we arrived in Evergreen in the dead of winter, with several feet of ice and snow on the ground.

If I knew then what I know today, I might have shared with Ligia a list of reasons she might reconsider my offer to spend the rest of our lives together. We can divide this list between "The She'd Reconsider List" and "The She'd Run Screaming from the Altar List."

The She'd Reconsider List

- I will constantly embarrass you in social settings with my horrendous grammar and constant use of foul language picked up in various slums and rural settings.
- I won't file taxes for the first five years of marriage, because I didn't make enough money.
- I won't even think about setting up a retirement fund or make a plan until it's too late.
- I won't have any medical insurance until the fifth or sixth year of marriage.
- I'll take you home to meet my family in the middle of winter, when it snows constantly and the temperature rarely exceeds the freezing point.
- Every three years, I'll ask you to pack up the children and all your earthly belongings and move to a different country, where you'll not know a soul.
- I'll be sued by local workers and have to leave Colombia illegally on short notice.
- My idea of fun will include visiting endless museums of every type all over the globe.
- I will always find you a job before you arrive in a new country or city.
- I'll idolize extreme do-gooders unknown to anyone in the room and speak about them as if they are colleagues.
- I will write a memoir that includes you, but you won't see it until it's finished.

- My idea of success is helping the maximum number of extremely poor people I had never met before.
- I'll think that having parasites is a viable weight-loss strategy and discuss them at the dinner table.
- I'll insist on speaking Spanish at home, despite your spending the day teaching it and my never remembering any of your grammatical corrections—for over forty years.

The She'd Run Screaming from the Altar List

- The honeymoon will include many twelve-hour drives in a Volkswagen Bug that will almost get squashed between two trucks carrying dynamite.
- Shortly after the honeymoon, I'll take a backpack and head off for four months alone throughout Latin America and rarely call.
- I'll bring the family to a training center in an isolated part of El Quiché, where the baby will contract amoebas and need hospitalization in order to rehydrate.
- I'll be threatened by local revolutionary guerilla groups and give you less than three days to pack up and leave the country.
- I'll take you to one country where green monkey disease, dengue, malaria, and other deadly ailments are commonplace.
- I will think that being absent for months on end is acceptable.

• • •

Ligia's best friend, Maria Rene "Mamane", lent us the yellow VW Bug that her parents had given her as a graduation present, and we headed out for a three-week honeymoon tour of Mexico. (Obviously I neglected to share the list of reasons why she should reconsider). We received a number of gifts, like blenders and a vacuum, but this was the best gift of all. I could easily drive twelve to fourteen hours a day. We stayed at the finest hotels money could buy during the entire trip—the best you could buy for less than three dollars a night, that is. Actually, they were fleabags, and we even spent a few nights in the Bug, which did not impress Ligia at all. I was constantly asking for her forgiveness because of the poor accommodations and would promise that the next place would be acceptable.

We entered Mexico over a narrow road through the mountains of Huehuetenango, which eventually would take us to San Cristóbal de las Casas, a community of mostly Maya then drove all the way to the northern border and back down the west side, to Oaxaca. The following postcard to my parents, dated July 29, 1973, refers to some of the highlights of the trip:

We went up the Atlantic coast and saw the ruins of Palenque, visited Villahermosa, Veracruz, and Puebla, "the Rome of Mexico," since it has hundreds of beautiful churches, and saw the art exhibitions. After 3 days in Mexico City, we took 7 hours to see the largest anthropological museum in the world, botanical gardens, a fine arts museum, floating gardens, University of Mexico with the Olympic stadium. Tonight it's the Mexican National Symphony Orchestra and tomorrow the ruins at Teotihuacan, and then up north to see most of the rest of Mexico . . . Things are really cheap! A good room with hot water for only 2-3 dollars!

On the last leg of our trip, we headed north, toward Saltillo, Monterrey, and eventually Torreón, some of the hottest places in the country. We departed first thing in the morning—we couldn't sleep due to the extreme heat. We were close enough to Texas to listen to English programs and Tex-Mex music on the radio. This provided a good opportunity to chat about the pluses and minuses of living in the U.S. Ligia's biggest question was, "You mean we can't have any *muchachas* to cook and help out?" That was a big negative for returning to my homeland right away.

Then we headed south, through the beautiful town of Guadalajara, then Morelia, and down south through Oaxaca again. As the little yellow Bug glided through the pines in the hills of Oaxaca, we saw a large truck coming right towards us as he passed another truck forcing us off the road, at which point I saw the sign on the door of one of the trucks

Cuidado, Dinamita A Bordo! (Be Careful, Dynamite on Board). I let out a few descriptive expletives and Ligia a scream of terror, but, under the circumstances, they definitely had the right of way, which was why I wisely let them career by.

Driving at night was a no-no even back in the '70s. Mexican truck drivers parked or broke down, right around a curve, in the middle of a road, in the middle of the night, and put a tree branch behind the truck as a warning. Most truck drivers didn't have insurance, and if an accident occurred, both parties could be taken into jail for interrogation, among other things.

• • •

T his nonstop trip through Mexico in 1973 would be just the beginning of an ongoing journey, through many parts of the world. Returning to Guatemala, we headed to the coffee plantation Francisco Miramar to relax and, for me, to get to know some of Ligia's family members. At one time, her family owned no fewer than eight plantations, but in the '30s her great-grandfather lost seven of them gambling and committed suicide.

Different Latitudes

Ligia's grandfather, Mariano, had reached his eighties but still kept a case of Johnnie Walker Black Label at the big house and would sip a few glasses of Scotland's best each afternoon. He often offered me a glass, which I gladly accepted. As he grew older, the issue of who should manage the plantation came up. Even though I had just married Ligia, I participated in a meeting in her father's home in Guatemala City, with Ligia's parents and Mariano's son, Tío Coco (Ligia's uncle), who lived on the coffee plantation. Tía Tita, Tío Mino, and Tía Regi were all present, with some of their children, as was Ligia's brother Roland and her cousin Edgar, to decide who should manage the operation.

Much to my surprise, they asked my opinion, and I let them know that I'd consulted an agricultural engineering firm, Sedinagro, who had given the Peace Corps volunteers in-country training. My contacts suggested that they could manage the plantation for a small percentage of the proceeds, which seemed appropriate, since they were qualified to do the job, as well as being motivated to make a profit.

In the end, the family took the more traditional route and asked Ligia's uncle Coco to manage the property. One consideration that led to this decision was his father's desire to continue living in the big house. Tío Coco was a personable guy who always treated Ligia, the kids, and me with respect and love. He really cared for the seasonal workers who came from the highlands each year to harvest the coffee. He provided schools for the children, a soccer field, bathrooms, and a concrete-covered area where the families slept. Permanent workers were provided houses made of cinder blocks with metal roofing, which was not usually the case at other plantations. He even brought in a tractor to carve out the soccer field, which is the first love of many Guatemalans. When the guerrilla groups began invading the plantations during the period of violence, they never damaged San Francisco Miramar because of the way they treated their workers, although many of the workers were forced to leave.

But as far as I could tell, Tío Coco had never really worked a day in his life off the plantation and had no degree or formal training other than his work on the plantation. Ligia told me that in the early '70s, before we met, she saw an invoice for $85,000 for three expensive bull-dozers and the soccer field when he wouldn't give her a small loan to purchase a used car so she could get to school. This, on top of paying some 200 workers, would result in a heavy financial burden, especially when the price of coffee dropped precipitously—which it regularly does.

Despite the economic threats, it was the period of violence in the early 1980s that did the plantations in. Guerrilla fighters recruited all the teachers during the day, and the military troops came in the after-noons to pressure the locals to tell them where the guerilla group went. Eventually, no workers were available to work on the coffee plants as they'd slipped back into the hills to avoid the confrontation.

One afternoon Turcio Lim one of the guerrilla leaders called all the plantation workers to the coffee drying platform and then brought out Ligia's uncle "Tio Coco" and asked everyone if he was treating them well—which he was—so nobody spoke out against him and Turcio let him go after saying, "We would have shot you right here if your workers told us anything bad about how you were handling them." Unfortunately the local teacher didn't have the same luck as he had spoken against the guerilla movement and they took him away with them later that after-noon and reportedly he was "disappeared" (tortured and killed).

By 1980 Ligia's family couldn't pay off their loans due to the lack of production, the low cost of coffee and mismanagement so they were forced to sell the plantation to a wealthy family from El Salvador. It was the last of the eight plantations in the family, and its demise reflected the poor use of considerable resources that had plagued the country—not to mention the impact of the period of violence—since the Spaniards arrived and began giving away the land to their soldiers and leaders in the form of *encomien-das*, which included not only the land but any families living on it.

Shortly after we returned from our honeymoon, I got to know Ligia better, especially when I was able to take part in some of her dreams. Evidently, both Ligia and her best friend, Mamane, spoke in their sleep. Mamane spoke in German, so her husband, Carlos, was clueless, but I didn't have that problem. Ligia would communicate in her sleep with her confidante, Mimi, her grandmother on her mother's side, who had died three years earlier. As a child, Ligia would stay at Mimi's when her parents went to the coast to manage the coffee plantation so she could go to a school in the capital city. Mimi was in fact Ligia's second mother.

One night, Ligia told Mimi she had considered dying so as to join her *abuela* and relieve me of the burden of her and our child. She also said she was hurt by my comment that it "takes more than love to have a family," as we'd also need money for the baby's clothes and food, as well as the apartment, and she wanted to give me the freedom she knew I desired to travel and learn. Dreams can be an important outlet for subconscious feelings and fears that might seem ridiculous during the day, with others around. I was being insensitive to Ligia's feelings and being way too pragmatic at all the wrong times, and this was a clear warning that I'd need to express how pleased I was at having our first child. After this, I began reminding Ligia that I thought that our first child wouldn't be our last.

On another night during our first months together, I decided to play along when Ligia was talking. I had to ask questions I knew Mimi might pose so I asked Ligia how Tío Coco was doing, and she responded, "*Babosiando como siempre.*" I would have fallen out of bed laughing, but that would have woken her up. *Babosiando* is a unique Guatemalan term indicating that he's goofing off, as usual.

She ended one dreamy conversation to Mimi with, "I'll write you a letter and visit you, and we'll never forget you—not ever." Which would probably be the case, as Ligia's mother and aunts held Mass for Mimi on the last day of every month for three years. Ligia would have named our child Mimi until I told her that one of my college girlfriends had the same name.

• • •

On December 27, I became the father of a six-pound, seven-ounce girl. The birth was a traumatic experience, since Ligia said she couldn't stand the labor pains, which began at three in the morning. We arrived at the clinic at 8:15 a.m., and the baby was born at 9:15 p.m. The clinic was just a few blocks from the Peace Corps office, but mum was the word, since the Peace Corps prohibited volunteers from marrying locals when still in service. Oops. But I wanted to serve my full term with the Peace Corps so I could participate in the inauguration of the new school in Calapté.

Initially, we couldn't find the doctor, which had something to do with his golf schedule. Eventually, he arrived and performed a cesarean because he claimed that the baby was suffering. I was waiting outside with Ligia's dad, Ricardo, so I had no idea what she was going through. At one point, I was struck by the realization that the child might die. I left the clinic and began walking, and the thoughts began running through my mind: *What if the baby dies? This little bit of life, which seemed destined for this world, might not make it?* My eyes filled with tears. But, subconsciously, there was another part of me reminding myself, *if this child lives, it means new responsibilities and less freedom of movement.*

Once our child was born, and after spending some time with Ligia in the clinic, my concern for the baby's health dwindled, and I was eager to see and hold her. The fear was gone, and now I was part of this mystery of life and would watch her pass through all the different life stages. And seeing Ligia's mom, dad, brothers, aunts, and cousins all pull together, concerned about Ligia's well-being during the operation, had also bound me closer to the family and made me more aware of what a strong, extended Guatemalan family was all about. I was amazed at the strength and cohesiveness of the Latin family structure.

Ricardo would cover most of our medical expenses over the years, including the births of our three children. I was a Peace Corps volunteer for part of our marriage, then a consultant with CARE in Guatemala on the one agroforestry assessment, followed by several years studying at the University of Texas at Austin, and then a few years helping to set up and obtain funding for FUNDECEDI (Foundation of Education and Development International). In all that time, we had no medical insurance of any kind. But when an emergency arose, Ricardo and Neta were always there, so we definitely benefited from this strong Latino family system and Ligia's parents' generosity.

We named the baby Michelle Germain (as in "Michelle, my belle" by the Beatles and the name of Ligia's favorite Belgian nun at her school), which was a nice change of pace since children are often named after one of their parents or grandparents. Once we took Michelle to our little apartment in Guatemala City, Ligia's family began to gang up on us to respond to the child's every whim. This was the part of the strong family tradition neither of us was crazy about. Everyone had his or her own opinion on how to care for the child, and I realized how important children were to this society. After the first week with our new baby, we were inundated with family pressure and second-guessing, even when we just left Michelle with the nanny in order to see a movie together. But we managed to ignore the guilt trip everyone tried to lay on us and we never left Michelle alone.

Ligia didn't have a lot of time to rest or recuperate. When Michelle was only ten days old, she went back to her teaching job in a wheelchair. Fortunately, the principal thanked her for attending the first teachers' meeting of the year, then sent her back home. But she was back to work in less than three weeks. I took care of the baby—with the nanny's help, of course—and wrote letter after letter to various universities, applying for a master's degree. Ligia was our only source of income at this point.

As soon as Michelle was old enough, we continued our treks down to the coffee plantation just before it was to be sold, in 1980. We got her a little green bathing suit so she could go wading in one of the small pools in the garden outside the big house on a hot day. She would splash around while great-grandfather Mariano looked on—and sometimes splashed him to everyone's delight.

The garden was filled with large and exotic tropical flowers such as bright orange birds-of-paradise and was perfectly pruned by several full-time gardeners whose key tool was a machete. No sit-down mowers here, despite the sizable property. Mariano kept six gardeners, old plantation workers, who received breakfast and lunch each day, then returned home, which seemed excessive and extremely inefficient until I realized that this was part of the plantation's "retirement" plan: to provide an easy task and a steady source of income to some of its older and more loyal workers. We always had at least one *muchacha* with Michelle all the time, so she had the run of the big house and the gardens without us worrying about where she was every second, although Ligia usually did anyway.

At the big house one afternoon in 1977, just before Christmas and Michelle's fourth birthday, I walked into the large living room with its high ceiling and shiny granite tiles. A large Christmas tree in the corner was covered with colorful ornaments, lights, and tinsel, and gifts piled underneath. Michelle wore a blue jumpsuit and held our new Airedale puppy, Tiki, in front of the tree, and out of the corner of my eye I saw no fewer than fifteen small children peering inside the room from behind the screen door off the back porch. These were the workers' children, who lived in the modest cinder block homes surrounding the big house,

many of which did not have indoor plumbing. They were all so innocent, so cute. And yet these children were relegated to peering in from
the other side of the screen and wouldn't dream of opening the door
and joining Michelle. This scene would be indelibly branded into my
brain because, although they too were nurtured by their families, it represented the sad and unjust disparity that existed in Guatemala between
the children of the haves and the have-nots, and the opportunities that
would or would not exist for them in the future.

• • •

B ut in my family, the children were protected, loved, and nurtured
by the extensive network of family members. We named our second
daughter Nicolle Kristine in honor of Ligia's Aunt Christi, who lived
in San Jerónimo and taught school for close to fifty years. Tía Christi's
daughter, Christabel, would also teach for fifty years, as would Ligia, for
over forty-five years, making for almost a century and a half of teaching
between them. Both Ligia and Christabel continue to teach. This was a
strong, determined group of women. We named our son John Henry because Johnnie Walker was popular in my new family, and John Henry was
a well-known folk hero in the U.S. Our son's official name is John Henry
Jerónimo for obvious reasons, and most Guatemalans have at least four
names anyway.

I was unprepared as a parent, so I depended on Ligia's good judg-
ment as a Latina, as well as her family and, of course, the ever-pres-
ent Catholic Church, to help bring up our children. We were living
in Guatemala City at the time. All three children were baptized in the
Catholic Church and had their First Communion there.

Ligia's parents would invite us on all expense paid weekend trips to
places like Antigua, the scenic colonial town an hour outside Guatemala
City. The Hotel Antigua was a colonial-era home outside the center of
town where several large bright red and green macaws would hang out

by the pool, screeching back and forth incessantly. The buffet had every-thing, and the service was top-notch. Several Maya women in their tra-ditional colorful clothing constantly stood next to an open fire, making fresh tortillas. Our other favorite place was the quaint little family-owned Nevada Inn, on top of the hill as you left the city. It was a simple home, with playground equipment for children, and the traditional fare was second to none. Ricardo would often order the pig knuckles, while I had *pavesa*, a clear chicken-based soup with a piece of bread and a soft-boiled egg in the center and cheese and ketchup on top.

One of our favorite stops on the way up to San Jerónimo, was the town of Esquipulas which was about three hours from Guatemala City, on the Honduran border. A magnificent colonial church off the central plaza was Central America's greatest pilgrimage center. Built in 1737, it was commissioned by Spanish conquistadors. The famous "Black Christ" was carved out of dark wood in 1594 and initially placed in a local church in 1595. It is now dressed in white satin and adorned with jewels. Major religious processions occur on January 15 and during Holy Week. Franciscan monks ran the church and provided a contemplative atmo-sphere. We'd always stay at a local hotel—Ricardo knew the owner—and we'd go to the church, enjoy the local cuisine, and walk around the mar-ket, with its stalls selling a myriad of trinkets, during the cool evenings.

We'd often stop at a stream, and Ricardo and the kids would put on their swimsuits and jump in. "Abuelazo" as he was known with the kids would walk out into the middle of the slow stream with Nicolle, and Michelle would float around on her pink inner tube. It was a great re-spite from the heat, as Esquipulas was in a very hot, arid area.

Ricardo had a small piece of land, where he grew tomatoes, next to a small river on the edge of San Jerónimo. San Jerónimo was my second site as a Peace Corps volunteer and where I first met Ligia. Her father would go up there almost every weekend, although it was a good three-to four-hour drive, to be close to the land he loved and his horses, of which he had several. His favorite was Zingaro, a spirited black Arabian known in the area for his high-stepping paces. Unfortunately, I always mistakenly called his horse Chingaro, which got a good laugh because, unbeknownst to me, it was a very dirty word—one of the few I hadn't learned by that time.

Ricardo owned a stable and a separate house with a few bedrooms and a dining area. The key feature was a covered porch with several hammocks where one could lie down and relax. At the end of the porch was my favorite bathroom: it had a giant tank like a small pool where one could cool off in the afternoon in the cold water from the mountains. Across the way, in a small house, lived the family who cared for the property when Ricardo was gone. Ricardo split the sale of the tomato crop with them. Chema was a faithful caretaker, a small but active guy with a great love of horses. His son Beto, no more than eight years old, would pull Michelle around the property in a tiny, blue-painted wooden car.

Ricardo would start the "barbi" with hot charcoal to grill some of the local beef, which he'd serve on a tortilla with a tomato sauce known as *chirmol*. Afterward, he and I would head for the hammocks for some undeserved rest. That was my idea of the good life. Michelle had her own small Brahma bull, and each child had his or her own horse.

When Johnnie was about six, he stayed with Ricardo one weekend and came back with a nasty rope burn on one of his hands. Evidently, he'd been told to hold the horse but forgot to tighten the rope on the saddle horn, so when the horse spooked and reared up, his hand was caught in the rope. Ricardo thought nothing of it and cleaned it up with some salve. Unfortunately, that didn't do the trick, and they ended up taking him to the emergency room due to the severity of the infection. Ligia informed me that he could have lost a finger.

This was in contrast with the majority of Guatemalans, who could not afford insurance. And when they had to enter a hospital, it was usually a public one, which meant it was crowded, filthy, and without basic medications and equipment.

Ligia always had a *muchacha* to help her take care of the children and the house, and they became an important part of our family, as we trusted them with the lives and well-being of our children. She regretted losing this advantage when we eventually moved to the States. Even when we moved to Bogotá, Colombia, with Plan International, one of the big five child sponsorship organizations, Neta paid for our *muchacha*, Marina La Tata, to accompany us. Marina had never left Guatemala before, so Ligia and her mom had to spend some time convincing her to move with us.

We had nine *muchachas* with us over the years. We'd pay them the going wage, which was minimal, and they'd get Sundays off. In Guatemala they were all from the coffee plantation, San Francisco Miramar, which provided the entire family with a steady source of well-trained household help. La *Naiya* had been with Ligia's mom and then came with us. She was a small lady with large dark eyes and short black hair, and she usually wore a light-colored cotton dress with simple plastic shoes. She was good with the children. Naiya would die in the 1978 earthquake, which caused over 27,000 fatalities.

Marina La Tata was smaller still, with long black hair and light brown eyes, and always got along well with the children. She was responsible for our youngest, John. She would be up first thing each morning and stay busy all day with chores, from cleaning the dishes to putting the children to bed at night. On Sunday most of the *muchachas* would head for the nearby park to socialize with their friends.

The children received the best education and nurturing wherever we went, as we always had a strong support system, and by this time I was actually getting paid a living wage. In Colombia and, later, in Sierra Leone, we always had a driver and staff to help us out. I remember my assistant in Sierra Leone, Steve, watched the children a few times, which was definitely not part of his job description. One day, when we left, Nicolle, who was only five or so, told him, "You need to spank us if we're bad." I don't know where that came from, but they were always well taken care of.

Ligia's parents Ricardo and la Neta visited us in Scottsdale, Arizona, where we currently live, several times over the years. They had been only to the southern part of Mexico and parts of Central America in the past—this would be the first time they'd travel to the States. We were able to bring all our children and friends together and take them to all the right cowboy and horsey places that Ricardo loved. We'd check out the Arabian horse event at West World, where we saw some of the most impressive horses in the U.S.

All of this travel and changing homes and friends every three years with Plan International had its downside. After departing Sierra Leone, it took me longer than I had anticipated to solidify a position in Denver, where I set up the regional office for CARE International. So Ligia and the children stayed in Guatemala, and when they finally arrived in Denver and we registered the children in local schools, Johnnie, who was six or seven, came home crying the first day because he couldn't speak English. Ligia requested special classes, but within a week he was speaking English like everyone else.

• • •

I always insisted on speaking Spanish at home, which is why I'm still fluent, not to mention that I married my own tutor, who has been patiently correcting my grammar for over forty years. To this day I read *Prensa Libre*, a Guatemalan newspaper, listen to the news on Spanish-speaking Univision, and read Spanish-language novels by some of the outstanding authors from Latin America.

My personal specialization in Spanish was in Guatemalan slang and profanity, as I had some excellent teachers in the slum areas and isolated villages I worked in over the years. Drinking the occasional beer with my professional counterparts in the highlands and spicing up my language with terms only Guatemalans know was always a sure way to get a laugh and connect with the locals. To begin with, I'd always use *vos*, which is the familiar form of the personal pronoun *you*, as opposed to the standard and more formal *usted*. I'd always refer to Guatemalans as *chapines*, which is how they refer to themselves, as opposed to Costa Ricans who are collectively known as *ticos*. Nuances that reflect a deeper understanding of how language is used differ from country to country.

Over the years, I'd use a number of terms of endearment for Ligia, like *mi amor* (my love), *mi amorcita* (my tiny love), *mija* (little girl), *muñeca* (doll), *amor de amores* (love of loves), but the one I stuck with over the years was *chubleta*, a nonsense word that started as *chula* (pretty), then *chulita* (a small, pretty girl), and eventually morphed into *chubleta*. Ligia, in turn, would call me *amorcito* (my love) and *cielo* (the sky).

Here are a few of my personal favorite Guatemalan slang terms:

- *a la gran*: oh my God (I have always used it in the form *a la gran puta*, see below.)
- *babosadas*: things (I use it to mean all kinds of "things.")
- *bolo*: drunk
- *cabal*: right on
- *caite*: sandal
- *canche*: blond (They also used it to describe the reddish-haired Ligia, so it can mean anyone with lighter-colored hair.)
- *chamaco, güiro, patojo*: child
- *ishto*: brat
- *pisto*: money
- *poporopo*: popcorn

My most frequently used expletives include:

- *a la gran chucha*: a female dog, bitch
- *a la gran puta*: the great whore
- *la chingada*: oh fuck
- *pisado*: bastard
- *que comes mierda*: eat shit
- *cerote*: a turd

And I could go on . . .

All our children spoke excellent Spanish, and Michelle became a certified simultaneous translator—a skill that is a real gift. All three children also learned French or German through the Rotary Youth Exchange program. I can get by in Krio, a creole spoken in Sierra Leone, and Portuguese. Speaking multiple languages opens one's mind and worldview as nothing else. Americans are at a major disadvantage against Europeans, most of whom speak three or four languages.

Over the years, we hosted several receptions for the "immediate" family in Guatemala. The first time was in 2000, after Ricardo died, when we invited most of Ligia's family to her mom's home in Utatlan II in Guatemala City, but we didn't tell Neta about our plans, as she would have freaked out at the thought of so many people at her home. She did freak out, in fact, but fortunately, her two sisters, Regi and Rosa, attended, as they hadn't seen one another for quite some time (although they both lived in Guatemala City). We had lots of Guatemalan finger foods, tamales, tacos, and black beans. The table, which we set up in Neta's driveway, was packed with small children, all chatting and having a great time. Naturally, I had a few beers, and the Johnnie Walker was in the back, just in case.

• • •

Thirteen years later, we'd organize a visit to Guatemala with Nicolle and John and their significant others, which was important if our children were to maintain their family ties and love of their first country. We headed to San Lucas Tolimán on Lake Atitlán and stayed at the Hotel Tolimán, which was run by our dear friend from World Neighbors days (a group I worked with for six years), Chati. We'd stayed in touch with Chati over the years; she's a lawyer and helped us with several property ownership issues. The hotel was quaint, with individual bungalows, each with its own fireplace, which was great during those rainy, chilly evenings. The restaurant looked off to one of the most spectacular lakes in the world, Atitlán, with massive volcanoes looming in the distance. All of us enjoyed the Guatemalan food. We started each morning looking off to the lake with our hot coffee, black beans and cream, tortillas, eggs, plantains, and papaya with a wedge of lemon.

During our week together, we visited Panajachel, Patzun, Chichicastenango, San Martín, Antigua, and Guatemala City. The highlight, though, was another family reunion, which, included almost 100 of our "immediate" family (just like at our wedding, all those years before). By then, some of our kids' cousins had their own children, so it was a great opportunity for everyone to catch up. We brought a collage of photos taken in Guatemala when the children were smaller. Ligia's Aunt Christi was almost ninety-six, but was up with the roosters to remind everyone that this was "Ligia's day" and they needed to head to Guatemala City, over four hours away, and the party. This was the first time in years that the three teachers—Ligia, Christi, and Christi's daughter Christabel—were together. We had a great *churrasco* (barbecue) at an event venue known as Las Orquídeas in the renovated home of a former plantation on the road to Antigua.

In the end, you can never tell how your lifestyle and values impact your children. I admit that I had the advantage of an attentive and loving wife, an extended family, and lots of good friends, who provided love and guidance for my children. I always felt that one of our biggest advantages of living abroad with the relief and development community is that we were in constant contact and interaction with people whom I'd consider the salt of the earth. But when my friends at Food for the Hungry put together a "Fifty Birthday Wishes and Stories for Mark Walker's 50th Birthday," all three of my children shared their thoughts, which were very moving. Michelle was twenty-six; Nicolle, twenty-one; and John, eighteen.

Querido Papi (Dearest Dad):
Remember when you would sing to me all those cowboy songs and play the harmonica to put me to sleep? Yes, I know you will try to deny it, but all those years living as a hobo on Amtrak really did pay off! No, really, Dad, I have very fond memories of those wonderful days. You are a great dad, always reaching out to your kids. I love our hikes every weekend; you do

a great job motivating me to get off my lazy butt! I am amazed you can actually accomplish the incredible feat of ungluing John off the computer seat to play racquetball, and I'm sure your other 2 kids [our Airedale terriers, Tiki and Luke] really love those hikes. You are el numero uno de los papis!!! I hope you have a great birthday and many mooooore!

Love, Michelle

For the past 20 years of my life, I've been lucky enough to have traveled with & gotten to know you. You have taught me so much about the importance of travel and knowledge of different cultures. You've always pushed me to go for my dreams, no matter how difficult they seem at first. For the past 3 years or so, my interests have been increasingly running towards travel. What better person to look to for inspiration than you? The biggest impression you've had on me has occurred over the past 2 years, when my dreams of travel have come into reality. Encouraging me to pursue my dreams of living in France and further encouraging me to explore Canada have broadened my horizons completely. I can't thank you enough for always pushing me to reach for the stars and see the world while I'm young. So much of what I do now has roots in what you taught me through your own experiences and through your constant support and encouragement to create my own adventures. I will never forget our stroll through Annecy in the French Alps or our Corona (beer) on the Seine in Paris. Maybe next time it will be a hike through the Amazon! Why not . . . you've taught me to be a dreamer & encouraged me to make those dreams reality. So, here's to another year of travel and adventure.

Cheers, Papi! Love, Nicky

Dear Daddy,

Now, you've always done fun things with me. Biked, hiked, thrown the football around, launched a rocket here and there, played racquetball, and other things. I've really enjoyed these things tremendously, but I've never really gotten a chance to thank you. Our recent plan of action includes playing rac-quetball and going to a baseball game occasionally. I just want to thank you

for giving me the chance to do fun, interesting things with you. I've always appreciated you, though not always said so.
With lots of love from your son, John

• • •

O ne thing I learned from my father-in-law was to invite our kids to do fun, interesting things, which always offers better opportunities to spend quality time with them. In our case, it's usually been traveling to different parts of the country and the world. We also tried to instill a love of reading and the importance of learning other languages and appreciating other cultures. And after all is said and done, our three kids turned out exceptionally well and took the best from each culture they experienced, so I can't really take much of the credit.

When Michelle was just months old and my relationship with Ligia deepened, my plans to travel throughout Latin America grew. I was indeed a rambling man and continued to work on a strategy to see everything south of Guatemala before settling down, although circumstances (the most obvious being our first child) would force some adjustments to this plan.

Four

A Tramp Abroad: The Journey from Guatemala City to Southern Chile and Back

Lord, I was born a ramblin' man,
Tryin' to make a livin' and doin' the best I can.
And when it's time for leavin',
I hope you'll understand,
That I was born a ramblin' man.

The Allman Brothers Band, "Ramblin Man"

What is life but a series of inspired follies? The difficulty is to
find them to do. Never lose a chance: it doesn't come every day.

George Bernard Shaw, *Pygmalion*

"Y ou're going where? For how long? And we've got a month-old baby?"

Ligia was not a happy camper, especially since I wasn't planning to leave her with any money (I just had enough for this trip, actually). But once we returned from our honeymoon drive through Mexico, I was still determined to fulfill a dream I'd held since joining the Peace Corps: using my knowledge of Spanish to travel throughout Latin America. Ligia's parents complained that I wasn't serious about the relationship. Her friends and cousins were appalled. Her aunt Regi said she could move into her large home while I was gone. Doña Lisa Jacobstal, the mother of her closest friend, Maria Rene, offered Ligia an apartment in their new apartment complex. She'd charge Ligia only half her salary, which wasn't close to the actual rent (including utilities) of the furnished apartment. Ligia's father would cover all the medical expenses, as usual, and provide any clothing they'd need.

I'll have to admit that I felt ambivalent about leaving my wife and child behind. I knew I'd miss them and that I had a responsibility as a husband and father, but I was still focused on my goal of seeing the world, starting with as much of Latin America as possible. Ligia was relatively philosophical about this rather bizarre state of affairs, and many years later, I would ask her what she was thinking when I headed out. She said that she adhered to the message of Chilean poet Pablo Neruda:

Well, now,
if little by little you stop loving me
I shall stop loving you little by little.

. . . .

and you decide
to leave me at the shore
of the heart where I have roots,
remember
that on that day,
at that hour,
I shall lift my arms
and my roots will set off
to seek another land.

In May 1974 I headed out alone with a backpack, with the goal to see all the major countries except Venezuela which was more inaccessible by land than most of the other South American countries, following most of Paul Theroux's "Essential Tao of Travel":

- Leave home
- Go alone
- Travel light
- Bring a map
- Go by land
- Walk across a national frontier
- Keep a journal
- Read a novel that has no relation to the place you're in
- If you must bring a cell phone, avoid using it
- Make a friend

I'd use the *South American Handbook* as my guide. This travel guide, published in the UK provides detailed information on each country, including what to see and where to stay. The most I ever paid for a hotel was $2.35, in Lima. I focused on visiting as many historic and scenic sites as possible.

Throughout Central America, I was amazed at the vast, commercial farmland filled with cotton and sugarcane—but no people. In San Salvador, my first stop, I thought that I was passing through a large public park, but it was the garden of a palatial home. It belonged to one of the famous "fourteen families" who controlled most of the land and the wealth of El Salvador.

There were actually dozens of families in El Salvador who, by the middle of the nineteenth century, were feudal lords. These wealthy landowners were granted an enormous majority of power in the national legislature and economy. Indigo, which was used as a dye, was replaced by coffee, making the farmlands quite valuable. As in Guatemala, the elite-controlled legislature and president passed vagrancy laws to remove people from the land, causing the majority of Salvadorans to become landless and clearing the way for these extensive gardens and vast fields of cotton and sugarcane. And yet in more recent times like the people in Guatemala City, the upper and growing middle class of San Salvadorans had access to large supermarkets, radios, televisions, cars, clothing, McDonald's, Dairy Queen, Kentucky Fried Chicken, and many other U.S. imports.

Crossing the borders at each of these small Central American countries was always an adventure that made me think Graham Greene's observations on seeing the U.S.-Mexico border for the first time: "The border means more than a customs house, a passport officer, a man with a gun. Over there everything is going to be different; life is never going to be quite the same again after your passport has been stamped."

Usually the border staff would mess around for almost an hour before they even inspected anything, in an attempt to leverage a kickback, or *mordida*. Since I was usually on foot or on a public bus and couldn't speak the best Spanish, I had to be patient as the guards positioned themselves to get a few dollars out of the gringo hippie. They would soon learn that this was like getting blood out of a turnip—and I learned the value of patience.

Panama was my last stop before heading into Colombia. I noted in my journal, "I was really impressed at the vigor and life that these people demonstrated in their celebrations and the distinctiveness of doing it. Maybe their culture hadn't been completely gringoized—not yet."

Panama City was a veritable array of tropical music, commerce, and vibrant nightlife. The Panama Canal—or Big Ditch, as it was called—was one of the engineering feats of the century. I jumped on the Panama Canal Railway and made the forty-seven-mile trip to Colón. The Railway was opened in 1855 and called an interoceanic railroad. It cost eight million dollars to build—eight times the initial estimate—and between 5,000 and 10,000 workers died from cholera, malaria, and yellow fever. Another 25,000 workers were killed on the joint construction of the canal by the French and Americans.

I sat by an open window as the canal and jungle slipped by and the damp, warm air passed through my hair. The train, which was pulled by a massive diesel engine, passed under a long line of trees with dark green leaves. As we arrived at the station, I noticed a large Johnnie Walker sign on top of one of the large buildings. Colón is a large port with colorful buildings covered with moss and plants hanging over the side rails of the porches above.

I was having such a good time wandering around this beautiful little country that I almost missed my flight out of Panama City by managing to choose a bus that stopped every few minutes. When I realized that my flight would be leaving in thirty minutes, I jumped off the bus and took a cab. I arrived four minutes before the flight was to depart. The airline staff said it was too late to board the plane, but I, along with two others in a similar situation, complained, so the clerk decided to talk with her supervisor. Five minutes later, she burst out of the office and began processing the tickets. The staff rushed us through, and I ran to the plane (which should have already departed but of course this was Latin America)—only to find that it was almost empty.

• • •

In Colombia, I headed immediately for one of the most beautiful towns in Latin America, Cartagena. It represents an eclectic mix of Caribbean, African, and Spanish tastes and sounds, some of which were due to influence of slavery on the Pacific coast. Then I went to the modern city of Bogotá, which is over 8,000 feet above sea level, making it the third highest in Latin America. Little did I know I'd be returning there with my family to live for three years. Then it was on to Cali, a sensuous, tropical center of salsa music, as well as the rumba. It boasted the most beautiful women in Latin America. The commercial streets were filled with lovely ladies of all skin and hair tones gliding along with their friends. All were dressed to the nines in stylish blouses, short skirts, and impressive jewelry. The city and everything about it was outstanding.

Since I was traveling alone and not given to look for company, I was fortunate to meet a taxi driver, Carlitos, whom I got to know. Instead of taking me to a cheap hotel, as I'd requested, he decided to take me to his home for a meal with his family. Carlitos had a basic education and was barely able to support his wife, Margarita, and daughter, Angela, with his earnings. Margarita prepared fresh bread that she sold at the local market.

Carlitos asked me to speak English to eight-year-old Angela, who was studying the language at school. Margarita prepared some chicken, along with what would become one of my favorite foods, *patacónes*, or *tostones*, green plantains that are cut, smashed, cooked in oil, smashed again, and cooked one final time, then salted. She also served *pan de bono*, which was like French bread with a cheesy flavor.

The family's kindness contradicted the stories I'd heard about tourists being ripped off. I had written in my journal, "I'll feel lucky if I can get out of Colombia with my camera and watch. I met one gringo who had his shirt and money bag cut through in order to take the money inside." I wore a money belt and kept my camera close by at all times. I left Colombia, and all the countries I visited on this trip, without any losses.

After breakfast, I said good-bye to Margarita and Angela, and Carlitos drove me to the bus station, where I'd continue my journey to Pasto, on the border with Ecuador. After a long trip south over relatively good roads, I arrived at the Central Market and soon found a family-run hotel. This little *pensión* overlooked the Central Market, so when I opened my second-story window in the morning, I saw a line of dead rats hanging there to be sold. My first reaction was "Gross!" The next morning, I had breakfast outside the hotel, next to the market, and asked the waiter about the rats. The waiter explained, "No, señor, those are actually giant guinea pigs we call *cuy*. They are very popular to eat both here and in Ecuador."

So there you have it—they're yummy, as well as cute and furry. I'd be confronted with this delicacy in Peru and Bolivia. They are usually fried and taste a lot like chicken. You eat them with your fingers and I always paid attention, as they have many tiny bones.

Ecuador reminded me a lot of Guatemala. A good portion of the population is Indigenous I actually went through Ecuador twice, once going down and again coming back. Quito is a beautiful city at 8,000 feet, making it the second-highest capital in the hemisphere. I admired the colonial district's architecture and monuments, including the Church of San Augustin, where the Ecuadoran declaration of independence from Spain was signed in 1809. La Ronda, one of the oldest streets in Quito, was one of my favorite areas. The narrow, cobbled pedestrian ways led to colonial homes with wrought iron balconies, as well as restaurants, bars, and cultural centers. I felt like I was in a time warp. I bought a short green and yellow poncho, or *ruana*, which would prove invaluable when passing over the often frigid Andes. The clear air and high altitude suited me as I wandered around, taking in so much history and culture.

The next leg of the trip, from Quito to the coast and the hotter, brasher, and more vibrant city of Guayaquil, provided some of the most spectacular scenery of my trek through Ecuador. I took an old steam engine out of Quito and went past some of the largest, most imposing volcanoes on the continent, like Chimborazo, which is over 20,000 feet high. The engine passed Riobamba and began to descend down to the Pacific coast. The stretch known as the Devil's Nose was so steep that the tracks actually went back and forth on some switchbacks. As the train descended, everything became greener. Then clouds engulfed the train, and coffee plantations began to appear. Finally, the train headed into the hot, humid, filthy city of Guayaquil, a busy industrial port surrounded by some of the poorest slums imaginable. This trip from the arid highlands to the lush green coastal area reminded me of my initial pickup trip from my village of Calapté to the imposing volcano Tajumulco and down to the South Coast of Guatemala.

Peru, like much of Latin America, has a diverse topography and culture. It's an imposing country off the Pacific Coast that is often shrouded in ocean mist. The three delicacies I enjoyed most during my stay were pisco sours, a rum-based drink with an egg and lemon thrown in; *escabeche de pescado*, a baked fish dish with tons of onions;and *ceviche*, raw fish with onions and lime. For the rest of my life, I'd have fond memories of Peru when tasting these traditional dishes.

My plan to head for Cuzco and the ruins of Machu Picchu were thwarted by a major landslide outside Huancayo, so I figured I'd continue south to Ica and Nazca, which is where the world famous Nazca Lines were etched in the desert by a civilization several thousand years before the Spaniards. Overlooking the town is Cerro Blanco, the highest sand dune in the world, at over 6,000 feet. The museums in the area displayed pristine pieces of pottery and mummies that were well preserved because of the extreme aridity.

Unable to reach Cuzco by train, I planned to head south, through Chile, and come back to Lima from Cuzco on my return from Bolivia, then head up north to Guatemala. Who would have thought that two months later the landslide would still not be removed? So I kept going until I hit Arequipa, which stands at the foot of the perfect snowcapped cone of the volcano Misti. The city has impressive Spanish buildings and churches. I learned that the city had been refounded in 1540 by an emissary of Pizarro but had previously been occupied by the Aymara and the Inca. This more circuitous route would help me avoid using the same roads twice in a row, a lesson I'd learned back in the States, between Crested Butte and Oklahoma City.

Throughout this part of the trip I kept hearing about the Shining Path (*Sendero Luminoso*), a fanatical Peruvian Maoist terrorist group that was started in the highlands in the 1960s by Abimael Guzmán, a Marxist philosopher who worked at the University San Cristóbal of Huamanga in Ayacucho. Their main objective was to kill as many local leaders and government officials as possible in order to throw the country into chaos and restructure based on their own form of governance. They claimed that the peasants were the essential revolutionary class because, unlike the industrial workers, who were limited in Peru, the peasants were better suited to establishing a Socialist society. Reportedly, over 30,000 Peruvians were killed during the fighting, mostly at the hands of the Shining Path, although a third reportedly died at the hands of government security forces that focused on peasant and union leaders.

My next step would be Chile which was also in the midst of a major political upheaval when I entered the country by bus. I knew that the *militares* would be wary of any longhairs with backpacks, so I got a haircut in Arequipa. When we reached the border, the *militares* pulled off a number of passengers with long hair and cut it themselves. This was not pretty, as the young soldiers had definitely missed hairstyling class and were obviously more familiar with submachine guns than shears. Although I joke about this now, I was petrified by these young, barely trained "soldiers" toting dangerous weapons—as were many of my fellow travelers.

On September 11, 1973, the Chilean military staged a coup to overthrow Salvador Allende. Like President Jacobo Árbenz in Guatemala, twenty years before, Allende was popularly elected, and, as in Guatemala, the CIA helped finance the coup that ousted him. President Nixon authorized ten million dollars for the CIA to overthrow Allende. General Pinochet's takeover initiated a period of political assassinations and disappearances that claimed the lives of 3,000 students and activists. This period would be dramatized in the movie *Missing*, with Jack Lemmon and Sissy Spacek, based on the true story of an American journalist who disappeared in the bloody aftermath of the coup.

I left Peru on a bus that careened south over the Atacama Desert, one of the driest in the world, until I reached Chile's capital, Santiago. The city reminded me of what I expected in Bavaria, Germany - old buildings and beautiful parks, with majestic mountains looming overhead. Santiago was under a state of siege, so I had to return early to my hotel. Soldiers were all over the place, enough to make me nervous, even though I wasn't involved with anything illegal or subversive. I was suspect by the local authorities on several levels: I was an outsider, traveling by myself, as well as being a young "hippie type". With the dangers and uncertainties caused by the state of siege, this was not a time to ignore government mandates, so I was in my hotel each evening well before the curfew.

I was always looking for cheap restaurants, but the *mariscos* (seafood) I had with wine must have harbored some bacteria because I woke up the next morning deathly ill with food poisoning. I ended up in a local hospital, in a room filled with beds behind curtains and nurses walking around. When asked if I had medical insurance (which I didn't), I showed them my Peace Corps Guatemala identification card (which had expired), and they didn't probe any further. The local Peace Corps office covered several days in the hospital. Fortunately, this would be the only time during the four-month journey when I'd fall ill, but it did provide an opportunity to reflect on my trip and appreciate how much I missed Ligia and my daughter and begin thinking about heading north, toward home.

I boarded an old steam engine from Santiago to the most-southern point one can go by land, Chiloé Island. The train kept a leisurely pace through some gorgeous green countryside. When it stopped to take on more passengers, I jumped off to gather some of the many wild blackberries growing beside the tracks. I stuffed as many as possible into my mouth, as I was craving fresh fruit—and it was free.

From Puerto Montt, I headed back up north, to the Lake District, between Chile and Argentina, which represented the most spectacular scenery on the entire journey. Transportation through the twelve lakes in the area included buses, backs of trucks, and boats. I was mesmerized as we floated past imposing waterfalls and snowcapped volcanoes, including Osorno. One of the islands had strange, barkless trees, which were the inspiration for some of Disney's fantasies.

The last part of this multi-vehicle journey through the Lake District only got better as we went through Nahuel Huapí National Park, the oldest park in Argentina. Our little boat glided past even more lakes, rivers, glaciers, waterfalls, rapids, torrents, forests, bare mountains, and snow-covered peaks. I definitely needed my *ruana* from Ecuador, as it got nippy at night. The lakes came alive during the day with swans, geese, and ducks, to name a few of the visiting waterfowl.

The spectacular ski resort of Bariloche is situated on the south shore of Lake Nahuel Huapí, at the foot of Cerro Otto. I was excited about checking out some of the many chocolate shops among its chalet-style stone and wood buildings and was able to stock up on chocolate for the remainder of my journey. The white chocolate was especially tempting and tasty. I really missed Ligia, as she would have loved all the rich chocolates bulging from the quaint little shops, and I was pleased to finally be heading back north.

At the heart of the city was the Centro Cívico, built in Bariloche alpine style, separated from the lake by one broad boulevard. On my way, I met a girl named Anna, who wanted to chat about my trip, as she was taking a boat ride later that day. Like many young people I'd meet, she wanted to speak English. Anna was about sixteen, with light brown hair tied back in a ponytail. She wore a white sweater, jeans, and light pink tennies. During our conversation, I began to appreciate all the things to see in her hometown, Buenos Aires: the best places to eat, where they dance the tango, and which museums to see. She said she was going home in a few days, so I asked if I could tag along. I saw her the next day, before she left on her boat tour, and she told me that her father said they wouldn't have enough room—although I realized it was my hippie-like appearance that caused him to decline.

Undeterred, I took the next bus to Buenos Aires, which was much like what I'd expect to see in a historic city in Italy with wide boulevards running into central plazas filled with large statues. Over sixty percent of the population is of Italian heritage. Years later, when Ligia and I were staying at a hostels in Venice, we heard *porteños* (a term used for those living in Buenos Aires) complaining bitterly about how dirty and old everything was in Venice. They were just as obnoxiously proud of their town as the New Yorkers I'd met during my Peace Corps training.

Along one of the broad boulevards was a big nightclub and movie theater so I watched a number of good movies and hung out, enjoying the nightlife in the warm evenings. I also visited a number of museums and art galleries. As I strolled through one of the history museums, I realized that almost all the art and history I was seeing related to the top five percent of the society. The largest homes, biggest businesses, newest modes of transportation, were developed for the upper classes and the products they produced. I never saw much on how the common people lived. That's often how history is interpreted—from the perspective of the ruling and educated classes—so if you want to see how the other half lives (well, the other ninety-five percent), you need to get out of the business districts and tourist centers. One of the advantages of not having any money was that I was forced to eat and sleep where the majority of the people lived. I never spent any time in the local Hilton, that's for sure!

Anna had given me her home phone number and invited me to partake in their afternoon *mate* hour—the Argentine version of the British afternoon teatime. Anna's dad, Javier, informed me that when Jesuit missionaries first came to Argentina, they tried to ban the popular indigenous tea, *yerba mate*, out of concern about its addictive qualities. Fortunately for all concerned, the missionaries reversed their stance and began cultivating *yerba mate* on the plantations in the provincial mission until their expulsion from the Americas, in 1767. By then, the popularity of the tea had permeated all levels of society.

Anna's family sat in a circle and sipped the *mate* through a silver straw from a gourd filled with hot water. The straw is like a sieve, so the tea is sucked without the leaves. The tea is slightly bitter, with an earthy taste. It takes some time to get used to, but I still drink it, to this day. I assumed that the water was hot enough to kill any communicable diseases. Soon it was "*che* this" and "*che* that" (a familiar way of saying "you," similar to the famil-iar pronoun *vos* in Guatemala). Javier learned that I was married, with a child, and traveling to learn as much as I could about Latin America, and he was impressed by my relatively good Spanish. Consequently, I passed the test and was invited to dinner and eventually spent a few nights in his modest apartment on the tenth floor of a housing complex.

Javier was a sales representative for a chain of automotive parts stores. He was a smallish guy with graying hair and a dark mustache. Anna was actually as tall as her father. On our last night together, they took me to a nice restaurant downtown where they danced the tango on the sidewalk. The juicy steak and dry red wine comprised what would be my favorite meal on the trip so far, and we laughed about Javier's initial concerns for the safety of his daughter when he initially met me in the Lake District.

After a quick breakfast the next day, I said good-bye to Anna and her family and boarded a hydroplane for the quick trip across the Río de la Plata, to Montevideo, and from there into the tiny country of Paraguay. Along the way, I stopped off at the most spectacular single feature on this journey, the Iguaçú Falls, located at the intersection of four countries: Argentina, Uruguay, Brazil, and Paraguay. When I saw the spectacular scene, I had to agree with Eleanor Roosevelt, who, on seeing the falls, declared, "Poor Niagara." Niagara Falls, which I'd seen as a child, was a third of the depth of Iguaçú Falls. For most of its course, the river flowed through Brazil, although the falls are on the Argentine side. The name Iguaçú comes from the Guarani word for "water." The falls are surround-ed by a lush jungle filled with birds and animals. I hung around for sev-eral days, watching the abundant wildlife and constant mist coming off the massive falls. One evening, while gazing over to Brazil and studying a map of the region, I realized, *I can't say I've been through Latin America if I haven't seen Brazil. It covers almost half of South America.* So I gave myself three weeks to see as much of the country as I could.

From the Iguaçú, I headed for San Juan Bautista in Paraguay, the home of Zapata and Luz, my former Peace Corps trainers in Ponce, Before I left Puerto Rico, Zapata let me know that he was returning to the field as a Peace Corps volunteer, and when I went through the Paraguayan capital, Asunción, I stopped by the Peace Corps office and found his site location. I took a bus up to his community and walked to his home, where I saw his imposing figure, with cowboy hat and Ray-Ban sunglasses, from a distance. Luz was as tall and slim as I remembered, with a beautiful face and brown eyes. They made an impressive couple. They'd both adapted well to the local community and introduced me to several friends from small ranches close by. San Juan was a rural community whose economy depended totally on agriculture. Zapata worked with some of the cattle ranchers on their extensive ranches.

A Vietnam vet, Zapata had been injured on the front and received a Silver Star. To him, the torture, brutality, and napalm he saw, as well as the shrapnel that mutilated innocent villagers, were all realities of war. He didn't condone the war but understood its laws. He believed that if one hostage could provide beneficial information that might save one American soldier, he should be tortured—whatever it took to get that information.

One evening, over *mate*, I told Zapata, "Isn't it a shame that the U.S. is always used as a model for so many developing countries while our country suffers from the destruction of our moral fabric, rising levels of alcoholism, drug addiction, and mental illness? In reality, Latin Americans could certainly teach us some important things about human relations."

Zapata didn't accept this line of thought. "Most Latin Americans would accept the problems in your country over the poverty and lack of jobs and opportunities they're facing in their own countries."

One day we visited one of the large farmers (*finqueros*) he worked with. He had 5,000 hectares (almost twenty square miles) with 2,600 cattle. I was expecting to find a big hacienda but instead found a modest home, a tiny Toyota, and no electricity. Zapata informed me that President Stroessner was one of the wealthiest men in the world because he'd made the country his fiefdom, which included controlling all modes of communication and the economy.

When I questioned the United States' support of Stroessner, Zapata countered with, "It's pragmatic. Our military was allowed to construct El

Pozo Colorado, a military base in the Chaco where nobody can enter, and it's strategically located between Argentina, Uruguay, Brazil, and Bolivia. The base was used to train anti-guerrilla groups. Bottom line," Zapata summarized, "money talks and bullshit walks." Obviously, our worldviews were worlds apart, although we were both part of the same organization and Zapata certainly helped me appreciate how things work in Latin America. But our differences of opinion would not change his being a gracious host.

Luz was a health worker with the poorer farm families. She was still overwhelmed by the unsanitary conditions and ignorance she found in the rural areas of Paraguay. Dishes unwashed for days because there was no clean water; flies everywhere, especially on food; and animals wandering in and out of the kitchen were all part of the problem. Often the children weren't cleaned up. Luz mentioned one child who was left in the kitchen alone with milk on his fingers, and a pig ate the fingers. Another baby lost an ear under similar circumstances.

Like Guatemala, Paraguay was a small country with a large Indigenous population. It was one of the most bilingual countries in the world, as everyone speaks Spanish and Guarani. In recent history, over a quarter of the population was forced to leave the country in search of a job. Over sixty percent were farmers at the time, although the majority of the land was unoccupied or underutilized for cattle grazing. As in Guatemala and El Salvador, the distribution of this land was skewed in favor of a few families. One study indicated that twenty-five Paraguayan families owned seventeen million hectares—almost half of the country.

President Stroessner's stranglehold on Paraguay was reflected by the circumstances of a teacher I met. His position had to be approved by the military boss of the district; the president's political party, the Colorado Party; the head of the police; and, last but not least, the ministry of education.

Luz was an excellent cook and had learned all the basic Paraguayan cuisine. A typical breakfast in Paraguay consisted of bread, butter, coffee, and milk (I skipped the milk, which might carry tuberculosis). For lunch we had yucca soup with vegetables and meat, a tomato and potato salad, a sweet *guayaba paste which one ate on a piece of bread* and a cup of strong coffee. We drank *mate* in the afternoons, and soon I had my own silver straw and gourd. My favorite meal was pizza de Paraguay, a yucca-based crust with tomato sauce and cheese on top, baked in a bread oven. I'd always think of Argentina and Paraguay while sipping a cup of *mate*.

Father Bellini of San Juan Bautista was a short, thin man with a dark complexion, black hair, and dark eyes, an Italian priest who had worked in the area for ten years. He received a BA in theology and an MA in law and had worked in rural, poverty-stricken areas of Sussex, England, as well as skid row in Paris. His mail was heavily controlled by the military, so he communicated with friends in Italian—with a code. He had documented the killing of three peasant activists by the government. I sat down with him for several meals and traditional passing of the gourd with hot water and *mate* before he trusted me enough to share his story.

The United States and USAID, as well as the Peace Corps, were all suspect to the locals, based on the strong relationship between Stroessner and the U.S. government. Between 1962 and 1975, the U.S. provided $146 million to the military government, and their officers trained at the U.S. Army School of the Americas. Stroessner provided refuge to such dictators as Anastasio Somoza, the dictator from Nicaragua. Three thousand to four thousand people were murdered, and 400 to 500 more disappeared. Years later, the military's complicity with the drug cartel would be revealed.

Historically, the priests, especially the Jesuits, had a strong influence on the Guarani population, especially in the Chaco region, which borders Bolivia. Father Bellini had recently sent five families to a 9,000-hectare kibbutz-like arrangement. Each family received the equivalent of sixty acres to live on and some basic social services not normally provided by the government. The priest shared stories of several white elephant projects financed by USAID. They sent an expensive harvester (bought in the U.S., of course) without checking out the local needs or ability to maintain such a sophisticated piece of equipment. On top of that, the crop harvested by the machine didn't even grow locally. This wouldn't be the last time I'd hear of, or see, examples of poorly conceived development programs supported by the U.S. government.

April 30ᵗʰ was *Día del Maestro* (Day of the Teacher), one of Paraguay's most important celebrations. Everyone in the town surrounded the basketball court, where a group played gringo rock music sung in broken English, as well as some romantic Latin music and a lot of polka, complete with dancing (that European influence again). Fortunately, my time in Crested Butte, which has a strong Croatian influence, had prepared me for this event, and much to the surprise of the locals I polkaed like everyone else, doing circles and cross steps.

People at the dance appreciated my participation at their fiesta. One old guy brought out glasses of whiskey to the dance patio three times, so I chugged them and thanked him. *"Gracias, Don Alvaro, muy amable"* ("Thank you, very kind of you"). I also topped that off with some of the weak local beer. Fortunately, I was able to rise early the next morning without being *de goma* (hungover).

Although I was enjoying life in this tiny place called Paraguay, I said *adiós* to Zapata and Luz and Father Bellini and hopped on a bus bound for the headwaters of the Iguaçú River, Curitiba. At the bus station, I met another friendly cabdriver, Alfredo. I had to use my bad Spanish, and even more broken Portuguese, to communicate, but, as my wife would find out the hard way, I never let grammar get in the way of communication.

Alfredo seemed to know everyone. A relatively small guy with well-worn brown leather shoes, he had a big heart and made it his job to hear the story of everyone he drove. He won me over by finding me a free place to stay for the night. I met some of his friends, and we chatted, drank a few beers, and listened to some Paraguayan music. That evening, I realized that I'd left my watch in a bathroom at Iguaçú. But I had rarely used it, other than to make sure I arrived on time for a bus or train, and they were usually late anyway.

Different Latitudes

In Rio de Janeiro, I found a cheap hotel in the Florida area, fairly close to the beach. I met some Peace Corps volunteers who all had met in Rio—seventy of them got together to party.

While talking with Jake, who had been in the country for several years, I noticed how poor his Portuguese was even compared with mine. He, like several of the volunteers I'd met, would never scrape the surface in understanding another culture. When I asked him what's next, he said he wanted to join a "fat capitalist" corporation because the pay was good. Obviously, we had totally different perspectives on what lay before us and how we'd impact the world around us. Not that making money and a profit are wrong—it just never motivated me much.

After this encounter, a short poem from a fellow Peace Corps volunteer, Jack Donnelly, came to mind:

Never have so few
Gained so much
For doing so little
For so many

Salvador da Bahia was the farthest north I'd reach in Brazil and was definitely a city worth getting to know better. It had a strong Caribbean/ African flavor (most Brazilians in this area are descended from people who were brought over as slaves). At the local market, El Modelo, I saw a group of black musicians playing percussion music and a large group of people dancing and drinking. I felt that I was really seeing things as they were for most of the local population. This included the *favelas* (urban slums), where trash was thrown out the front door, open sewage emptied into the ocean, and poor children played outside cardboard homes.

After a two-day ride over potholed dirt roads, the bus pulled into the capital. Brasília, which is in the middle of the country, was planned as a bow and arrow, with large government buildings lining a broad boulevard (the arrow) that runs through the center. The city was too

organized and empty to feel Brazilian. But at least the government leaders were trying to overcome the typical Latin American demographic
distribution pattern that concentrated all the resources and population
into a few large cities on the coast.

Due to Brazil's immense size, I felt the need to hit it hard and therefore spent thirty-nine straight hours on buses. This included eighteen
hours overnight from Brasília to São Paulo and, the next day, another
thirteen hours and a second night from São Paulo to Campo Grande. I
wanted to get to Bolivia on Friday, and the only train for Bolivia would
depart early Friday, and then nothing until Monday, not even a bus. At
this point, I was more than ready to begin heading north to Guatemala
and Ligia and our daughter.

The train trip to Bolivia passed through a number of swamps filled
with gorgeous, bright pink flamingos. We stopped every few miles, it
seemed, to pick up passengers and were offered the local delicacy, ar-
madillo, from several women who had booths with small charcoal grills
and sent their children to take orders from the passengers hanging out
the windows.

At a restaurant in Santa Cruz, I met some Brits, who provided me
with film when I ran out. The Bartons were a young couple traveling
through Latin America using the *South American Handbook*, as was I. Ligia
and I would eventually visit them six years later, in Bognor Regis, on the
south shore of England.

In the capital, La Paz, I met Günter Morales, a Bolivian who moved
to Chicago to make his fortune and returned home for a visit with his
own chauffeur. Günter, who spoke perfect English and owned a chain of
car washes in downtown Chicago. He invited me to travel with them to
Cuzco, Peru, and the ruins of Machu Picchu. The high point of this trip
was when we crossed the border. I'd been harassed or hit up at almost
every border in Latin America, but this arrangement was the strangest.

The Bolivian and Peruvian authorities had customs and passports in
two different cities, with two different office hours. One of the offices
was in Puno, a really dismal place. If you don't make it to the customs in

Puno before 6:00 p.m., you have to wait until the next morning, when they reopen. And when leaving Peru, you must first go to the Policia Judicial, then to Peruvian immigration for your exit stamp. The officials are usually gone because of some holiday, and they don't work on Sunday. Sometimes the Bolivian officials in La Paz would purposely give you the wrong visa, so the officials on the border wanted to send you back to La Paz—a day or so of travel away—to get the right document. Günter was used to these games and found out where the customs people lived, so we could visit them and share a bottle of Johnnie Walker in the form of a *mordida*, or kickback. This approach beat getting upset or returning to La Paz for the "correct" visa.

Once we crossed into Peru, we headed for Cuzco, the ancient Inca capital, said to have been founded around 1100 AD, which also became a colonial center when the Spaniards took over. Most of the small, stout people in this area spoke Quechua. The colonial churches, monasteries, convents, and extensive pre-Columbian ruins were interspersed with countless hotels, bars, and restaurants. Almost every central street has remains of Inca walls, arches, and doorways. The curved stonework of the Temple of the Moon, one of three temples, is said to be unequaled in the world. One can only be amazed by how the Inca could have hauled those gigantic stones, weighing tons, to one place and have them fit so perfectly with other stones that they didn't even need cement.

Günter seemed especially proud of his heritage and insisted that we travel together on the eight-hour train trip to Machu Picchu. All along the train route, we stopped to pick up a few passengers and would be surrounded by women selling food. I usually avoided such roadside delicacies, which is why I was only really sick once during my four-month journey.

I experienced a tremendous feeling of awe when I first witnessed the massive green peaks of Machu Picchu. The ancient citadel straddles the saddle of a 6,000-foot mountain, its steep terraced slopes falling away to the fast-flowing Urubamba River, snaking its hairpin course far below on the valley floor. Towering overhead is Huayna Picchu, with green jungle peaks providing a spectacular backdrop for the whole majestic scene. Amazingly, this Inca city was buried in the jungle for centuries, until Yale Professor Hiram Bingham stumbled upon it in 1911. We needed the entire day to hike around the staircases, terraces, temples, palaces, towers, foundations, and the famous Inti Watana (the Hitching Post of the Sun). I hiked partway up Huayna Picchu, although the steps were slippery at best. It was one of the major religious sites of the Inca, was built over a period of eighty years and then mysteriously abandoned.

After thanking Günter and his driver for their hospitality and help, I realized how much I missed Ligia and Michelle. I had sent an occasional postcard to let Ligia know I was still alive but hadn't received any mail during the trip, because Ligia's letters probably arrived after I'd moved on. Our phone conversations had been brief. I was tempted to take a bus directly to Lima or Quito and from there fly to Barranquilla, Colombia, then back to Guatemala. I was truly lonely and wanted my loved ones around me. I wanted to return to Colorado to feel the mountain breezes and the traditional North American foods of Thanksgiving and Christmas. After four months of traveling alone, I was definitely ready to return to my new family in Guatemala.

From Cuzco, I headed posthaste back north through Peru to Ecuador and Colombia and then got a flight in Panama to Guatemala. My trip through the highlands of Peru was delayed by a bus that broke down at night, on a mountain, in the middle of a snowstorm. I preferred to sleep through much of the journey, which wasn't easy, since the heater didn't work, but I didn't want to look over the side of road to the abyss below. I would remember this trip years later, while on another bus. I was leading a donor trip from La Paz to Las Yungas, a hilly countryside filled with tropical forests and vegetables, when a truck ran into us on a dangerous, narrow road. The truck was filled with local farmers on their way to work, and the driver's only excuse for hitting us was that he was driving a truck without brakes.

Different Latitudes

Back in Cali, I looked up Carlitos and Margarita, and, as before, their hospitality knew no limits. After lunch and a cold shower, I felt recharged and ready to finish the trip home.

My journey, which had spanned a continent, was finally over. I'd seen some of the most spectacular scenery in the world, hiked through the jungle and over massive peaks in the Andes, and gained a new appreciation of a history and culture that would stay with me forever. I'd made new friends, several of whom I'd reconnect with in future travels, but it was time to return to Guatemala City and fulfill Ligia's belief about our future, expressed in the second part of Pablo Neruda's poem:

But
if each day,
each hour,
you feel that you are destined for me

. . . .

my love feeds on your love, beloved,
and as long as you live it will be in your arms
without leaving mine.

Five

On the Front Lines: Developing and Managing Overseas Programs

Plan International USA is part of a global network that believes the promise of children far exceeds the poverty they were born into.

— Plan International website

Do-gooders are different from ordinary people because they are willing to weigh their lives and their families in a balance with the needs of strangers.

— Larissa MacFarquhar, *Strangers Drowning: Grappling with Impossible Idealism, Drastic Choices, and the Overpowering Urge to Help*

Care International, Guatemala, 1974

The Peace Corps was the beginning of a long journey around the world, serving those most in need, as it is for many volunteers. The transition from the Peace Corps to my new career was almost seamless, as I had gotten to know some of the CARE staff when I was involved in a Calapté school garden program for which CARE provided the vegetable seeds. When my Peace Corps term was up, I contacted CARE's executive director, Bill Salas, and his assistant, John Rutin, both of whom were graduates of the Thunderbird School of Global Management. Bill was a tall, lean, rather severe guy. John, on the other hand, was more personable, and we even kidded around about some of the crazy things we'd seen that very morning, like someone from the passenger side signaling what the driver is about to do—whether it's legal or not. These antics always provided some laughs if they didn't run you over first.

CARE hired me to develop an agroforestry initiative, which would eventually include Peace Corps volunteers. So in 1974 I started my first three-month stint as a consultant, for a whopping $500 a month, beginning a forty-year career with various international development agencies. I would return to CARE International a second time—you never know where those dots of curiosity will connect.

My job was to search the highlands to identify best practices for land management for small farmers, and then develop a program around the appropriate technologies. It was a perfect opportunity for a young former volunteer eager to learn more about which programs and organizations were having the greatest impact in the field with small farmers. The lack of land management, leading to erosion and low crop production, was perhaps the most crucial problem facing the indigenous population of Guatemala and would lead to such tragic consequences as river water levels dropping up to sixty percent, according to a study prepared by the Organization of American States and the Technical Center for Forest Evaluation.

Mark D. Walker

One of the first experts I interviewed was the founder of an experimental farm, a Scotsman named John Hibbits, whose technologies and approaches with the indigenous Maya highlands groups became my model. He had a demonstration farm and training center outside Quetzaltenango, the highlands capital of Guatemala. I spent a few weeks in the highlands, talking with other groups' leaders, involved with agroforestry practices with the indigenous people. When I returned to Guatemala City, I learned about CARE International's "food for work" calculations to determine how much food would be appropriate to give small farmers in exchange for introducing specific types of erosion control. The most important land management and conservation techniques the final report would recommend included the construction of terraces, correction of drainage through the construction of small dams, and the improvement of soil productivity.

After writing a thirty-five-page report describing the problems and basic program plan, I spent two days with Bill Salas, breaking it down into the CARE format so the organization could submit it for funding. Unfortunately, much of the information would be distorted once we fit it into the restrictive, complicated CARE format. In my journal, I noted, "It was nothing more than a mental game of putting the project words into the forms of CARE. Many times the narrative sounded impressive but meant nothing—and Salas admitted it." Basically, the CARE report focused on the technical responses while I had emphasized that the obstacle to successful development projects was of a cultural nature and that working effectively with the indigenous communities meant respecting their organizational structure and values. Welcome to the world of overseas development agencies.

The official title of the study was, "Highlands Integrated Agricultural Development Program." I was asked to sign another CARE release form in which I acknowledged that all my work was now officially CARE's property. That made sense at the time, since what else was I going to do with the information? At least now I had some field experience in program development on a paid basis, and it would open the doors to other consulting jobs.

Birth of A Guatemalan Development Agency, 1977-1980

Seek always to do some good somewhere. You must
give some time to your fellow man, for remember,
you don't live in a world all your own.

— ALBERT SCHWEITZER

After my brief stint as a consultant with CARE, Ligia, Michelle, and I went to Colorado to spend some time with my parents in Evergreen. It was the dead of winter, under two feet of snow, which was difficult for Ligia, but Michelle couldn't slide down the hill in my parents' back-yard enough. Although Ligia could understand my parents, she wasn't confident enough to speak English, so she wrote her questions and responses down on a pad. Her English would improve over the next six months, when we took on apartment-management responsibilities for a low-income housing project with 120 apartments in twelve buildings in Arvada, a suburb of Denver. I forget how, but Roy Crowe, an Aussie I met in Bolivia, turned up in Arvada, which was fortuitous because I detest maintenance work and he was able to fix everything that broke in the apartments while we helped clean up the hallways.

My Peace Corps experience kicked in, and I asked the management company Howard Bishop for a three-bedroom apartment to set up an "action center" to involve the residents, which included over 200 children. The key projects included—you've got it—a community garden, which provided fresh vegetables and kept some of the children involved, cultivating the vegetables. We obtained playground equipment, which the residents installed. All of this enhanced the feeling of community and pride, and this motivated families to stick around and pay their rent, which made for a win-win situation. The job helped enhance Ligia's command of English as she showed the apartments and dealt with many of the resident's disputes. It also provided some of the initial funding I'd need to move our family to Austin, Texas, and enroll in the master's program at the University of Texas Institute of Latin American Studies.

I was offered an internship for *The Latin American Review*, a public radio program anchored by Jim Angle, who would become an accomplished journalist and eventually a reporter for Fox News. We interviewed Latin American leaders, including Orlando Letelier, who had been Chile's minister of foreign affairs and defense minister under Allende and the ambassador to the U.S. Several months after our interview, he'd be assassinated by agents of the Chilean secret police (DINA) in downtown Washington, D.C. President Pinochet directly ordered the killing, according to declassified U.S. intelligence that would surface years later, although most of us knew this was the case at the time. These types of politically motivated assassinations occur in Latin America all the time but not usually on the streets of our own capital. Letelier was a handsome, intellectual diplomat who had been promoting meaningful change in Chile for years during the Allende regime. His commitment, vision, and intellectual capabilities impressed me, and he would be greatly missed by many of the Chilean people.

Most of my professors in the program were from Latin America, and I even learned Portuguese since a third of them were from Brazil—it was exactly the challenging educational experience I was looking for, and I'd have my master's degree in a year and a half from a prestigious Latin American studies program, which would provide the credibility I needed to land a job with an international development NGO (nongovernmental organization).

Since I was an intern, my tuition was covered, and Ligia managed apartments (a result of my policy of finding her gainful employment before hitting the ground in our next site), so we didn't need my student loan, which allowed us to leave three-year-old Michelle with her grandparents in Guatemala City and launch a four-month trek through Europe.

One memorable moment on our journey occurred at the road leading into the mountainous Lake District in North West England. Ligia, who was furious with me, threw her wedding ring into the grass on a roundabout where we were trying (unsuccessfully) to hitch a ride down to the Lakes. I had managed to time our arrival during peak tourist season, and no rooms were available in the Lake District, nor was anyone interested in picking up a couple of hippies stranded on the side of the road. Even worse, I had vastly underestimated our budget, and we had to hitchhike all over Europe in order to see all the places on my travel agenda. Ligia had never hitchhiked in her life, and this was not what she was expecting at all, so after three months, she was totally exasperated and I was lucky she only threw her ring at me. We were able to find it before moving on to Scotland.

Our first stop in Scotland was the quaint little home of Agnes and George McCormick, relatives of my mother's, where we were able to relax and mend fences. We just needed some downtime and an opportunity to soak in my Scottish heritage, which included drinking lots of tea and milk with scones and meeting some of the locals at the pub. After our visit with the McCormicks, Ligia and I spent close to a week in and around the cobbled streets of Edinburgh, with its iconic castle on the hill. After a final trek through the Highlands, from Inverness to the Isle of Skye on the western coast, we made our way back to Guatemala, where we had Michelle back in our arms again. We spent the first week getting reacquainted, as Michelle barely recognized us when we returned.

In Guatemala I began looking for a job. I met several missionaries who were involved with disaster relief work after the earthquake of 1976. They were working in conjunction with a number of churches in the States and Canada and Calvary Chapel in Guatemala City. They had spent an incredible amount of time and money trying to build a road from the town of Canillá, in the middle of the department of El Quiché, to Joyabaj, on the other side of the mountain. Quiché was one of the more isolated and poorest provinces in the highlands of Guatemala. None of the missionaries were really engineers, and they didn't know much about community development. The road was finally completed but was soon impassable due to the rainy season and a lack of maintenance. But they'd recognized that a long-term, sustainable development process was something the Evangelical church should be involved in. With that began the social action/development component of the church, known as the Foundation for Education and Development, or FUNDACED.

Alan McDougall was a Canadian missionary and sociologist who invited me to help them out. Alan would become my mentor and taught me a lot about development and mission work. He had been a pilot in World War II and spent thirty years as a lay missionary in several Latin American countries. He had previously worked for the Canadian Broadcasting Corporation, making him a communications expert. A tall, slim man with boundless energy, Alan pushed himself constantly and pushed everyone else just as hard. He'd stay out in the sun for endless hours, cutting back brush and weeds with a diligence that amounted to penitence. He was like the Hermanos Penitentes, who beat their backs with whips to atone for their sins. Over the years, I'd meet a number of such do-gooders who open themselves to a sense of unlimited, crushing responsibility. Alan would be one of those extreme do-gooders, who went out of his way to help those in need no matter the consequences. What would this world have been like if he'd simply followed his career as a communications expert? In the end, if there were no do-gooders like Alan, humanity would be in even worse condition.

As someone entering the do-gooder business myself, I'd have to find that balance between the desire to help strangers in need and my responsibilities as a husband and father, a process I was slow to learn. Alan would be an incredible inspiration, but he was single and wasn't able to help with this particular balancing act. At a certain point in my career, I'd need to acquire a degree of blindness in order to get by. I'd realize that do-gooders must have strong stomachs, as they are constantly confronted with human suffering and death. Although I didn't realize it at the time, my own happiness and success would depend on my ability to relieve the pain of strangers without ruining the lives of my family and friends in the process.

Different Latitudes

Alan took Ligia and me on a fund-raising tour through Mexico City and the Coachella Valley and Indio, outside Palm Springs, California. He provided many church contacts and an understanding of how to raise money from individuals and churches, which kept us going during my early career. One such group was comprised of Hispanic farmworkers from the Coachella Valley who spent time with us in the program area around Canillá in Guatemala. They complained about the discrimination and lack of opportunities they had in the U.S., how they weren't hired for positions they were qualified for, how their children were held back in school due to their race. While helping the small farmers we worked with in Canillá, I noticed a whole new perspective on what real poverty and discrimination were. When we eventually visited with them in Coachella as part of our fund-raising efforts, some six months later, several of the group were more conciliatory and appreciative of what they did have in the U.S. That overseas experience widened their worldview and gave them an appreciation of how lucky they were here in the States.

When I was in Canillá, the center of the program, a Spanish priest in San Andrés Sajcabajá, accused us of "stealing his sheep," since we were with the Evangelical Calvary Chapel. The Evangelical church in most parts of Central America can be found only in the areas the original church leaders designated for each denomination. So one's choice of church depends on where that church historically was established in your community—and it usually doesn't function outside that community. The vast majority of the church leaders are illiterate will little formal theological training of any kind.

Although I met many good people among my Evangelical brethren, by far the least inspiring member of this group was the Guatemalan president, José Efraín Ríos Montt, who ruled Guatemala for nearly seventeen months during 1982 and 1983. Like many upper-class Catholics Rios Montt turned charismatic in the late 1970's and many of these charismatic Catholics defected to Evangelical churches once their new sense of empowerment collided with unsympathetic priests. Also in the rural areas I was working in the violence between the army and the guerilla groups grew to the point that the priests had to abandon a number of provinces including Quiche which resulted in considerable growth in Evangelical churches which up to this period of violence had been small islands in a Catholic sea. But by the 1980's the number of Evangelical churches would swell as Maya church members fled from the prosecution of the Catholic Church.

Rios Montt would join the new "Church of the Word" which according to Anthropologist David Stoll who did a survey of the Church in northern Quiche states that this church was "organized for members of the elite by California hippies turned Evangelical missionaries." I remember Rios Montt preaching the Gospel to Guatemalans on television every Sunday evening. Despite those inspirational sermons, he was instrumental in the armed force's brutal attacks against the Maya population and forcing many into resettlement camps in the northern part of Quiche around Nebaj.

According to David Stoll's book, "Between Two Armies in the Ixil Towns of Guatemala" the Catholic Church estimated that between 1981-1982 alone, "1.5 million people were displaced, which would be a fifth of the country's population." Both Ríos Montt and his chief of military intelligence, José Mauricio Rodríguez Sánchez, were finally put on trial in 2013 and convicted for genocide and crimes against humanity. The charges arose from systematic massacres of the country's indigenous population carried out by Guatemalan troops and paramilitary forces, as well as the related forced mass displacement. I never cease to be amazed at how far from one's professed religion we can get sometimes.

Unfortunately, the Guatemalan board of directors of CEMEC, Calvary Chapel's outreach group, didn't share Alan's vision for a social/development outreach as it didn't include the preferred conversion outreach where success is measured by the number of new converts, so they weren't very supportive of our efforts. Finally, Roger Layton, the head pastor, stepped down from the board, and his son-in-law, Alvaro Muñiz, took over as executive director of CEMEC, which would eventually become FUNDACED. The foundation would establish a large urban renewal project called Carolina in the slums of Guatemala City, as well as programs in several rural areas. The program I managed in Canillá was the largest.

Alvaro was a large guy—about six feet tall, which might be why he was on a national basketball team—definitely not a typical *guatemalteco*. He had greenish brown eyes, black, curly hair, and a great sense of humor. He and his wife, Gloria, had a son, Josef. Alvaro's father was a former minister of agriculture and held other high-level positions in the Ministry of Agriculture. Alvaro had a nice home on the road out of Guatemala City to El Salvador. He didn't have any problems letting me know when I was blowing hot air, but we always respected each other and have remained good friends over the years.

Networking became one of my key pastimes in those days. My favorite group was the Missionary Bible Study breakfasts, held each Tuesday morning at six thirty at the Hotel Pan American in downtown Guatemala City. Whenever missionaries came out of the boonies, they'd meet at this breakfast. I met the pilots of Agape Flights, who would fly us into the project region, cutting a twelve- to fourteen-hour trip in the backs of trucks and on buses to a forty-minute flight. Some of these missionaries were quite conservative.

One fine afternoon, after participating in the inauguration of the school outside Canillá with Save the Children—an international child sponsorship organization, with programs in more than thirty countries— the Norwegian country director and I climbed into the small Cessna of our Agape pilot, Don. The Norwegian director was pleased with what we'd accomplished. He pulled out a beer the locals had given him as a token of thanks, and opened it. Don went ballistic and began shouting at, and blaming, me for defiling his plane, saying that I was a corrupt hippie Peace Corps volunteer. (I resented his reference to corruption.) That was a rocky flight back to Guatemala City, but we arrived safely. I had had no idea that the Norwegian director had brought a beer on board, or I would have warned him to keep it stashed for a more appropriate time and save us all from possible destruction at a few thousand feet over mountainous terrain. I asked Don for forgiveness over the miscue, as I didn't want to make the twelve-hour trip back home over horrendous dirt roads and we did show disrespect for his tightly held missionary values.

Unfortunately, FUNDACED couldn't pay me much money, and the funds for the program were dwindling, as reflected in this January 1978 journal entry: "I expect that our faith in the Lord and the knowledge that our work will benefit Guatemalan peasants are what helps us enjoy life and look forward to the next day despite our rather precarious economic situation." Several of my journal entries refer to the fact that we were down to our last fifty dollars.

I got to know several staff members of World Vision, the largest Christian child sponsorship and development agency in the U.S., which eventually provided $120,000 a year for several years for the agricultural work in Canillá. Dr. Lee Huhn managed the preventive healthcare component of the work; the entire program was the Integrated Development Program of San Andrés and Canillá. I recruited several Peace Corps volunteers, who did much of the agricultural training and agroforestry work. We hired local "promoters" who spoke the local language, K'iche', to do most of the village-level training.

Alan McDougall and I designed, and helped build, the agricultural training center and model farm in the valley of Canillá. I often had to fly in and couldn't get out because the small runway was clouded in. The pilots needed a "hole" to come down and get us, so I often spent an additional week away from Ligia and Michelle. Shortly after Nicolle was born, I moved the entire family up to the agricultural farm. This proved a bad idea: Nicolle became ill with amoebas and almost died of dehydration. Again, Ricardo helped us out, and we were able to put Nicolle in Aurora y Grande, one of the best hospitals in the country, where most if not all the doctors were trained in the U.S. or Europe.

One of the highlights of our time in Canillá was Thanksgiving, which was not a Guatemalan tradition, but it was my favorite holiday. I prepared a turkey, or *chompipe*, stuffed with onions, garlic, and fruit, and popped it into a large clay oven. After four to five hours, we had one of the tastiest, most tender turkeys I'd ever eaten. We were joined by several members of a USAID team who were out evaluating some of their programs, and we talked about the condition of the roads, weather, and crops, and our families back home and what they were eating.

Although most of the local population in Canillá were *ladino* and wore Western clothing, all the people we worked with were from the surrounding hills and spoke K'iche'. One afternoon, during a hike with Nicolas, one of our bilingual promoters, to do a needs assessment survey, we climbed straight up a hill for some forty-five minutes until we finally arrived at a home that could only be described as a hovel. Much to my amazement, they had some of the plumpest and juiciest peaches I'd ever eaten. Nicolas took care of all the preliminary salutations and explained that we represented a group called FUNDACED and wanted to improve the quality of living. Could we see their home? It was made of adobe and had dirt floors and only a few small windows with wooden shutters. The eating area was separate, in a round, thatch-covered room, and there was a small traditional steam bath. I asked where they fetched their water, and the *señora* said they hiked an hour to the stream below. I also learned that the children had to cross two streams on their one-and-a-half-hour journey to school each day, making attendance sporadic at best during the six months of the rainy season. Although the surrounding area was heavily forested, this family was eking out a living, growing crops such as corn, beans, and some vegetables, as were many of their neighbors.

Many of the K'iche' population were not only abandoned by their government, but also suffered greatly during the thirty-six-year period of internal fighting, which was especially hard from 1981 to 1984, just after I left the area. The army established a military garrison at the Catholic convent in San Andrés and began a campaign of killing and repression. When I was still there our bi-lingual promoter Nicolas told us the military would roam through villages looking for young men to recruit and would burn down homes when they left, calling their owners subversives.

None of our staff were compromised, but I never traveled at night and always checked in with our local staff and support groups like the Peace Corps volunteers to find out if any violence was imminent.

Although I didn't witness political violence in the field when I returned to our home in Guatemala City I did receive several "death threats" which I decided to ignore based on input from Ligia's family members who considered a scare tactic but this showed that someone was unhappy with the rural development work I was involved in. Upon arriving at our home in Guatemala City after several weeks in the field I found that all my books were gone. When I asked Ligia she told me that she'd burnt them all! I was furious and flabbergasted so I asked Ligia for an explanation. "Well first off many of your books are Marxist." (Okay so I did have a few of the classics plus NACLA studies "North American Congress on Latin America" and Susanne Jonas's, "Dependency and Imperialism" among others) and if the "Judiciales" (basically government sponsored death squads) they'll take my family especially my cousins and "disappear" them (torture, kill them and dump them in a mass grave) so it's not just about you. Suddenly the light went on and I remembered that my good friend Rudolfo who was one of my Spanish teachers in Puerto Rico with the Peace Corps had studied in Russian and was a confirmed Marxist and his library was a lot more extensive than mine and if he was discovered the connection between us could very well lead the "Judiciales" to our doorstep. So I took this as another lesson learned about the underlying violence swirling around me.

Country Director with Plan International 1980-1986

Guatemala, 1980–1981

Through networking, I linked up with staff members from Plan International, which was headquartered in Rhode Island. After several interviews, I was hired as an assistant director. For the first time, I'd receive a decent salary and medical benefits. I would be responsible for managing a slum program across from the Puente Incienso in

Guatemala City. We established a local cooperative, Chapinlandia, which provided small business loans. When I left, about a year after taking the position, the community presented me with a handwoven wall hanging, with the inscription "Mark Walker, *recuerdo* (a memento) from the staff of the Chapinlandia Cooperative, June 1981," which hangs on a wall in my study to this day. I was proud of the progress the cooperative made in promoting small business development, but Plan International had offered me a position as director in Bogotá, Colombia.

This might have been an opportunity to share my "transparency list" and warn Ligia what she'd be getting into by leaving Guatemala, her parents, her friends—that extended family and everything she knew and loved—for a career in overseas development work. Here are a few of the reminders she would have checked off over the next couple of years:

- Every time you come to a new country, the chauffeur, my secretary, and the nannies will be your best, and often only, friends.
- You will wait up to a month before the household goods, including furniture, arrive in order to set up house.
- Although a beautiful city, Bogotá can be a cold, damp place.
- Even before you've set up the house, Mark will have found you a full-time job at the British School, where you'll teach the Queen's English.
- He will be sued by local workers and have to leave Colombia illegally, on short notice.
- He'll be threatened by local revolutionary guerilla groups and give you less than three days to pack up and leave the country.

Once again, I decided not to share the list at that time or over the next couple of years for that matter, so we packed up and headed to Colombia with three children and our Guatemalan nanny. Our departure meant that the ongoing balance between helping those in need and looking out for the best interests of my family would begin in earnest.

Mark D. Walker

Colombia, 1981–1983

Bogotá would remind us a lot of Guatemala. You can find yourself in a different ecological zone by driving a half day in almost any direction. We tried to see as much of the beautiful country as possible. We lived in a colonial-style neighborhood on the north side of the city, and Ligia's mother, Neta insisted that we take our *muchacha* with us, so Marina, "La Tata", who had been born on the family's coffee plantation, became the nanny and kept track of our son, John, as much as possible. The girls went to the British School.

Colombia had been plagued by civil unrest and violence for centuries. I asked a Colombian friend, Jaime Victoria, the director at Save the Children—(one of the groups I also worked with in Guatemala) about the basis for this streak of vengeance and violence. He gave me a series of books in Spanish with historical passages and stories from those visiting the country, beginning with the first colonists, the Spaniards. I read many of the stories and learned about an eleven-year civil war called La Violencia, during which 300,000 peasant men, were killed. The battle divided villages down the middle and was similar to the nineteenth-century Hatfield–McCoy feud in the Appalachian Mountains of the U.S. The killing was part of a crisis of this coffee republic in which a weak government could not mediate property disputes.

One weekend, Ligia and I spent a few days at Jaime's family's coffee plantation, a few hours outside Bogotá. According to Jaime, this small town was engulfed in violence for many years, and all families in the area had been affected in one way or another. The highlight of this visit was a meal the *muchacha* made, chicken and yucca fried in olive oil with tons of garlic and onion. The yucca took on the flavor of the crisp chicken skin and was unforgettable. I follow her recipe for this scrumptious meal to this day.

The *bogotanos* had some of the best food imaginable, and they specialized in restaurants with all different kinds of indigenous dancing. The dances ranged from the accordion polka–type dances of the highlands to the hot salsa dances of the coastal areas. Our favorite foods included *arepas*, thick, cornmeal tortillas with butter on them;

patacones, fried plantains; *pan de bono* a cheese bread that goes especially well with *guayaba* jelly (my staple diet during my first trip through Colombia); and *ajiaco*, a chicken stew filled with vegetables, including yucca, topped off by a few pieces of avocado. I look forward to these delicacies to this day.

One community provided us with boiled potatoes and grilled meat served in newspaper which I thought was a joke. But it saved the need for plates and silverware.

Our favorite restaurant, Tramonti, was on the top of a mountain overlooking the city. The wood from orange crates was the basic building material, and the view was unforgettable. We especially appreciated the music of Rene Betancourt, so after one of his sets, I went up to get acquainted. Rene said that he was one of the first artists to use the organ and synthesizer with popular Colombian music. I purchased one of his tapes and listened to it often, when we had a tape player.

One afternoon, I piled our family, plus the nanny, La Marina, into Plan International's Toyota Land Cruiser for a memorable road trip through Cali, to the colonial capital of Popayán, and from there over the Andes, to the Inca ruins of San Augustin. I'd been through Cali, a beautiful agricultural center in Valle del Cauca and, as I've previously mentioned, home to the most attractive women in Latin America. Every type of plant and flower imaginable flourished in the valley.

We spent a few days in the well-maintained town Popayán. The city is a colonial replica, like only a few other Latin American cities, including Puebla, Mexico; Antigua, Guatemala; Cartagena, Colombia; and Cuzco, Peru. Popayánwas founded in 1536 by one of Pizarro's lieutenants. We spent hours wandering around the many churches and museums. One of my favorite photos was taken when the three kids and Marina sat on the side of a fountain with an Inca symbol in the middle. Four-year-old Nicolle, or Nicky, as we called her, wore a traditional maroon jacket from Guatemala and red pants. In her little shoes and blonde pigtails, she looks as relaxed as she can be. Michelle, with her arms crossed and a blue bow in her hair, looks down at Nicky, while John, only a year or so old, is all wrapped up in a blue sweater, with his little legs hanging over Marina's lap. Little did any of us know that we'd soon be on one of our most dangerous journeys.

The next leg of our trip was across some barren mountains to our next destination. As we drove, Ligia asked, "Where are the other cars? How about the buses—where are they? And why aren't we seeing any gasoline stations or towns?"

I was clueless but took note of her concern. After an hour or so of this isolation, I stopped the car to get a better view of the terrain and realized that those extensive green fields were coca, the key ingredient in cocaine.

"Yikes," I said to Ligia. "Let's get out of here! It's too late to turn back, so let's just keep trucking and pray that nobody stops us, asking any questions."

The kids were asleep in the back, unaware of the potential danger. Colombia was one of the world's largest cocaine producers, and the U.S. Drug Enforcement Administration has spent millions of dollars in an attempt to dismantle the cartel's ability to process and send the drugs north by bombing cartel members' homes and spraying their crops with defoliants, making this a less than hospitable place for a U.S. citizen.

But ignorance was bliss, and we made it safely to the ruins of San Augustín. This site is a monument of the splendid cultures that predated the Spaniards' arrival in Colombia. The kids were now awake and eager to crawl around the many statues and ancient ruins.

Marina was invaluable throughout the trip, keeping the kids comfortable and safe. She was a short, stocky lady with black hair and brown eyes who often wore simple cotton dresses and sandals. When Nicolle got sick after we took her to the program in Canillá, Ligia's mother contacted a cousin who worked at the U.S. Embassy to help Marina get a visa to Colombia and the States. Ligia and Neta had to do a lot of convincing to get Marina to leave her family and friends to come with us. We liked her so much that we tried to convince her to come with us to our next site, in Africa, but she said, "I'm sorry, Doña Ligia, but I'm afraid the natives will eat me." She never did use her visa to enter the U.S. and, tragically, died of cancer at thirty-eight. By then she had two children of her own who did immigrate to the States.

Personally, I never looked back, as I saw the moves to new and different countries every few years as the inevitable result of my experience with the Peace Corps and having obtained the master's degree to enter the world of international development. I thought that despite the inconveniences and occasional dangers, meeting new people from all over the world and learning about new cultures would be the best thing for the entire family. In the end, I think I was right, and Ligia concurred.

Resistance to change can exist on many levels, from the target community, the government, or the very organizations we'd been hired to manage in order to promote that change. I learned this the hard way in Bogotá, where the local staff formed a labor union. One day, as I was in the office bathroom, which was located directly above the meeting hall, I heard a commotion below. I heard, among other things, "We need to get organized just like oil company workers do in order to control our working situation. Why shouldn't we be allowed to negotiate a fair wage and decent benefits? Alfredo's uncle has worked with the petroleum union for years and can help us get organized."

I sat there for a while, taking in the storm that was definitely brewing, thinking, *Oh, shit, this is all I need! As if I don't have enough going on, hiring new staff, filling out reports, visiting programs, and trying to get along with everyone.*

The program had been set up twenty years earlier, as Plan International's first field office in the Western Hemisphere. Shortly after my arrival, I became the director for the Bogota program, with the charge of promoting changes in a program that was already in flux. I decided to accelerate the ongoing process to decentralize the operation. My goal was to take the offices and staff into the slums and closer to the communities we were serving, where we'd be more in tune with the local needs. In the past, all the families from the three program areas would converge on a central office complex to receive services. My predecessor, Tim Allen, had informed me that some families had been receiving services for three generations—a clear sign of the creation of dependence on outside resources that wouldn't last forever, nor would they promote local leadership or businesses that would lead to a sustainable development process.

After some initial research about the group that was organizing the union, I learned that its secretary, Alfredo, was the nephew of one of the leaders of the most radical petroleum union in the country, and that it was affiliated with the local M-19 guerrillas, who used violence to get their demands met. Alfredo was one of our best young social workers, an articulate and motivated leader, but instead of becoming fast friends, we were on a path of confrontation.

The M-19, like most guerrilla groups in Colombia, emerged from the era of La Violencia, which had ended in the mid-1960s. Having established itself as an urban guerrilla group, the M-19 reportedly set up units in each of Colombia's major cities. One of its founders, Jaime Bateman Cayón, had been a member of the FARC-EP, the major guerrilla group in the country, but many M-19 members came from universities or unions, and many had families with deep roots in the system they wanted to overthrow. This was part of the country's dilemma: members of the same families were pitted against one another.

Officially, I'd be sued by the Plan International staff members who formed the union, as part of a civil litigation process, for infringing on their right to free assembly, which was a smart move. This approach meant that, under the Napoleonic Code used in Colombia, I was guilty until proven innocent, required to sign in and provide a deposition at a local courthouse weekly, and couldn't legally leave the country. And since most cases weren't resolved in less than five years, I would need three lawyers, including a labor lawyer, to deal with the charges and additional legal maneuvering. But the Plan lawyers only antagonized the union leaders and their legal advisers. After all, that's how they made their living. In the end, the staff wanted higher wages, more in line with the for-profit groups they were familiar with, but that wasn't an option for a not-for-profit group whose major goal was to support the children of the slum areas around Bogotá.

I tried to get the union members to appreciate a major difference between Plan and the petroleum corporations their unions attack: we were a not-for-profit organization, and our donors would not be happy if they learned that an increased amount of their monthly $21 gift was going to salaries. Finally, after I'd been giving testimony at the local courthouse for four months, my secretary was contacted by one of the union leaders, who said, "This is the M-19. Tell the senior director that he has seventy-two hours to leave the country, or we'll kill him and his family."

My secretary's face was white with fear when she told me. I checked with the local authorities, who thought it was a legitimate threat but assured me that they'd provide a team of four bodyguards for me and my family. I was thinking, *Do I really need this? Is it worth the risk to my family's lives? Maybe I'd go with security like this if I was making a fortune with one of the petroleum companies, but that's not my line of business.*

The Plan International executive staff in Rhode Island took immediate action, and we were out of the country in seventy-two hours. Several staff members would pack up our household items and store them until my next assignment was determined. I had been threatened several times in Guatemala, but Ligia's family and our friends determined that it was meant only to scare me out of an area where I was causing "trouble." This group in Colombia seemed to take violence and innuendos of death and destruction to new levels.

The day of our departure was nerve-racking because we knew my name was on the official no-fly list, based on the pending litigation. However, no computer control existed at the time, so we presented our passports and boarded the plane—Ligia and I, the three kids, and our nanny. Once we took off, the plane take a severe turn, and Ligia clutched my hand and said, "They're taking us back to Bogotá! They must have found out."

Fortunately, the Colombian authorities weren't that well organized, and our flight continued north.

Soon after, I checked in with some of the former Plan staff and learned that the Bogotá office, which had existed for over two decades, had been closed. All the staff and those they served were out of luck.

Different Latitudes

Next stop: Sierra Leone, Africa, where I was given a director position with Plan International.

• • •

I might have pulled out my still-unshared transparency list, which would have included the following considerations for Ligia:

- Instead of a cuddly dog or cat for a house pet, we will have a large monkey.
- Freetown has the second-highest precipitation rate of a capital city in the world. It could rain for six days straight—nonstop—meaning that any leather left in the closet for a week might turn a bright green.
- We will need a four-wheel-drive vehicle to get to our house in Freetown.
- One of the two guard dogs in our compound will be struck in the eyes by a spitting cobra.
- Although many of the government officials speak English, we will need to learn Krio in order to properly interact with our staff and many key village leaders.
- The International School is anything but international.
- One must often be medevacked out of Freetown to receive the necessary medical care.

But once again, I failed to mention these minor inconveniences, and we packed our bags in snowy, frigid Evergreen, Colorado, and headed for the sweltering tropics of West Africa.

SIERRA LEONE, 1983–1986

When Plan International's program director offered me the opportunity to be the country director in Sierra Leone, I was at my parents' home in Evergreen and had to get a map to find the place. After ten years overseas, I thought that I knew what underdevelopment was. Little did I know that Africa would be an entirely new ballgame.

On first landing in Sierra Leone, I would be introduced to the concept of WAWA, "West Africa Wins Again." In other words, if it can go wrong, it will. The Plan International driver was waiting for us at the so-called Lungi international airport and after brief introductions, he threw our luggage in the back, and we headed slowly for Freetown. I was eager to see my new office and became impatient with our snail's pace on a perfectly well-paved road, so I told the driver to step on it. He complied, only to stop in front of the ocean (the airport was on an island). There we sat for several hours waiting for the ferry to come across and pick us up. The driver calmly explained that it often didn't return because of a lack of fuel. So much for being in a hurry in West Africa!

During my first year, I went far up-country, to Kambia, at the border with Guinea, to spend time with several missionary families. The roads to their homes were almost impassable. There were times I actually had to guide the driver of the pickup across several logs that spanned a river. All the roads were dirt and in horrendous condition. When I complained, people could only say, "They were paved and perfectly maintained when the British ruled." Sierra Leone gained its independence from the British in 1960.

The missionary homes had electricity, produced by solar panels, for just a few hours each evening. And when the lights went out on my first night there, all I could hear was the beating of drums in the distance—an eerie feeling for someone not accustomed to Africa. As I listened to the steady, incessant drumming I thought, *What are they saying anyway? Are they letting everyone know that the missionary folks have some visitors? Are they planning something other than a welcome bash?* I decided to abandon fruitless speculation and hope for the best. The next day, we checked out some local programs and then headed back to Freetown. I had a whole new appreciation of these missionaries' dedication and willingness to live in such isolated areas in an entirely different culture than any of us had ever experienced.

Different Latitudes

Like many African countries, Sierra Leone was divided into a number of tribes that had tremendous influence over their members. When I hired a new staff person, he or she usually had to bring part of his or her extended family along—whoever had the job supported everyone else. Although the country was incredibly rich in resources, almost all the diamonds, shrimp, and minerals were sold on the black market, so the government was virtually bankrupt.

Although the American-German film *Blood Diamond* was set almost fifteen years later, during the civil war of 1996 to 2001, it was realistic and reflected many problems facing the country (like much of their wealth, especially diamonds, being sold exclusively on the black market). On our way out of Lungi Airport one afternoon, we were watching the planes come in while waiting for our flight. I noticed a Learjet on the other side of the runway, and I pointed out the Swiss flag on its tail to Ligia. "I wonder what that's about," I said.

Two men stepped down and walked across to the terminal. After about ten minutes, they emerged with what looked like two metal-plated briefcases.

"Hmm," I said, "Must be sending some important documents to Geneva for those crucial negotiations going on." But I was really thinking, *There goes the next shipment of diamonds to a Swiss bank. So what else is new?*

The level of corruption was mind-boggling, even after having spent years seeing it in action in Latin America. Sierra Leone was ranked way down, at 119th in corruption out of 175 countries, with a score of 29 out of 100, according to the 2015 report of Transparency International. Scores range from 0 (highly corrupt) to 100 (clean). The Corruption Index ranks countries/territories based on how corrupt a country's public sector is perceived to be.

We had to mark all the parts of our office vehicle engines with chalk before bringing them in to be repaired: more than once, an NGO staffer would send a vehicle out for repair only to realize afterward that the defective part had been replaced, but three other engine parts had been switched out with used parts. I eventually brought in a diesel mechanic from the British International Voluntary Service to set up an inventory system for spare parts and train our staff how to maintain the equipment. We became virtually self-sufficient. I wasn't surprised when an audit revealed that the government of Sierra Leone had "lost track" of thirty percent of the funds, or $5.7 million, sent to combat the outbreak of Ebola in 2014. And of course, the number of people dying from the deadly disease would increase as a result.

Many times we had to resort to the same strange superstitions that were prevalent among the locals to get any results. When a typewriter was stolen from our office, Ligia called in the police, but after she talked with some of our senior staff, we also invited a witch doctor. The witch doctor passed along a kettle of hot oil from one staff person to another in the belief that the culprit would be burned when the kettle passed his or her way. And it worked! I was never one to argue with what worked, and this would not be the last time that Ligia's cultural sensitivity and sixth sense would win the day.

Mark with original Plan International staff in Freetown

Different Latitudes

My expat staff was excellent. Rose Sherman, an assistant director, was from Liberia—the next country to the south—and had worked with higher-level government functionaries there, so, while she had a heart for those in need, she knew her way around the bureaucracy. Her husband was a construction engineer, but because of job limitations, he had remained in Liberia. Her children got along well with ours—the two youngest were the same age. Her son, Kapakai, was a thin little kid with glasses. We have a photo of Kapakai between two blond-haired, blue-eyed Walker kids, in a canoe on the sand. I remember John and Kapakai beneath an umbrella, playing racing cars on the beach, with steering wheels and stakes for the stick shift.

Steve Albrecht, my other assistant, a lanky Texan with black hair and a substantial mustache that hung down on the sides, was located up-country, in Makeni. He had a nice place, where I stayed overnight on several occasions. Since part of the population was Muslim, we'd be awakened at the most outrageously early hours by the town crier in the minaret of the local mosque. Once again, another eerie sound for the unaccustomed.

Florence Bangali was my very competent administrative assistant. A Ugandan, Florence was in Freetown because her husband, Andrew, was a Sierra Leonean diplomat. We were lucky to get someone with Florence's broad background. Even in the land of WAWA, she could figure out how to get things accomplished.

For the first time in the program's history, I hired several university-level staff, which was a challenge, since most university-trained Sierra Leoneans were in London or some other foreign city. John Kenaba was an experienced program manager with a master's degree in sociology. He helped develop training programs for our staff and monitored their progress. Cecilia Koroma was a graduate of UCLA and had a degree in social work. She brought a new perspective on how to best promote health programs for women and children and how to monitor their impact.

Our most impressive partnership was with a local group called the Work Oxen Programme. It helped small farmers purchase an ox and taught them how to use it to greatly increase their rice production and add much important income to their meager budget. Most consequentially they converted a warehouse into a metal shop and taught farmers how to produce plows, which became an important source of jobs and income as one of the few local industries in the Makeni area. The group even produced a white T-shirt with red sleeves and a large ox and plow on the front, which I wore with great pride.

We were able to build on the program to benefit over 20,000 families through a child sponsorship model. Each child would be visited periodically by a social worker to see how he or she was progressing. They'd all attend school and be expected to get passing grades. The entire family would have access to a number of preventive health services, as well as some small industry development programs. We had three program areas—in Makeni and in the coastal towns of Wellington and Freetown.

For the first time in my overseas experience, I succumbed to some serious, unknown diseases. This was the land of Lassa fever and green monkey disease. I was stricken with large boils known as furuncles that appeared under my arms and kept me bedridden. I went to Abidjan, Ivory Coast, for a Plan conference and had the French-trained doctors do extensive blood tests, but there was no clear diagnosis or cure found. Eventually, I had to be medevacked to a tropical disease center in Manchester, England, where they never figured out the cause of the problem, but the rest and cooler climate did the trick. Personally, I think it was the beer that cured me. My hotel had a pub down in the basement, and I tried as many of the local brews as possible.

Nicky fell once when we were in Freetown and hurt her leg. We thought it was broken and took her to a hospital that had one of the few X-ray machines in the country, only to learn that we couldn't use it because of an all-too-frequent blackout. A great example of WAWA. No wonder Salone—the Krio term for Sierra Leone—was known as the white man's grave. Fortunately, we avoided what could have been a life-threatening injury when our personal physician informed us that Nicky's leg was not broken but badly bruised.

Different Latitudes

We began learning Krio as soon as we arrived. This is not a trading language like the creoles of the Caribbean, but an official, written language. The staff loved to hear me say "Howdy body?" or "How di go de go?" each morning. Rose, my Liberian assistant director, also felt the need to learn some Krio because of the positive impact it had on my relationship with our local staff. Rose was a well-educated West African, whereas I had never worked in Africa and still was not fluent in Krio so I had some making up for lost time to do. I'm sure that more than one staff member was thinking, "Here comes the white man taking over for a competent local staffer."

Rose did have some fun with me at a school inauguration. We were being honored by the community with a local delicacy, monkey brain soup, and she never gave me a heads-up on what to expect. She probably saw the look on my face when I reached the bottom of the bowl only to find a monkey hand, which is a lot more unnerving than the chicken leg I'd find at the bottom of a Guatemalan stew. I never had any problems keeping my weight down in Sierra Leone. The favorite local dish was cassava stew (potato leaves with a little dried fish) called *plasas*, on top of white rice. And you ate with your hands, which, along with the salty fish taste, was something I never looked forward to.

I did enjoy the groundnut stew, a peanut butter–based sauce prepared with chicken or beef. I also occasionally drank palm wine (fermented coconut milk), but I always checked that it hadn't been mixed with water, because that's where the amoebas get you. Most of the Peace Corps volunteers had orange-colored palms and bottoms of their feet due to the excessive use of palm oil in the cooking. Most Peace Corps Volunteers (PCV's) had a distinct, pungent odor about them as well. I remember admiring these PCVs, who endured circumstances even more extreme than what I had encountered in Ixchiguán, Guatemala.

My savior was the local Star beer, as well as Heineken and Guinness. Although many villages we worked in didn't have refrigeration, and a warm Guinness (it resembles dirty car oil) in the tropics is not my idea of refreshing, I always enjoyed a cold one after a hard game of squash at the Aqua Club in Freetown. The children would swim in the pool with their friends, and I would play squash. Ligia also became an excellent player. Squash is a popular sport in many Commonwealth countries and is referred to as the chess of racket sports due to the need for precision when striking the tiny ball, which almost dies when it hits the floor. The Aqua Club was a gathering spot for all the expats. Many of our friends were Irish, British, Dutch Russian, and Armenian.

Only two restaurants in the entire country could be considered decent. One was the Lighthouse, which was run by some Armenian friends. The kibbeh and hummus were great. Alex's Bar was another favorite place. It served delicious, large lobsters for six dollars, and the tables were right on the beach. Alex's became the watering hole for many of the expat community. Lots of Guinness and gin and tonics flowed in order to ward off malaria, among other unknown ailments, lurking in Salone.

Our home was on the outside of town. The first thing I did when we got there was to buy generators for our home and the office, as electricity was sporadic at best. We had a large tank to store water, which was also cut off during most of the day. We had a driver, Santigi, and a nanny, Musu. Ligia did a great job keeping the children alive and well—not an easy task with all the diseases and poison-spitting cobras around. Our home was next to the Russian ambassador's. The Russians could be seen playing volleyball on the beach but kept to themselves.

The guard to the gate to our home, Cole, was the most unassuming of all our house staff. He had little formal education, and he never wore a shirt, only tattered old shorts and plastic sandals. When we left the country, he presented us with two tables he had carved out of local hardwood. Each stood about two feet high and a few feet wide, with two perfectly carved elephants as the base. The tabletops were carved with alligators on the sides and an elephant in the center. Cole also carved two wooden panels with a person climbing a palm tree to harvest the fruit for palm wine, and another tree with a snake coming down. Two men were imbibing the palm wine from a jug. We brought most of the pieces with us and have them in our living room today. Cole gave twelve-year-old Michelle two small carvings of a village man and woman.

Different Latitudes

Years later, when I asked Ligia why the front gate guard would give us these elaborate carvings, she told me that Cole had brought one of his young daughters to our compound when she was deathly ill from an infection caused by genital mutilation, and Ligia and Musu had nursed her back to health. Ligia and I were appalled at this practice. Sierra Leone has one of the highest rates of genital mutilation in the world. Its part of an initiation ceremony that gives membership to a women's secret society called bondo, which has considerable influence in rural Sierra Leone.

Our favorite times were at the beach, where we paid a whopping five dollars a month to rent and maintain our own palm-covered beach house. The ocean was pristine and clear and blue. The children ran around as free as larks, and the local children were always ready to join in and play. Despite the challenges we'd faced in West Africa, when I asked the children, after we'd returned to the States, where they'd most like to live, they all said Sierra Leone!

Graham Greene wrote several classics that give one a feel for Sierra Leone and West Africa. His best-known book about Sierra Leone is *The Heart of the Matter*, which takes place in Freetown. I even had a few beers at the downtown hotel where he reportedly wrote the book. It was just as run-down as it probably was when the book was written, some forty years before. The other book is *Journey without Maps*, about Greene's trip with his brother from Sierra Leone to Liberia at a time when no roads existed and they were carried in hammocks by several men. They were the first white men whom some of the villagers had ever seen. The primitive conditions and odd customs they observed were strange.

Getting anything accomplished in Sierra Leone was a struggle, and I would never know what impact, if any, I had on Plan International's operation. My boss, James Byrne, the international program director, summed up what he thought I accomplished in this recommendation letter of January 1985:

Mark's most outstanding quality is his ability to analyze a situation, identify what is wrong, set a plan of action and then implement that plan. Mark went to Sierra Leone as a Plan Field Director. He had inherited a program which was poorly planned and poorly implemented. In a short period of time, good contacts were made with the public and the government of Sierra Leone, and he set the program on a solid footing. Mark is a serious person who brings to any task experience, intelligence and dedication. In a phrase, Mark gets things done, efficiently and effectively.

Life in Sierra Leone was incredible, but after fifteen years of working abroad, it was time to move on. Michelle would need to go to England to a boarding school if we staying in Sierra Leone, and we might see her once or twice a year, so I needed to make a career change that wouldn't entail living in countries with no educational infrastructure, and I'd need some time to figure out my next career move. At this point, the do-gooder instinct would need to give way to our children's education. So Ligia took the children back to Guatemala, and I headed to the States to look for a job, probably as a fund-raiser for one of the groups I'd worked with over the years, since I was committed to this work. Our pet monkey, the endless beaches, and the beach hut, plus the friendly people, seemed to allay some of the inconveniences and challenges we had faced. But even though I would begin working with NGOs stateside, I would continue to do a series of field surveys and evaluations, which would be interesting but less stressful than bringing my family with me and being responsible for the entire operation on a day-to-day basis.

Six

GLOBAL SURVEYS AND EVALUATIONS

*A leader is best when people barely know he exists. When his work
is done, his aim fulfilled, they will say: we did it ourselves.*

- LAO TZU

Overseas Travel with the Cooperative Housing Foundation
GUATEMALA, 1986

Upon arriving back stateside from Sierra Leone I connected with
CARE International since they were my first consulting client in
Guatemala. Eventually I'd be named the new Regional Director for
the Rocky Mountain Regional Office, but before starting this position
I obtained a consulting job with the Cooperative Housing Foundation
(CHF), which would bring me back to Guatemala three times over the
next twelve months which helped me stay connected to my kids but allow
them to finish up their school in Guatemala where most of their classes
were in Spanish and they were really doing well. When not working I
spent all my extra time with my family, who was living in our home in
Residencial V, a gated community within a few blocks of Ligia's mother,
Neta, and her brother, Roland. By now all three children spoke excellent

Spanish and Johnnie didn't speak much English at all. Ligia and I were able to leave the kids with the *muchacha* in order to get out for dinner together and to catch up.

Mike Viola, a former CARE International Director I'd worked with in both Bogota and Freetown, was instrumental in my landing this consulting position with CHF. Initially, I met Mike when he was with CARE in Bogota. His wife, Cecilia, who was Filipino, taught at the British School, where Ligia also worked. We enjoyed hanging out together with our similar cross-cultural marriages and had dinner together a number of times over the years. Mike was a large guy with white hair and glasses. While serving in the Philippines he played rugby, which makes our football look like a non-contact sport —they don't wear protective equipment and are always pushing, pulling, clutching, grabbing in the middle of a large "scrum" of players. Mike was a great complainer, and was pessimistic to boot, but that never stopped us from having a good conversation.

With Mike's help, I was hired to set up a property management system for a low-income cooperative housing program in Escuintla, Guatemala. Escuintla was a large, commercial center on the hot and humid South Coast, on the road to the major port on the Pacific coast, San Jose Champerico—meaning that I'd be putting in a lot of "sweat equity" of my own. The timing was ideal, since these would be quick trips, and CARE didn't pay for their fundraising staff to see the work overseas firsthand which I considered a big disadvantage and my visits allowed me to report back to CARE donors about the field work in Guatemala, which would add to my credibility with the larger individual and foundation donors.

When I arrived in Escuintla the first time, many of the cooperative members hadn't paid any rent or had sublet their houses and moved to the U.S. Consequently, little income was coming in, so the maintenance of the common grounds and parks was minimal. Over the next two trips I completed an assessment, wrote the program, and designed the training materials and maintenance manuals so the local staff could manage the housing project once CHF left.

Different Latitudes

One of the highlights of this consulting gig was getting to know Ray Ocasio and his wife, Michelle, and their three kids. Ray was from my native New Jersey, so we had a common link to the Garden State and its basic "cut the crap" approach to life. Michelle, like Ligia, was a teacher, and they were both bringing up the kids, so they had lots to discuss in that regard. We also brought our families together for different activities and we've stayed in touch to this date. Ray's specialty was low-income housing, and since Ligia and I had managed some government subsidized housing in Denver in between overseas gigs, we knew a lot about the challenges of providing affordable housing for those with limited resources.

While in Guatemala, I took Johnnie, about five at that time, up to the Chimaltenango/Tecpan area to visit one of CARE's program sites. The CARE driver was amazed at all the intelligent, insightful questions Johnnie was asking—in perfect Spanish, of course. Upon arriving in Tecpan, I began interviewing some of the participants of CARE programs and afterwards I found Johnnie—blond hair, blue eyes, with his jeans and cowboy boots, playing with a miniature helicopter and thinking, "He's so small, but no doubt he's going to grow up fast and be way more mature than I was at that age!" And as it turned out, I was right. On the way back to Guatemala City we stopped off at Katok's, a large restaurant with a thatched roof that specialized in tasty sausages of all sorts. The owners were German and produced all kinds of excellent smoked meats. This trip allowed me to find out more about how John was doing and his thoughts about heading to the States.

Indonesia & The Philippines
1992

Bali, Indonesia, and the Philippines would be my next overseas trip as part of an interdisciplinary program evaluation team to determine what World Neighbors and its Area Representative, Larry Fisher, had accomplished, and what direction programs should take in the future. Fortunately, Larry and his wife, Lucy, chose the exotic island of Bali as their home and the site for the initial workshop. Bali is an amazing island, not only for its natural beauty, but also because each village foments a specific art form. Some villages specialize in dance, some in carving, others in weaving, still others, music. Combinations of Buddhist and Hindu traditions permeate all levels of society. Our group stayed in a small complex of quaint, thatched huts with a pool and great food. Tons of fresh fruit was always available. My bedroom was on the second level, so when I swung the porch door open I was faced with endless miles of green rice fields with a volcano on the horizon. Truly a Shangri-La type of place.

Larry gathered an extensive network of development experts from many different organizations, including the Ford Foundation, Save the Children, OXFAM, Peace Corps, and the Canadian Peace Corps, as well as a number of indigenous groups and foundations that actually implemented the programs. We began the workshop assessing the needs, challenges, and future of the region, which would include Indonesia and the Philippines, where World Neighbors had a number of programs throughout the archipelago.

Next we split up into small groups and visited program sites to see the work first-hand and talk with the local program leaders and villagers. I was part of Larry's team, which started off on the small island of Sumba (one of over 13,000 islands in Indonesia). Because Larry had worked with the Ford Foundation for a number of years, we developed what would become a very successful fundraising strategy with the Ford Foundation around the world. They became one of World Neighbors' most loyal supporters, and funded programs on every continent we worked on, and these team visits of fundraising and field staff were an important part of the relationship building process. After the survey visit Larry and I even took off for a week to network and do fundraising in Singapore and Japan, although I don't remember any immediate funding coming out of those trips.

Our first stop was the island of Sumba, in the eastern Indonesia province of East Nusa Tenggara. Most of the original forest had been cleared for planting of maize and cassava, among other crops. This and the growing population were a threat to both the forests and bird life.

Larry had spent so many years visiting and living in local communities like the ones we'd visit on the island of Sumba that he wasn't aware of the needs of an outside group not used to these conditions. He provided us with thin, cotton bed covers as our only blanket, and we slept on bamboo floors each night. The first night we slept in a lean-to on the top of a mountain where the temperatures dropped rapidly when the sun went down. Between this and the constant walking, my back really suffered. I would have suffered even more if my friend and World Neighbors area representative for Latin America, Ed Ruddell, hadn't brought along a "space blanket," an aluminum foil-like covering which the astronauts supposedly used to keep body heat in, and it worked well. I got a solid night's sleep.

During the day we hiked from community to community, visited the farms, local experiments, and extensive agroforestry work being done. These efforts were important since the dense population had devastated the local ecosystems and forests had almost disappeared on some parts of the island. When we were leaving one village in the afternoon, I caught a scene out of the corner of my eye that prepared me for that evening's meal. Some villagers were skinning, and cooking a dog over an open fire. Nobody could figure out why I wasn't chowing down on that evening's tasty barbecue, but I am an Airedale fanatic and have raised six over the years, so I couldn't stomach this canine delicacy.

After a short program visit to East Timor, the island of Cebu in the Philippines would be our next stop. Like Sumba, this island's forests were being destroyed as a result of poor land management techniques, the impact of loggers, and simple population pressure. The local cooperative had an office with a very talented and committed staff. I left my program evaluator mode to spend time with the local staff discussing how they could increase their funding sources beyond World Neighbors, an important step in becoming a viable, local organization. Local embassies and European funding agencies were an important in-country funding source if the local staff could develop and maintain good relationships.

We were welcomed in every village we visited. Larry and his staff had done an incredible job establishing a positive partnership with local groups and villagers. He even took a group of the local leaders to Honduras where they met Roland Bunch and his Guatemalan staff, who actually developed many of the appropriate technologies, including the use of "green manure," (nitrogen fixing cover crops planted to manage soil erosion, soil fertility and water conservation) that the Philippines and Indonesian staff were introducing.

We then went to the main island of the Philippines and rested up for a few days in the capital city of Manila. Larry took me to meet his close Ford Foundation friends and we enjoyed some local cuisine, which included lots of rice, shish kababs, grilled fresh fish, and plantains, and lots of their local beer, San Miguel. I thoroughly enjoyed visiting several museums and cathedrals in the area because of the strong Spanish influence and similarities to what I'd seen in South America (the Philippines was a Spanish colony for some 300 years). They spoke English and Tagalog, and also used a lot of Spanish words. We also went through several slum areas, which were some of the largest and nastiest I'd ever seen. Former President Ferdinand Marcos and his wife, Imelda, were famous for developing massive monuments and hotels right on top of extensive slum areas—the contrast between wealth and poverty was stunning.

We completed this leg of our trip at a sister agency, IIRR (International Institute for Rural Reconstruction). I had met the staff members of this group in Guatemala and visited their headquarters in New York City. Their founder, Jimmy Yen, was Chinese and the father of "barefoot doctors." He was one of those "Extreme Do-Gooders" who would impact the way international NGOs work with the rural poor. We discussed development issues and approaches with them at a small resort overlooking a gorgeous lake set in the middle of an extinct volcano.

We returned to Bali to complete the workshop, where we summed up our findings and helped develop an overall strategic plan for World Neighbors in the area for the next ten years. By this time my lower back was causing me a lot of pain and loss of movement. One of the participants, Dr. Hari, whose father established World Neighbors' programs in India over forty years before, tended to me, using acupuncture. The pain was relieved somewhat, but one session couldn't do the trick, so I stretched out each morning and used lots of Advil.

Since I was already in one of the most gorgeous places in the world, I took off for a few days of vacation and went skin-diving. The water was crystal clear and the reefs teeming with fish. The local restaurants were also excellent, and the fish couldn't be any fresher. I stayed in Denpasar, the gateway to Bali, and visited the surrounding towns, which specialized in artwork, pottery, textiles, and silver. Since Ligia appreciated the multi-color textiles from the Maya groups of Guatemala I purchased a "sarong" which is a large length of fabric most women in South Asia wrap around their waists, in this case brightly colored by means of batik (a dying process) with printed designs depicting local animals and plants. She loved it and hung from our office wall.

Guatemala & Honduras
Site Surveys, 2004

Twelve years would pass before my next two opportunities to participate in a site survey and as part of a multi-disciplinary team developing a monitoring and evaluation system for the use of essential medications on the quality of health in isolated rural communities. Ligia was in Guatemala visiting her mother and our children were all grown up so I invited her to join me on a program site survey in Guatemala with MAP International and she provided cultural and historical context and insights throughout our time on the road. The purpose of the visit with MAP in Guatemala was twofold. To provide field level input on the successful distribution of essential medications for our corporate partners and in my case to bring back reports and photos to our individual donors on the positive impact of our health care related activities.

Kipp Branch, who was responsible for monitoring MAP's distribution of $400 million worth of essential meds, led the visit. Kipp was a big bruiser of a guy. Short hair, big build and, not to my surprise, a big Georgia football fan. When I first joined MAP (which is located in the Deep South - Georgia) he helped me learn how to pronounce "Dawgs," the University of Georgia's mascot, which was a rite of passage in that part of the country. His wife was from El Salvador, so we often discussed life in Central America and the immigration issues facing those in the U.S., although both our wives were legal citizens.

Operation Blessing (OB) was our key program partner in Guatemala and they had the field staff and local relationships that allowed them to successfully distribute MAP meds to those in the greatest need. OB is based in Virginia Beach, run by Pat Robertson, with whom I'd met several times, along with his son, Gordon, as part of my fundraising activities. Their notoriety comes from the "700 Club," which is produced for Christian audiences around the country and the world. They had a viable radio ministry in Guatemala, as well as the health-related activities we were checking out on this visit. Like many of the heavy hitters I'd meet over the years, I wouldn't agree with much of their politics but they had access to the resources which could meet some of the immediate needs of those marginalized in the places where International NGOs work.

Our first stop would be a public school in Chiquimulilla, close to the Salvadorian border. As soon as we arrived we were surrounded by little girls in their blue and white school uniforms. Both the children and their lunch program received MAP support. Close by, we also visited a clinic run by Dr. Jaime Aguilar that was inundated that day with families looking for basic medical support. One little girl was almost ready to pass out because she was undernourished and dehydrated. The little girl had black hair with two ponytails, and her eyes were just barely open. Ligia looked over to me and said, "She looks like Nicky when she had amoebas, so listless, although we were able to get her into one of the top hospitals in the country, while this little girl is stuck in this backwater clinic." (which usually had few if any medications with a line of fifty people waiting to see the one physician).

Different Latitudes

These are the types of local medical centers that MAP tries to support. We started our visit at the place where the meds were labeled and stored in the back of the Operation Blessing supervisor's home—not ideal for control purposes, but little or no warehouse space was available in this little town of Pasaco. From there we visited a clinic partially built, funded, and supported by the local Rotarians. Four Rotarians greeted us in their white knit cotton Rotary shirts. They had all participated in Rotary's Polio Plus initiative, vaccinating children and providing the equipment to maintain the cold chain, which is the temperature the vaccine must be kept at or it will spoil. The clinic had a full-time pharmacist, and the inventory checked out based on the list of gifted medications Kipp brought.

• • •

After returning to Guatemala City we headed up the "Pan American Highway" (don't let the term highway fool you!) past Cuatro Caminos, where the road forks off in the direction of either Quetzaltenago, or, in our case, to Totonicapan. Since most of the highlands bus traffic goes past this intersection, it's filled with small shops and food stalls, and is a natural place for people to pick up a bus going closer to their destination. Since this area is known for its outstanding potato tamales, you can find every variety imaginable, like "sweet" ones with prunes and raisins mixed with chicken or beef, or my favorites, which are "salty" ones with a tomato sauce and beef. Ligia has the sweet tooth, so she purchased the prune and raisin version while I went with the salty version, which melted in my mouth.

For the next few hours we followed the ever-curving road through oak and pine forests. This area is the home of the threatened Guatemalan fir called *Pinabete*. Finally we arrived at a village known as San Bartolo Aguas Calientes, outside of Totonicapan, and met the OB local leader and physician, Dr. Imelda Champet, a small but stocky Guatemalan lady with round wire-rimmed glasses and black hair. She wore a green medical scrub and a black skirt. She invited us into her humble, relatively small, clinic, which was actually part of her parents' home, where she lived.

Imelda was with a lady and her three daughters, plus a son who was running a high temperature. She had the youngest daughter, about five years old, in her arms. Her seven and nine-year-old daughters wore white blouses and grey sweaters. The boy was about eight, with a blue shirt and slacks, and shoes that already had holes in the soles. The mother wore a colorful red, white, and green embroidered blouse called a *huipile*. Imelda asked the mother in the local dialect, K'iche, about the symptoms—what had he eaten? What was their source of drinking water? Had he been ill previously? She learned that the mother had gotten the children up at 4:00 a.m. in order to catch a bus, which was a five-hour walk away. The bus took them to Totonicapan, and from there they took a smaller bus here to San Bartolo. Obviously, she was well motivated to assure her child's quick recovery.

Different Latitudes

After the consultation, I went with Imelda to her small stash of meds, which she kept in the back. She had all the basic meds that MAP provided, such as oral rehydration salts, exam gloves, Nystatin Cream, Ibuprofen, aspirin, wipes, Iconazole Nitrate, pre-natal and multi-vitamins. But Imelda was also familiar with the many home and traditionally Maya herbal remedies, which are far more accessible and economical for her patients.

Imelda studied medicine in the U.S. and worked with a private clinic in Quetzaltenango, and had been offered a number of lucrative positions at hospitals in Houston, Texas. I asked her why she didn't take advantage of the opportunity after all her hard work and studying. Not many Maya doctors get a chance to leave and make their fortune abroad.

"No," she replied. "The indigenous community doesn't have enough physicians to come close to meeting their needs, and I speak their language, know their culture, and appreciate their challenges like few other doctors could."

Like Dr. Federico Alfaro, the founder of Heartbeat International, this humble, indigenous doctor stayed home where the need was greatest and she could be most impactful saving lives.

We had driven through Totonicapan (Toto) in order to see Dr. Imelda. Toto was a special part of the Maya area of the highlands. In 1820 the local indigenous residents revolted against the government because of the excessive tributes imposed by the Spanish King, Ferdinand VII, and the unfair demands by the American-born Spanish elite, or *criollos*. The rebel government only lasted twenty days and the rebels were captured, whipped, and imprisoned, but it is widely celebrated as the opening volley in the independence struggle.

Since we were in Toto, we passed through San Andres Xecul to see their funky yellow church, which is like none other I've ever seen. Statues of saints catch your attention initially, but then, with an explosion of color, angels and flowers abound. Many of the images are unconventional at best. Some figures are resting and thinking, others singing, and a few murals represent sacred scenes. The church was restored in 1999, but its actual origin is unclear.

Once our site survey work with MAP was completed, Ligia and I headed up to Huehuetenango to visit her nephew, Carlos Sosa, and his wife and two daughters. Carlos had stayed with us years earlier in Oklahoma City when I was with World Neighbors, while he was studying to be a diesel mechanic in Tulsa. We went up to the Mirador at about 8,000 feet with the entire family, where we would overlook the spectacular Cuchamatanes Mountains, which I'd hiked around years prior as a Peace Corps volunteer.

When I learned that Carlos had never visited one of my favorite indigenous Mayan communities, Todos Santos, I insisted that we drive down and see it together, since it's only a few hours' drive from Huehue, depending on the road conditions. I think that Carlos's lack of interest might have been based at least partially on a lack of appreciation of the Maya culture, as he was a Ladino, which meant he spoke Spanish and wore western attire. This lack of interest is fairly common among Ladinos and is part of an underlying racism that permeates much of Guatemalan society.

The road from Huehue to Todos Santos includes one sharp curve after another. The key for survival is to be aware of large *campo* buses filled with up to fifty locals, some hanging from on top of the bus with the chickens and goats (the ones that wouldn't fit inside the bus). The bus drivers take it for granted that they have the right-of-way no matter what, due to their size and weight. Todos Santos is at 8,000 feet and they produce potatoes, broccoli, and coffee on the lower mountain slopes. The population speaks the Maya language of Mam.

An annual festival is celebrated October 31-November 2, and is centered on All Saint's Day on November 1 (*Todos Santos* translates to "all saints" in English). Festivities include traditional dances, marimba music, and the famous horse races. The horse races are often the scene of mayhem and bloodshed due to the riders' penchant to drink alcohol for days leading up to the races.

The men still wear their traditional attire, which includes round broad-brimmed hats and cotton shirts with broad collars that have small pockets with zippers on the back of the collar to put money in. The shirts are pure cotton and do remarkably well in hot, as well as cold, weather. I wore one for a number of years (custom made, of course, since the women don't make sizes for *gringos*). They're white with blue stripes and red/blue embroidering where they button up and on the cuffs. The pants are deep red with white stripes going up and down. Most wear sandals made out of old tires. We spent most of our time there in the local market admiring the incredibly colorful embroidered shirts and *huipiles*, as well as the incredible variety of fruits and vegetables that are part of any village's central market place.

Todos Santos was an insular community that mistrusted outsiders. While we were in the central marketplace, I took a photo of a local Mayan lady selling bananas, and she began yelling at us and demanding we pay her for the photo—which I did. After all, I'm the visitor. In the past I remember the indigenous women wouldn't let us take photos of their children for fear they'd lose their "spirit" but with tourism and the need to make ends meet women now demanded to be paid for their images.

On the way back to Huehue, we stopped over with Mario and Raquelita Sosa, Carlos's parents. I always misspoke her name and said *la Raqueta*, as in a tennis racquet, but she was always very good-natured and ignored my obvious and consistent mispronunciations of her nickname. Mario owned a bus line and had invested in several hotels in Guatemala City that his two daughters managed. We always stayed at one of them, off Roosevelt Boulevard close to where Ligia's mother and brother lived. We paid forty-five dollars a night for a very clean room with tile floors, a nice bathroom, and Wi-Fi. During our stay, Mario's hotel hosted a fundraiser to support groups helping small children.

On the night of the fundraising event at the hotel to benefit orphans in Huehuetenango, one of Mario's daughters displayed the paintings of artists from Huehue throughout the lobby and hallways of the hotel. One of the painters had a very surrealistic style, with horses and birds in pinks, oranges, and turquoise blue, which would have made them perfect to market in the state of New Mexico. Unfortunately, he was fairly drunk and didn't carry business cards, so I lost contact with him. I was impressed that Mario, a relatively humble local man from a rural part of the country, was able to develop a considerable business empire. He and Raquelita were able to travel wherever they wished, and had recently returned from a trip to China, making them true world travelers.

In route to Guatemala City from Huehue on the Pan American Highway we ran into a fairly frequent traffic stoppage caused by peasant farmers blocking the road in protest, usually a new tax or the government's inability to fix or build new roads. The bus driver wasn't surprised and just opened the bus door for us to file out and wait with everyone else. The lines of pickup trucks, buses, and other vehicles went on for miles. Several men sat down on the grass as local women with their colorful *huipiles* and multi-colored skirts walked by with cold drinks (in plastic bags), fruit, and tortillas. It all looked like a tranquil picnic scene. We did the same and chatted with a few of the local women going by.

• • •

Ligia and I had never visited the incredible Maya ruins of Tikal in the jungle area of the Peten together, so I made reservations at the Camino Real, a four-star hotel. After landing at the local airport we headed out to the hotel, whose entrance was surrounded by gorgeous jungle flowers and foliage. All the furniture in the lobby was made of the hardwoods, like mahogany, found in the Peten area. On the mid-level of the hotel was a large open area covered by a traditional thatched roof overlooking Lake Peten Itza, where we'd have our traditional Guatemalan breakfast. The pool was below that and all the rooms were built like separate huts, except they were all air-conditioned and had nice bathrooms.

We took a hike up the hill behind the hotel, which had an even more impressive view of the lake. The hotel manager knew of our hiking plans and insisted we take two soldiers who followed close behind, "just in case." On our way up we saw innumerable local colorful birds, a few monkeys, and a large ball-like thing hanging from one of the trees—oops! That would be a hornet's nest, so we moved right along. I don't do that well in the humidity of the tropics, but do far better when I can jump in the pool in the afternoon, as we did on this particular day.

The next day we wandered around the archeological site of Tikal, which is filled with so much history, as well as every imaginable variety of plant and animal. We climbed up Temple IV, which overlooks the entire jungle with two other temples poking their stately heads above the jungle's green canopy. These are the same temples used as the backdrop of the *Star Wars IV* ships shooting over an extensive jungle with the tops of massive temples sticking out of the trees.

Back down on the ground I took a picture of Ligia between the massive roots of a 200-foot Ceiba tree. The trunk was a favorite for making canoes that can hold up to forty men. All the branches are at the top of the tree, where they radiate out like the ribs of an umbrella. This massive tree is the national tree of Guatemala. It's called a "cotton tree" because of the fluffy white stuff that comes out of its pods.

This was the trip where Ligia and I hosted our first family reception in her mom's home. We put white tablecloths over five tables and provided yellow cups so everyone could share in a champagne toast for the three matriarchs present—Ligia's mom, Antonieta, and her sisters, Regi and Rosa. The tables were packed with young and old as well as a few nannies caring for the kids. This was a great excuse for us to get most of the family together so we wouldn't forget our ties to this incredible country and to Ligia's family. I hung out in back of Antonieta's home with a few of Ligia's cousins telling jokes and sipping a glass of scotch whiskey. These are the same cousins we'd continue to connect with each time we visited the country.

MAP International/ PQMD
(Partnerships for Quality Medical Donations) Survey
Honduras, 2005

Several people in the Honduran capital of Tegucigalpa looked at us as if we were from a different planet when we pointed our bright yellow GPS units to the heavens in order to get a signal. Danny was a young intern from Loma Linda University, a lanky student with blond hair and blue eyes. He had an orange T-shirt, with shorts down to his knees and tennis shoes. He would provide much of our technical support. He had his right hand extended to the sky while looking down at the GPS unit as we tried to get a signal. Brett, who was with Direct Relief International, was next to him with his arm extended out, also trying to get a signal. David, the Pfizer representative, also had his right arm extended to the skies. David had little experience in Central America but he did represent the corporate sponsor of this program, so he was treated with deference.

Different Latitudes

We were a four-member team working on a prototype gizmo that would allow us to simultaneously check our location and pull up a medical survey. The entire initiative was part of the PQMD (Partners for Quality Medical Donations) a global alliance of over 30 corporations and nonprofit organizations (MAP was one of the founding groups in 1996) which promote high standards in medicine and medical equipment donations. In this case we introduced a proto-type GPS unit to record the location of gifted medications in order to confirm they had arrived safely and match them with the health issues and needs we'd identify with five organizations at nineteen sites we'd visit over the next week. Such a monitoring program would add credibility to both the pharmaceutical partners as well as the international NGOs like MAP International.

Danny and his cohorts from Loma Linda University had developed the medical survey, while David represented the pharmaceutical company that helped underwrite the program, and Brett and I represented two of the agencies on the ground responsible for distributing the meds. Since I was the only one who spoke Spanish, I did all the medical surveys and translated the results to the other participants. I soon realized that the health survey was far more hospital/curative oriented than what I would have preferred, given the basic health needs of the local populations we were serving, so we recommended that more questions about clean water, use of latrines, and the basic intestinal ailments, like worms, needed to be included on future evaluation surveys.

Our first test site was San Pedro Sula, where we met with the Director of Project Hope, whose staff helped coordinate some of the visits. We interviewed staff and visited programs of World Vision and Project Hope, both of which received essential medications from MAP International. We also visited a state hospital outside of Copan, the site of the Maya ruins. The hospital was relatively clean and seemed to be well equipped, and they had all the meds that MAP had provided them. As we departed, we passed by a workshop at the back of the hospital that was producing small wooden boxes. The hospital representative who was showing us around explained quite proudly that the hospital had helped develop the small casket business because no less than three to four babies die each and every day in this small community and many more throughout the country. This sad state of affairs explained the considerable growth of this particular cottage industry. As we passed by the row of a half dozen small coffins I thought of how vulnerable my own children were during their early months and felt a somber reminder of how much more work was left to do here and throughout the country.

Honduras was one of the poorest countries in Latin America and also had one of the world's highest murder rates. More than half of the population lived in poverty and per capita income was one of the lowest in the region. Poverty rates were higher among rural and indigenous people and in the south, west, and along the eastern border than in the north and central areas, where most of Honduras' industries and infrastructure are concentrated. Although primary school enrollment was nearly 100%, educational quality was poor, the dropout rate and grade repetition remained high, and teacher and school accountability is low. Honduras still has one of the highest child mortality rates in the world, which is one of the reasons that every NGO (Non-governmental Organization) I've ever worked with, starting with the Peace Corps, had a presence there (until recently when the drug trade and violence forced the Peace Corps out).

The Evangelical Hospital in Siguatepeque, which is between the capital, Tegucigalpa, and the key manufacturing center, San Pedro Sula, was our next survey site. The hospital was founded in 1949 by Dr. Marion McKinney of CAM International (Central American Mission), which, like many church-based groups, found the support of such a large program difficult, so in 1969 they established a local non-profit organization that was self-sufficient. The hospital was very impressive, with several operating areas, X-rays, a full-time pharmacist, and a sixty-six-bed capacity. The facility included nice homes for ex-pat Christian physicians who visited for extended periods of time working and, most importantly, teaching the local medical staff.

Bob Hamman, a MAP donor, had invested a million dollars in this facility, which is one of the reasons it was so well developed. Over the years I'd meet Bob and his family at the hospital, as well as at their residence in California. The hospital also had a strong outreach initiative that included a clinic outside of town and a team of social health workers focused on prevention. We entered the hospital and climbed a set of stairs to the library where I was able to interview several staff members. Naturally, since the questions were more curative oriented, the hospital fared the best of any program we saw, and their commitment to educating and training local villagers in the area of prevention resulted in them doing well in the preventive health care part of the survey as well. They also had a very well-organized pharmacy, which included some MAP International meds, but also meds from a number of other sources, which assured they would be able to charge a minimum to those locals with limited funds and no insurance.

My favorite and most inspiring staffer at the hospital was Dr. Enrique Martinez, the Director. Enrique was a stout Honduran with black hair, glasses and a full beard, which was beginning to whiten. He met his wife, Norma, an Argentinean missionary nurse, in Buenos Aires, when he was studying there. They had three children, one of whom, their son Guido, was following his father's footsteps, studying in medical school. Both Enrique and Norma would take the path less traveled and focus on providing basic medical services to the medically underserved. Norma was a committed professional in her own right, and was the Director of Agros International, which helps poor farmers access the land they need to farm and trains them to be successful in producing food for their own needs, as well as for earning a living. Enrique also obtained a degree in Public Health at Loma Linda University, which explained his effectiveness in developing an efficient preventive healthcare outreach program.

I'd put both of them in the "Extreme Do-Gooder" category and give them special mention for the excellent job they did bringing up children who would become professionals making a difference in the lives of the poor in their own right. Both Enrique and Norma appreciated the challenges of funding the hospital, so they invested in farming together with the Osorio family, and subsequently others who shared a similar vision. Omar Osorio was a board member of the hospital and the Director of the local coffee cooperative which produced coffee that would be processed in Phoenix Arizona, sold online as "Café Por Favor" to various church groups and individuals with part of the proceeds going towards the extension program of the hospital. Eventually Omar's daughter would be the MAP International manager of Honduras. Their dream was to produce sufficient resources to augment their hospital stipend, and also for the myriad community projects and ministries among their target populations.

Enrique continued as Director of Hospital Evangelico de Siguatepeque, intent on grooming next generation leaders at the hospital. He was also the founder and past director of the National Board of Directors of the Honduran Scripture Union. He was the local group coordinator of the Latin American Theological Fraternity, founder and past president of CEE (Evangelical Community of Learning), and a Sunday School teacher, as well as serving on the pastoral staff for ten years at Bethel Church (founded by CAM). Having helped raise three children myself, I was inspired by all this couple had managed to accomplish and the many lives they impacted while successfully raising their children.

These overseas program development and management experiences provided a good basis for everything else I did as part of the international NGO community. I saw the needs first-hand in several different countries and saw both successful and less than effective programs. Most importantly, such first-hand contact with those in need, their leaders, and the staff of the entities we worked with, as well as those we collaborated with, provided a lifelong fire in the belly desire to make changes where change was possible and to offer opportunities for those who aspired to a better quality of life for themselves and their families. And these visits would generate invaluable stories and examples of how the programs impacted the lives of those we serve which was the primary interest of the donors of the organizations I'd raise funds for over the next thirty-some years.

Seven

FUNDRAISING FOR INTERNATIONAL NGO'S

If you want happiness for an hour, take a nap.
If you want happiness for a day, go fishing.
If you want happiness for a month, get married.
If you want happiness for a year, inherit a fortune.
If you want happiness for a lifetime, help someone else.

— CHINESE PROVERB

In 2014, CARE's programs reached almost 3 million
people in 59 countries with information and tools to
facilitate women's empowerment and promote equitable
enjoyment of rights, roles and opportunities.

— CARE ANNUAL REPORT

Denver, 1986-1988

With Ligia and the children settled in Guatemala to complete the school year and my study with the Cooperative Housing Foundation (CHF) completed, I was able to focus on my new position with CARE International and on becoming a professional fund-raiser. When I decided to pursue a career of working with international NGOs abroad, I had no idea how complex they were. Then I began working in their state-side fund development departments, where I saw the demands from the board, donors, overseas staff, partners, and those they serve in the field. They all compete for attention and resources, and they all represent totally different backgrounds and worldviews.

In 1986 I headed out for the CARE regional office in Kansas City. Much to my surprise, it was still in the basement of a department store where the original CARE packages were packed and sent to Europe to alleviate hunger and show solidarity with the people of that war-torn area during and after World War II. Originally known as the Cooperative for American Remittances to Europe, over the subsequent four decades, CARE had shifted its focus from helping Europe to delivering assistance in the developing world.

A clear mandate for this office was the generation of resources. The Kansas City office seemed to be stuck in the post-WWII era, and its larger donors and volunteers really weren't active, so I decided to move the office to Denver. I found a place in the center of town, next to the capitol building. *Colorado Business Magazine* ran an article that helped attract some interest from the business community. "Plug into CARE for international trade help: CARE has 5,000 staff members in 39 Third World countries," the article stated. "They can help market Colorado products abroad." Okay, a bit of a stretch, but First Interstate Bank of Denver ended up helping underwrite our forty-first anniversary and national TV special by inviting its clients to preview the program, as well as funding a photo exhibit from CARE staff abroad.

I was shocked to learn that some of the CARE fund-raisers who had been with the organization for over twenty-five years had never visited a program in person. I couldn't imagine how anyone could promote this type of work based on what came out of the marketing department. Although I couldn't change this long-standing policy at CARE, I was fortunate to have been in Guatemala with CHF, and I took several days to visit one of the programs I was expected to raise funds for at CARE and produced new photos and stories of its impact.

Different Latitudes

I decided to focus on funding the Highlands Integrated Development Program of San Andres and Canilla because it was the same one I had done research on thirteen years earlier, as part of my first consulting gig. I found out through my Peace Corps contacts that the executive director of Food Industry Crusade Against Hunger, George Scharffenberger, had served as a Peace Corps volunteer and eventually a country director. FICAH promoted anti-hunger programs that this CARE program, which helped small farmers, accomplished. I flew out to their offices in Washington and got to know George. We hit it off, as we had a good deal in common. He'd been a volunteer in three countries, two of which were in West Africa, and CARE had since expanded the prototype program in Guatemala to Ecuador, where George had served. I wrote up the proposal and FICAH gave us a $70,000 grant for community land use management in Ecuador and the agroforestry program in Guatemala.

To accomplish this, I had to work with CARE staff in several locations. Our *CARE Express* employee newsletter put it like this: "Thanks to the collaborative spirit and hard work of CARE staff in the U.S. and Latin America, including Denver's Mark Walker, Kirsten Johnson of CARE-Guatemala, John Mosher of CARE-Ecuador, and the New York–based Resource Development Support Group's Lisa Habernickel and Tom Gibson, readers of the *Express* can welcome FICAH to the growing family of major CARE donors."

What the article didn't mention was that some CARE staff responsible for foundation giving at the New York City headquarters were livid that someone would come out from Denver and successfully get this grant. This was when I began to learn about the importance of "territory," even within international NGOs. I decided to claim ignorance of these divisions and get the funding, after which I could profusely ask for forgiveness—a tactic I'd use many times over my professional career.

Once I had an office in Denver, I was prepared to hire some staff. Roslyn Fogel, my administrative assistant, had worked with the Jewish community for her entire adult life and knew many of the key donors in the philanthropic community. I could always depend on her to organize local events—she knew where to go for everything. Thanks to Roslyn, I was able to invite the international president, Phil Johnston, to Denver several times a year to meet with key donors. Roslyn handled all the event logistics for these visits, which allowed me to focus on Phil and the donors. Most large donors want to meet the key leader no matter how many great stories the regional rep might have. I also hired a major-donor representative, and between the two of us, we traveled 4,100 miles by air and 1,300 miles by land during the first few months of our new office.

Despite the relatively short period of time since the Denver office was established, income would exceed that of the twenty-year-old Kansas City office by five times. By the end of the year, we'd exceeded income by more than $124,000 over the previous year—a clear indicator that our team was making things happen.

Different Latitudes

Oklahoma City, 1988–1993

*That little army—some long-since departed—who
helped me beat the raw metal of a good idea into
a worthy instrument of effective service.*

— John Peters, founder, World Neighbors

Tom Moore contacted me from Dallas about a small international development group in Oklahoma City looking for a senior director of development, so I checked it out, and it seemed to be an ideal fit. After some forty years, World Neighbors was working in a dozen countries, helping people develop, manage, and sustain their own programs. The organization didn't give away food or material aid, nor would they accept U.S. government funding. Instead, it provided training so that people could gain the skills and leadership to work together for change. The result was self-reliance rather than dependence on external aid.

I was fortunate to meet the founder and visionary of the organization, Dr. John Peters, and his wife, Kay, who were living in Denver at the time. John asked me a number of questions about my fund-raising experience, which was limited, unless you counted the funds I'd raised abroad.

John would be the first of several extreme do-gooders I'd meet over the years who sacrificed their personal comfort, and sometimes safety, to help the most needy and vulnerable at the far ends of the earth. John told me that he'd been a chaplain in the Philippines during World War II and couldn't get over the images of poverty and depredation he'd seen there. On April 22, 1951, at St. Luke's United Methodist Church in Oklahoma City, he gave a sermon, titled "Let's Deal with Basic Issues," that started a grassroots movement called World Neighbors. I was amazed by how many of WN's key donors were at St. Luke's that fateful April morning. John's message was simple, yet revolutionary.

John had spent time with the poorest of the poor and had seen their suffering first-hand, which is another characteristic of the extreme do-gooder: he had *felt* the troubles the rest of us only understand intellectually. Throughout his life, John received countless honors for his work with World Neighbors. He was elected to the Oklahoma Hall of Fame and nominated three times for the Nobel Peace Prize. I was impressed by how unpretentious and humble this man was and looked forward to becoming part of a team to carry his vision forward.

Many of WN's key donors came from multigenerational giving families—that is, starting with their grandparents, they had been giving for forty years—so they were very committed, but, of course, they also gave to other charities. Our largest individual donor, Beth Ann, was also committed to Oral Roberts, founder of Oral Roberts University in Tulsa. Oral once told his donors that God would "call me home" if he didn't raise $8 million for the university. I thought, *How do I compete with* that? Of course, he exceeded his goal, and Beth Ann made a seven-figure gift, so what can I say? We organized a capital campaign and were able to recruit Beth Ann's two children, both of whom would become board members for World Neighbors (one would even be the board chair).

The fastest way to move the organization's fund-raising program forward and to enhance its visibility in the community was to develop a $4 million capital campaign to celebrate WN's fortieth anniversary. This would include a new headquarters in order to change how the organization was perceived in the community. WN's existing office, a rather dingy medical clinic, in no way reflected its needs or mission.

The campaign offered the opportunity to evaluate and recruit new, young, committed donors with connections and experience in philanthropy. Our executive director, Bill Brackett, hired an architectural firm from Texas, Rand Elliott, to create an award-winning design for the office, which included using recyclable materials and designing it as an African village so the "path" would take you to all departments. Fundraisers and program staff were situated together since they needed to constantly interact on program needs and funding opportunities. The central meeting room was round, like the United Nations' main meeting hall, and the bathrooms featured leather strips to open the doors instead of doorknobs. One of our retired overseas staff designed a giant globe made of wicker with red markers where WN's programs were located. The office design would be recognized in several architectural publications.

Soon schools and churches were sending groups of students to the office to learn about hunger and global-related issues. The new office changed the tone and level of professionalism, as well as the image, of the organization, not to mention that we exceeded our income goal. One tradition we introduced was to ring a large ship bell when a gift of $5,000 or more came in, to celebrate our donors' generosity and to remind everyone of the power of philanthropy.

My five years in Oklahoma City were a great experience, and the entire family enjoyed our new Okie friends and neighbors. Ligia taught Spanish to law enforcement and medical personnel at one of the many vocational schools. Our children loved the local schools, and Michelle successfully applied to become a Rotary Youth Exchange student. I learned a lot about fund-raising with WN and qualified to join the Association of Fundraising Professionals.

SCOTTSDALE, ARIZONA, 1993–1999

He upholds the cause of the oppressed and gives food
to the hungry. The LORD *sets prisoners free.*

— PSALMS 146:7, WHICH INSPIRED
FOOD FOR THE HUNGRY'S NAME

Wherever I am, though far away at the ends
of the earth, I will cry to you for help.

— PSALMS 61:2, FROM THE FLYLEAF OF LARRY WARD'S BIBLE

The founder of Food for the Hungry, Dr. Larry Ward, was living in Arizona when I arrived in Scottsdale. He was in his mid-seventies, with the smile of a man who had spread goodwill and kindness to the ends of the earth. Larry had left his position as executive vice president and overseas director at World Vision in 1970 and headed out to help impoverished people in Haiti with resources purchased with his personal credit card. What followed was an adventure of a man who dared to put his life in jeopardy—under gunfire and threats—because he had a vision based on Scripture: "But Jesus said, 'You feed them'" (Mark 6:37). Like a number of the founders of large development agencies I had the honor of meeting over the years, Larry was an extreme do-gooder. And as was often the case, he struggled to balance his personal life with his wife, Lorraine, and two children while roaming the globe saving lives of the dispossessed, as depicted in Norman Rohrer's book about Larry, *This Poor Man Cried.*

I was recruited by the Executive VP, Rory Starks, who had worked at World Vision, and their key marketing agent, Russ Reid, a real marketing guru. I would learn to appreciate Rory's many skills, which included being a tremendous jazz piano player. He put together a team that would grow the organization like never before. When Ligia and I visited him, I explained that, because I'd never saved much money after living abroad for so long, we'd be pressed to purchase a home in Scottsdale's relatively high real estate market. So we worked out a loan, which I'd eventually pay back, that allowed us to purchase our first and only home. This afforded us a level of stability we'd never known before—more than twenty years in the same place.

Rory and I traveled together to a number of overseas conferences, which provided opportunities to integrate his knowledge of direct marketing with my major-donor experiences, resulting in some powerful fund-raising initiatives. During one conference, in the Dominican Republic, I was able to get to know the country director and his staff, and learn about their funding needs and the logistics necessary to organize effective major-donor tours. Checking out the hotels, restaurants, and roads before bringing in large donors is a prescription for good planning and a successful tour. In this case, I'd bring the daughter of FH's board chair and her husband and children, which not only generated a major gift from multiple sources but led to a new, dynamic board member.

Many of the issues that impact good philanthropy, such as corporate culture and structure, were beyond the control of the fund-raising staff. Also, anything impacting how the CEO and board function—or, in this case, don't function—can be a danger to one's career and longevity on the job. FH lacked a true fund-raising culture, and its CEO was rarely available to meet with key prospective donors.

I explained to an executive officer the importance donors place on personal contact before they'd consider a major gift. He responded, "Okay, I'll give you one week a year for you to organize all our major-donor visits."

"How's that?" I said, thinking, *You've got to be kidding! This is an international organization with large donors all over the country. And by the way, if they're worth their salt, ten to twenty other agencies are also trying to set up visits. So what makes you think anyone could line up our top twenty donors when you are available?*

I didn't say that out loud—which is why I lasted six years there—but I knew I was going to need a small miracle to improve the poor fund-raising culture.

So I hired Craig Hammon, who I considered one of the best major-gift consultants in the country. Craig was on the board of several potential funding organizations. After meeting with our key executive officer and sharing the industry standards of fund-raising and how other executives operated, Craig helped me renegotiate the fund-raising process with him. Consequently, the executive officer agreed to work with ten major donors and report back on what he'd learned on his visits. He also participated in two "Philanthropic Quest" events with major donors, which I'll describe in more detail later on. Even with this headway, one formidable challenge remained: the CEO's wife was also his administrative gatekeeper, and she wasn't enthusiastic about major-gift fund-raising either.

Africa, 1996–1997

On my second visit to Kenya, I participated in a Food for the Hungry planning conference in Mombasa, on the Indian Ocean. As was typical of these conferences, the organizers tried to fill every waking hour with endless speeches and meetings. Consequently, I slipped away in the afternoons to Tuskerville with several of the overseas staff. Tuskerville was a small beach bar on the fringes of the resort where we stayed, and Tusker was the excellent local beer. The first batch was tasted by the residents of the historic Stanley Hotel, and Tusker's slogan was *Bia yangu, Nchi yangu,* or "My beer, my country" in Swahili. These were the types of unofficial meeting places where I'd get to know the international program staff and find out what plans and funding needs they anticipated. And after a few Tuskers, it was easier to get a positive response for a special report I needed for one of our foundation donors.

Over the years, I tried to model the importance of treating our donors as partners. At a planning conference in Entebbe, Uganda, I sat in the back, writing postcards to key donors, thanking them for their support and providing them with an idea of the issues we were dealing with. Seven years after this conference, FH country director Shaun Walsh was traveling in the back of a truck in war-torn Afghanistan with Ray Buchanan, the president of Stop Hunger Now. In the past, I'd helped Ray, as a consultant, to organize a successful $500,000 capital/financial campaign. Shaun and Ray were checking out damage done by horrendous flooding, and, as they careened along a bumpy dirt road, Shaun noticed that Ray was writing postcards. Shaun said, "That reminds me of a friend at Food for the Hungry who always sent postcards to his donors. Who are you sending those cards to?" Ray went on to explain that a consultant friend had convinced him of the importance of writing personal notes to key donors because the only way to raise the big bucks was when fund-raising and overseas program staff work together and share their passion for making a difference in the lives of those in need. At that point, Ray and Shaun realized that they were talking about the same person and had a good laugh.

SCOTTSDALE, ARIZONA 1993

After returning from my initial visit to Guatemala, I knew I needed to build an integrated team to manage and develop the major-gift program for Food for the Hungry. I found several committed staffers who bought into putting donors first. One of my assistants, Kelly Hurt, would soon develop into a first-rate foundation coordinator. Kelly wanted to obtain her bachelor's degree, so FH provided her books and supported her efforts until she graduated. Our focus was always that relationship building was as important in foundation giving as it was with individual donors. We invited foundation staff on our donor visits in an effort to develop the same level of personal relationships and trust. Our foundation income would increase from $250,000 to more than $650,000 over the years, with a focus on Christian-based foundations.

We needed someone with serious fund-raising experience, so I recruited John Scola, who had worked with a number of large charities and eventually would be recognized as the Fundraising Executive of the Year by the Association of Fundraising Professionals. He was the ideal candidate from my perspective, but he was Catholic. Many of my Evangelical brethren don't consider Catholics "Christians" and have no time for the pope. With a wife and three kids who were baptized in the Catholic Church, I had a slightly different perspective on the subject, although I never shared it with my coworkers. But I wouldn't concede that John wasn't the most qualified candidate. I brought in additional local references that won them over. As the years went on, John often wondered why he was always sent to places like Antler, North Dakota, to track down donors while I was leaving for Newport Beach in Southern California. But he kept his sense of humor and became an effective road warrior for FH.

Executive VP Rory Starks and I often made donor visits together all over the country. After one such visit, he made the following observations in my "Fifty Birthday Wishes and Stories for Mark Walker's 50th Birthday" booklet:

> *Mark never stops working . . . or so it seems! I was traveling with Mark to visit some donors. After being on the road for a few days we got on the plane to head home. I was tired and looked forward to relaxing on the flight. Knowing that Mark seems to never stop working, I hinted: "Boy, this has been a tiring trip. I'm looking forward to relaxing now." I made a critical mistake, however. I sat next to Mark on the plane! Soon after takeoff he pulled out several file folders and said, "I just have a couple of things to go over with you." So much for relaxing on the way home!*

So much had been accomplished over the previous six years or so, but many feathers were ruffled in high places. I had disrupted the status quo by pushing the key executive and board members to get out of their offices to occasionally visit donors and encouraging a commitment from everyone in the organization to pay more attention to relationships with donors, not just with those we served abroad. I began feeling pressure from the executive officer to move on. A new senior staffer who became my supervisor made it a point to give me grief, although I doubt this was in his official job description. But as this complicated situation unfolded, I was recruited to join one of the largest relief and development agencies in the country, MAP International.

MAP INTERNATIONAL 1999–2009

I met Ray and Beth Knighton, the founders of MAP, in a small office at the organization's headquarters, in Brunswick, Georgia, where they volunteered every Thursday. Ray was a large teddy bear of a guy, a real optimist who never could ignore an opportunity to help someone in need. His commitment under any circumstances would classify him as an extreme do-gooder, in my opinion, and he, too, would travel the world helping the unrepresented and ignored while struggling to bring up his family.

"Have you written down your stories about the organization and those you've served over the years?" I asked Ray.

"Of course," he said.

"Where are they?"

"In the attic," Ray said.

"Not exactly what I had in mind," I said.

Sharing Ray's story would be important to the donors who had supported him and MAP over the years, as well as to those who would come later. We hired a ghostwriter to help Ray organize his stories into a book, *Serving the Servants*, which included many photos of collaborators such as Billy Graham. Ray often told us how, in 1954, he answered a call in his tiny office at the Christian Medical Society in Chicago. The caller was the executive of a major pharmaceutical company who wanted to donate $25,000 in surplus medicines, and that conversation marked the beginning of MAP. As the director of a nonprofit organization that co-ordinated fellowships for Christian medical students and doctors, Ray had a reputation for knowing seemingly every medical missionary in the world.

I'd work with both Ray and Beth over the years, reconnecting with their original donors, some of whom were willing to include MAP in their estate plans and benefit the organization far beyond the Knightons' expectations. I also participated in a meaningful tradition of joining all new staffers for pizza at the couple's home, where each of us was asked to introduce ourselves to the group. Ray asked questions about our past work experience and personal lives, so we went away feeling like part of the family. When I finished sharing my story, I felt that the Knightons and the MAP staffers were comfortable with their new fund-raiser, and I felt part of the team.

Since the 1950s, MAP had delivered more than $4 billion in medicines and other essential supplies to nonprofit partners, mission hospitals, clinics, and medical mission teams, shipping to more than 115 countries annually. By the early '80s, MAP had broadened its scope of activities to include community health and preventive healthcare through multiple offices in Latin America and Africa.

I had never spent much time in the Deep South, so visiting MAP's Georgia headquarters became another cross-cultural experience. Brunswick is just north of the Florida border, and when you get there, you get a sulfurous whiff from a leather-tanning factory. I'd never experienced the humid weather of the South, nor the marshes that were part of the Golden Isles, right off the Atlantic shore. I'd catch the locals off guard when I called their beloved marsh a "swamp", but sometimes I couldn't help playing the uppity Northerner. A few hours after arriving, I was able to understand most of what they were saying, and Southern specialties like catfish, okra, and grits were a welcome change of pace from Arizona cuisine.

Paul Thompson, who had worked for many years at World Vision and had ample experience in the Christian relief and development field, had recruited me to MAP. At MAP Paul was confronted by a massive debt and deep divisions among the leadership. Ray's successor and a VP were actively vying for the new leadership role. When the board took sides, many key donors were turned off by what they perceived as a jockeying for leadership that ignored the organization's mission. For years I was to deal with the fallout of this internal struggle because a number of key supporters totally withdrew their giving from MAP. Much to my surprise, after my fourth month with MAP, Paul announced that he was taking a new job, on the West Coast, so all we had discussed and negotiated went out the window.

Paul had identified a fairly typical split between the program staff and the fund-raisers in his initial report shortly after he joined MAP. I repeatedly heard stories of how overseas program staff expected the fund-raisers to raise money for their programs without working side by side with their fund-raising colleagues to make the programs more "fund worthy."

Eventually, a decrease in funding and the internal strife resulted in almost half of MAP's staff leaving or being let go. Most, if not all, remaining staff inherited responsibilities to fill the gap and, in some cases, weren't doing what they were best at. As I came on board, it was clear that we'd be digging out of a hole.

GUATEMALA, 2001

MAP International brings passion, science and focus to seek solutions to disparities that should not be tolerated. They want equity to be more than a slogan.

— DR. WILLIAM FOEGE, FORMER CDC DIRECTOR

Since Guatemala was my favorite place in the world, it didn't take long for me to help organize a visit there with several headquarter-based staff and some of our NGO and corporate partners. The new CEO, Michael Nyenhuis, was a journalist who had seen our work first-hand in Honduras and was never the same. John Garvin, the essential med program coordinator, who had been with the organization for over twenty-five years, accompanied us, and we met with my friends at Food for the Hungry—including Phil Sandahl, the FH Country Director—to get the lay of the land and focus on identifying FH's health and medication needs that MAP could help with.

The next day, we met with the First Lady of Guatemala, who traditionally heads up SOSEP, the government agency responsible for authorizing all incoming medications from international NGOs. That year SOSEP had distributed vaccines to 1,400 childcare centers, which is where we needed SOSEP's help.

We had lunch with the regional director of Merck to thank the company for the hepatitis A vaccines, worth about $800,000, that MAP had successfully distributed through SOSEP's childcare centers. At the end of lunch, John reminded the Merck representative that the initial vaccine wouldn't work unless the children received a second dose, so the rep agreed to a second donation for the same amount. I was thinking, *Now, why didn't I think of that?* But donors liked to get this field-level information directly from the program staff whenever possible. You could tell John had been doing this work forever, so he brought a lot of credibility to the table. This was another example of the important relationship between fund-raising and program staff.

Once we announced the second donation, we worked with the First Lady to set up news coverage on a local TV station of SOSEP, MAP, Merck, and the vice minister of health signing the agreement. The ceremony went off well. The next day and as Michael, John and I got into a cab at our hotel, the driver recognized us and said, "*Uds. estuvieron en la televisión con la Primera Dama de la Corrupción*" ("You were on television with the First Lady of Corruption"). Everybody in the country, including the cabdrivers, were aware of the incredible levels of graft and corruption so common in the government. President Portillo would become the first president extradited (from Mexico) to face charges of corruption and would spend time in a U.S. prison (among the hundreds of millions he stole, the president made the mistake of ripping off some USAID project funds). And I realize today that I never did learn the First Lady's first name, as she was known popularly as the First Lady of Corruption.

Phoenix, 2009–2010

We grant the wishes of children with life-
threatening medical conditions to enrich the human
experience with hope, strength and joy.

— Make-A-Wish mission

Jody Edwards introduced me to the Make-A-Wish Foundation, one of the highest-profile charities in Arizona, which helped children with life-threatening illnesses. After ten years with MAP International, I decided to move on. Jodie's recommendation was a big plus since she was the executive director of the Make-A-Wish office in Phoenix at the time and a past president of the Greater Arizona chapter of the Association of Fundraising Professionals. I'd also done some work with the office years earlier, introducing the staff to the Philanthropic Quest a paradigm shift in organizational development leading to breakthrough giving, so I was in a good spot to land the position.

Founded in Phoenix, in 1980, when a group of volunteers helped a young boy fulfill his dream of becoming a police officer, Make-A-Wish is one of the world's leading children's charities. After the founding of the organization in the United States, interest in granting the wishes of children with life-threatening medical conditions quickly spread to other nations. In 1993 Make-A-Wish Foundation International was officially formed to serve five countries outside the U.S. By the time I became its VP for development, MAWFI was in over 35 countries.

When I researched our board members, who were from all over the world, I was excited about Annie Simpson in New York City, who was well-positioned in both the financial and philanthropic communities, as well as a generous giver in her own right. We met in a restaurant in the SoHo section of Manhattan, and it didn't take long to figure out who was going to be running the show. Annie was very direct and somewhat abrasive and had her own way of doing things, thank you very much. My counterpart for corporate giving, Stacy Harris, also went to meet with Annie and came back with a similar impression, so I realized that it wasn't a personality issue as much as a question of who would call the shots.

I worked with several board members, trying to promote major gifts, especially with local foundations. The greatest opportunity was with the board member in Singapore. Gene Ho was a brain surgeon, and he had a personal relationship with the family member who headed up the foundation in Singapore we wanted to work with. I hired my friend, Kelly Hurt, from Food for the Hungry days, who now had her own grant-writing company, and she put together some reports and a proposal. My boss, John Stinson, called me into his office to say that Gene had found some problems with the details in the proposal—this after we'd asked him to review it for accuracy and he'd approved it.

We made some additional changes to keep Gene happy but would be hampered by his need to control all interaction with the donor and his reluctance to approach her for the larger-size gift we considered appropriate. But what could we do? He was a longtime board member—and a brain surgeon, no less—so he must know fund-raising, right? In my own mind, I asked Gene, *Okay, I walk into the operating room one day and tell you to step aside so I can complete the operation and sew up the patient's head. What would you think about that?* But of course I decided not to go there.

As we developed an annual giving program, I realized that MAWFI had not been soliciting its donors by mail—or any other way, for that matter. And I was astounded to learn that we couldn't solicit potential donors from the United States, even though over 96 percent of our donors were U.S. citizens, because, according to the agreement between MAWUS and MAWFI, all U.S. citizens are MAWUS's. That meant that even though a donor might express interest in supporting a child in their country of origin or somewhere they'd traveled, we'd be limited in how we could interact with them. These turf battles were never productive because they ignore the interest and motivation of the donor. But this was what we as fund-raisers often must deal with.

World Wish Day, a global celebration of wish granting occurring all over the Make-A-Wish world on April 29th, was by far the most important initiative our team developed. Working with the marketing staff, we developed a website that could track the number of wishes each office around the world was fulfilling on this special day, which gave a sense of the foundation's global impact on the lives of children with life-threatening diseases. This global effort also allowed us to solicit special gifts from individual and corporate sponsors, to unite the worldwide MAW team around a common theme and an effort to generate more recognition and funds for our cause, and to break down some of the differences and nuances that kept us divided. The first year was a big success, although we didn't generate a lot of new income, which would have to be a focus in the future.

Before the year ended, I joined our team in Argentina with members of some thirty affiliates from around the world to learn what the office in Buenos Aires had accomplished and share best practices. My presentation on "Best Practices in Global Fundraising" allowed me to focus on what was working in different parts of the world, but the highlight was the affiliates' own stories of success. Since the level of English of some of the attendees from Latin America was somewhat limited, I spoke Spanish when necessary to engage the participants, and we enjoyed a rich sharing of experiences. For the first time, I think, some of the affiliates realized they were doing a good job but could do a lot better by adding some new strategies.

Monica Maradona, the director of the office in Argentina, had been there for some fifteen years. She was a well-heeled lady who knew many well-to-do Argentineans. We toured the office and a wish event where we saw its work in action. All was very well done, but the Argentina office's focus was on special events. The staff was engaging volunteers who would buy tickets or obtain gifts in kind to fulfill a wish, but when I began probing about who knew whom, or why one donor was giving a few thousand dollars when they owned two yachts and just sold their company, the discussions would get more complicated.

One of those donor families hosted a dinner that included a tour of their home, where the works of art alone gave one an appreciation of their giving potential. Philanthropy, especially among individuals, is a lot less developed in Argentina than in the United States, and it takes a long time to develop the relationships necessary for someone to consider a breakthrough gift of any kind. As Monica told us, "Our work raising money, my efforts and that of the rest of the board, is totally voluntary, and we obtain donations based on our personal relations and the reputation of Make-A-Wish in Argentina."

In the end, those personal relationships were key, and most staff and board members wouldn't jeopardize it by asking someone to make a special gift to a cause the donor wasn't enthusiastic about. But at least we were identifying potential major donors and beginning to discuss possible strategies to approach those donors with larger needs and opportunities to impact the lives of more children.

Three months after a very positive performance evaluation—we had increased donors and income, established an annual-giving program and World Wish Day, developed materials for a major gift campaign, and increased the number of foundations providing funding—I was called to John Stinson's office. John and the CFO, Peter Wright, were sitting at a table.

"Mark, I'm afraid we're going to have to let you go."

"But John," I said, "I just successfully completed the evaluation process, and you didn't identify any real problems."

"I know," John said. "It's not your fault."

"Okay," I said. "Then what's the issue?"

"I can't say," he said.

I knew it was an issue with some of the board members, like Gene and Annie, who wanted things their way or the highway, and I knew I was in Arizona, which is an employment "at will" state—which means your boss can fire you whenever he wants, no questions asked.

John said, "We'll allow you to resign in order to keep your record clean."

"Sorry, John," I said, "this was your decision, so you can pay for it accordingly."

As John and Peter knew, according to state law, I wouldn't be eligible for unemployment insurance if I willingly quit.

That's the way we left it, and I did eventually need to tap into unemployment insurance for several months, but I was able to leave with a good relationship with John and the staff, and he provided a positive recommendation: "Mark Walker brings an expertise in fundraising that is second to none. He put a structure in place for us that will help us to cultivate our donors to a higher annual gift!"

C'est la vie. You can only do your best, even though the odds for success can be against you.

Different Latitudes

When I shared my experience with Jodie Edwards, the former director of the Phoenix office, she told me that she had resigned not long after I joined the organization because several staff members made her life miserable in order to take her position. "Make A Wish US is filled with type 'A' personalities who will do anything to meet their goals and elevate their position, and sometimes it's just not worth the hassle," she said.

As past presidents of the Greater Arizona chapter of the Association of Fundraising Professionals, we were both aware that the majority of job announcements for fund-raisers were from Make-A-Wish. The openings were due partly to the foundation's growth but were also emblematic of the dysfunction that results in constant staff turnover, among other things.

Although I was annoyed, I would never get bitter and would look for the next door to open. Over the years, I had worked with some incredible international NGOs as the head fund-raiser, but soon I'd be given the opportunity to take up the reins of leadership as the CEO.

Eight

Poverty is slavery.

—SOMALI PROVERB

We are an international organization dedicated to the recovery
of women and children who have endured extreme human
rights abuses, particularly human trafficking, gender-based
violence, and sexual exploitation. We do whatever it takes
for as long as it takes to restore life in all its fullness.

—HAGAR MISSION STATEMENT

A few months after taking the CEO position at Hagar USA, I headed off on a twenty-six-hour journey to its international headquarters, in Phnom Penh, to see the organization's work first-hand in Cambodia and Vietnam, as well as participate in its International Conference. Although the trip was arduous, I was able to review some of the program reports from the office and Cambodia and was inspired by their simplicity and the difficult circumstances facing the survivors:

Different Latitudes

Hagar Cambodia welcomes the toughest of human conditions. Since 1994, our ministry has been committed to serving women and children who are the most rejected by society. This includes women who have been forced, tricked, or coerced into forced prostitution, and children who have been sold into brothels, trafficked for labor, forced to beg on the streets, or sold into domestic servitude. Because we believe in a redeeming God, we believe that each of these who have suffered egregious abuse can become whole again.

In the fight against the scourge of human trafficking, there must be many players. In fact, we feel it is our privilege to journey with women and children from complete darkness and to help lead them toward the light. On a daily basis, we see evidence that holistic, Christ-centered care really does restore broken lives. Women and children who have suffered extreme injustices really can become what God intended them to be. But it's not easy, and it doesn't happen quickly. It's the result of patient, long-term, painstaking work.

As was the case with all the other groups I'd worked with, I made an effort to meet the founder, but Pierre Tami wasn't available. I was also impressed with the story of Hagar and her son, Ishmael—recounted in the Bible, the Torah, and the Koran—which inspired Pierre to launch the organization for the millions of exploited, trafficked, disabled, and abandoned women and children. I was impressed that Pierre was a doer: "The world is over-managed and under-led. We need vibrant leaders: they go out with great passion and just do it. And my advice is: if you have an idea, if you have a dream, be passionate about it. Don't talk about it—just go and do it!" Sounded like good advice to me.

When I arrived in Phnom Penh, one of the first staff I'd meet was Sreyna, who had worked for over five years in the Aftercare Program for Trafficked Girls. Hagar's model of care was intensive and focused on the individual's needs, delivering protection, counseling, economic empowerment and social integration. The goal was that the girls move from trauma to a deep-seated resilience and ability to live independently back in family and community.

I was impressed with Sreyna and wasn't surprised on my next trip, a year later, to learn that she'd been made a supervisor overseeing fifteen staff members. Her father had molested and abandoned her, and yet she was so determined to help other girls in her situation that she managed to obtain a university degree and join Hagar as an Aftercare Program co-ordinator. Now, that takes guts. Here's her response to several questions I posed during my first visit to Phnom Penh:

Mark: Why do you work for Hagar?

Sreyna: What Hagar does is very important to help people, especially children. When I was a student, I dreamed that one day I could be a counselor or have a chance to work with children because the children are in crisis. Because of my background, I had some difficulty when I was a child. I was abandoned by my father, so I can understand how it feels, that the child needs support and help during that time. That is the way that I can see that Hagar is involved in those cases. So I want to be a part of Hagar to help children who have been abused.

Mark: What's most important to you in the story of Hagar?

Sreyna: When Hagar and her son were abandoned, with nowhere to go and no food to eat, it was very hard. They cried to God, and God helped them and kept them alive. So that is meaningful to Hagar's clients. When people need help, they just cry for help, and He helps them.

Since most of Hagar's donors were Christians, and many were Evangelicals, they're interested in the spiritual healing aspect of Hagar's work. But Buddhism was the state religion in Cambodia, and you can be thrown out of the country if government officials think you're converting anyone, so Hagar could only work through local church groups in handling this part of its curriculum. All of this was more complicated when working with the Communist government in Vietnam, and further exacerbated when working in a Muslim-based society like Afghanistan's.

Human trafficking, according to the International Justice Mission, is "a form of modern slavery in which someone coerces another person into commercial sex or exploits a child in the commercial sex trade. Simply, it is sexual violence as a business. The nightmare of forced prostitution thrives when law enforcement cannot or does not protect vulnerable children and women."

The primary program focus at Hagar was on protecting the survivors, many of whom were suffering extreme trauma. We couldn't show their images for fear that a perpetrator might try to track them down or do them harm (and one of the reasons I'm using only first names). Everyone who visited Hagar's programs went through an extensive security check, including the CEO of Hagar USA. We also needed to limit the number of donors we brought in, and they, too, were required to go through the security check. These were all new challenges from a marketing and fund-raising perspective.

One of the clients whose circumstances moved me most was Channa, a twenty-year-old surrounded by alcoholism, physical abuse, and family members ravaged by HIV. "Before I came to Hagar," she told me, "I was hopeless." She went on:

My parents divorced when my mom was two months pregnant with me. My mother was a farmer, and my stepfather was a fortune-teller. Our daily life was so difficult. We did not have enough food, and my stepfather was violent. He abused us all, even my grandmother. I love her so much because she is the only one who cared and loved me. My stepfather never loved me as his own daughter, and my mother didn't love me either. During that time, I lived in fear every day. I had no hope for my future.

To make matters worse, my stepfather wasted what little money we had on alcohol and his nightlife with other girls. Because of his lifestyle, he became HIV positive and infected my mom and two sisters. One day my mother brought my sisters and me to Phnom Penh because my youngest sister was very sick. A week later my sister died from HIV. After that, my mom asked a taxi driver if there were any organizations that could help us. The taxi driver gave her Hagar's address, and the three of us were accepted into the shelter in 1999.

One year later, my sister and I began living with a Hagar foster care family. My mom was so sick, and three months later, she died of HIV/ AIDS. I continued my studies at Hagar's catch-up school, and I realized the importance of education. Education brings us knowledge, a job, and value in the society. If we have a job, we can support ourselves, and a job teaches us how to work in a team. This makes us stronger.

I've learned that we may experience bad things in our lives, but we must not let this experience control our future. What happened has already passed. What we need to focus on is the journey forward.

• • •

According to the United Nations, four billion people live outside the protection of the law. That means that their public justice systems—their police, courts, and laws—are so broken, corrupt and dysfunctional, that there is nothing to shield them from violence.

—INTERNATIONAL JUSTICE MISSION

My visit to Hagar's Community Learning Center, in Phnom Penh, which provided catch-up education for children who had received little or no formal education in their lifetime, was encouraging. We saw twenty of the 200 students who passed through the program each year. The boys and girls wore their white uniform shirts and blouses with red collars and sleeves. Most of the children were Hagar clients, but many children from the local marginalized community also participated in the program—an approach that impressed me. The marginal community where the school was located was filled with abandoned and abused children. Engaging and educating communities about how to identify and support abused and trafficked children greatly enhances the long-term impact of the Community Learning Center.

One young boy's story says it all:

My name is Sam. I am now 14 years old and I study third grade at Hagar's Community Learning Center. I came to Hagar in 2010 with my twin brother. My father died when we were still very young, leaving my mother to care for her seven children. Because of our poverty, my siblings and I didn't have the chance to finish school.

In our free time, my brother and I would go to the pagoda that was near our house. One of the monks was very friendly to us, but one day he abused us. The police found out, and they brought him to prison.

When I first came to Hagar, I was very nervous because I did not know anyone except my brother. I didn't trust the teacher and counselors. But after a short time, we began to adapt with the new environment because everyone was so nice and friendly. What I like most about Hagar is learning from mentors. They are friendly, and they teach me a lot. They are good at football, know how to play music, and they teach us how to use the computer. I want to be like them.

Hagar has provided me with a lot of the most important thing: education. Education gives me knowledge, and it could help me have a good job. Now I know how to protect myself from abuse. If someone comes to me and wants to abuse me, I will run to the crowds and ask for help.

When I go back to my community, I will try hard to study and pursue my higher education. In the future, I will be a police officer and find justice for kids who are abused. I want to help vulnerable people.

From there we visited the House of Smiles program, which operated a community-based rehabilitation center through integrated classrooms in government schools where children with intellectual disabilities and their families received support. We saw many of the 100 participants in the program. One group received food preparation classes in a kitchen while others were in a computer lab. Other students were working in a garden, which provided some of the food the first group prepared. Educating and training parents how to properly deal with, and care for, their children was important to providing a more stable and positive environment for them. In all cases, the parents and community members were present, obviously involved, and supportive of the program.

We also visited the Aftercare Center for girls, age four to fourteen, from backgrounds of human trafficking and sexual exploitation. These were just some of the hundreds of girls who passed through those doors on their recovery journeys. Boys who suffered sexual exploitation were also accepted. The day we were there, the girls were making bracelets and simple jewelry to sell in order to generate some income.

Here's one of those girls' stories:

My name is Srey, and I am 13 years old and love studying and spending time with my friends. I dream that one day I will be successful and I can live with confidence in the community.

My life in the past was difficult because I grew up in a broken home and lived with very poor conditions. My siblings never had enough food to eat, and we never had the chance to study in school. We felt hopeless.

When I came to Hagar, I did not speak, only cried a lot. I was so scared, and I did not trust anybody. But in time I started to love the shelter, and I began to see change in myself. I especially love counseling sessions, when I can share everything that I feel inside. Whenever I do this, I see all my problems go away. I also love going to school and meeting new friends at school. I learn a lot about protecting myself and knowing my own rights. I want to study hard because I want to be a good model to my classmates.

Today I live with other girls in a group home. Here I can learn many things from our foster mother, like cooking and cleaning. I know these skills will help me become more independent in the future. I know that, when the time comes, I will be ready to live on my own.

Different Latitudes

I am now a strong girl. I want to live my life in all its fullness. It will be a wonderful future if I can live with my own family with love and peace. Today I do not live in fear anymore. I live in hope.

As we left the center, I reflected on the fact that most of these victims were just about the same age as my two lovely granddaughters.

On my initial visit to Phnom Penh, I participated in an international planning conference, which allowed me to interact with the directors of the other fund-raising offices from the United Kingdom, Australia, New Zealand, and Singapore. Toward the end of the conference, all the directors went to a small resort in Kep City, on the coast of Cambodia, for a two-day retreat. The resort was on the side of a hill with a great view of the Gulf of Thailand. The meeting schedule was limited leaving us time to get acquainted and do some personal reflection. Temperatures were high, as we were in the tropics, so the small pool came in handy, and occasionally a cold beer was in order.

The meetings were held in a bungalow that had tile floors and hardwood panels and furniture—very relaxing, so everyone hung out in bare feet. One of the Hagar board members, a North American minister of a church in Phnom Penh, facilitated a session in which each member of the team shared his or her life story. Many of our staff had been victims of sexual and physical abuse themselves, or were very close to victims of human trafficking. My one thought at the end of our time together was, *I really have not suffered nearly enough to be part of this crew!*

When we got back to Phnom Penh, we spent our last evening together on a riverboat on the Mekong, a massive river that pours through Southeast Asia from China. This historic river is used for transport and is a key source of water and food for several countries. Our time on the Mekong was a great opportunity to learn more from the other country director as well as to try some Cambodian food. I had a legendary soup called samlor korko, which is part of a thousand-year tradition from the Khmer Empire, which was centered on Angkor. I was told it included Asian eggplant, bitter melon, fresh pumpkin, lime leaves, lemongrass, mushroom sauce, and coconut milk, seasoned with turmeric and paprika. I enjoyed it and felt I was tasting some of the country's rich history.

• • •

My experience with eBay demonstrated that
you can do well by doing good.

—Pierre Omidyar, founder of eBay and Omidyar Network

Over the past twenty years, Hagar has developed a unique model of social enterprise to meet the needs of its clients. The goal, simply put, was to offer women a safe, income-generating opportunity so that they could move toward economic independence. In 2009 Hagar International formed the Hagar Social Enterprise Group, which was tasked with supporting the organization's social enterprise investments. I got to know HSEG's director, Wesley Nguyen, and several board members. The activities had to fit the needs of the clients, most of whom were traumatized, illiterate, and lacking any marketable skills. The mandate was for the enterprises to reinforce Hagar training, craft a supportive organizational culture, build social capital, and facilitate career progression. I had actually interviewed Wesley before he was offered the position. He was Vietnamese American, a returned Peace Corps volunteer in Mongolia, where he met his wife. His last job was with USAID in Afghanistan, working on income-generation projects, so we thought he could do the job leading HSEG.

Over the years, Hagar developed three wholly owned social enterprises: Hagar Crafts, which generated employment for twenty-three women by exporting handmade textile products; Hagar Soya Co. Ltd., which made soy products for street cart operations and employed 112 staff at its peak; and the Hagar Catering & Facilities Management, whose focus was altered early on by Hagar founder Pierre Tami who hired 120 staff to provide the low paid garment workers cheap and nutritious meals.

Different Latitudes

During a meal with Wesley Nguyen, the HSEG director and Li, the catering manager, Li informed us that the catering service was feeding over 20,000 garment workers every day and its little restaurant was generating jobs and a profit. Li was from Cambodia but had worked in several other countries. She was a small, attractive lady who seemed comfortable managing a family as well as a large business.

My own involvement with the program occurred on my first trip to Hanoi. I met Michael Harder, one of the Canadian owners, and Jim Blair, manager of the Hanoi operation of Joma, a bakery and eatery. Michael and Jim started Joma in Laos, where they had six outlets, and shared the challenges of dealing with the Communist regime of Vietnam. I was impressed by the great service in a North American–style café environment.

Hagar staff had approached Michael and his partners about replicating Hagar's holistic model of rehabilitation and social enterprise through their firm, which provides superior-quality bread, pastries, fresh salads, gourmet sandwiches, fair-trade local coffee, and delicious treats. Michael and Jim's company had grown to employ 175 people, with $1.5 million in sales, so they were onto something. They wanted to up the social ante, and this seemed like an ideal business partnership. They would start by expanding from Laos into Vietnam and eventually into Cambodia.

On this trip, I brought a Hagar board member, Frank Thomas, and a Canadian donor, Brian Rooke, who were both businessmen and possible Joma investors. I wanted to find out what the synergy might be between Hagar's business-oriented donors and its social enterprise program. We checked out the Joma production house, where Hagar clients produced and measured all the key ingredients and items they sold at the bakery. A number of the ingredients were secret, so the staff couldn't see the recipe but could mix the ingredients and measure them out into plastic bags of various sizes to be delivered to the outlets. All the staff wore white chef jackets and white hats and looked quite professional.

One evening the international CEO, Toliman Painter, along with Frank and Brian, met with Joma owners Michael and Jim at a high-end restaurant. As Michael and Jim explained the business model, and Toliman explained why it was ideal for Hagar's clients, Frank and Brian got quite animated, and by the end of our dinner Brian had told them he was very impressed. He had developed several successful franchises in Canada and wanted to talk to his brother about investing in Joma.

Evidently Brian's brother was equally impressed, and they made an offer to invest. Clearly, a synergy was created between businessmen when learning about Hagar's social enterprise model. Their solid business investment could eventually lead to sizable gifts generated from the successful businesses these men had already developed.

PHNOM PENH AND HANOI
NOVEMBER, 2012

Phnom Penh is jam-packed with motorbikes and tuk-tuks, which are like motorcycle-pulled chairs on wheels. It's hot and humid and often raining, but such is life in the tropics. Frank, Brian, and I went down to the river for a boat ride up and down the Mekong, the physical and cultural center of the city. Every size boat imaginable travels up and down this massive river.

To really understand the culture, and what made Cambodia what it is today, one must visit the Choeung Ek monument, on the site of the best-known of the country's Killing Fields. As you enter the memorial, there is a pagoda-like tower, and you're confronted by the grisly scene of human skulls piled one on top of the other. As you walk around, you also find marked mass graves, which hold hundreds, if not thousands, of victims' bodies.

Just as I'd felt the need to understand the La Violencia period in Colombia, I tried to understand the nature of the regime that turned Cambodia into horrendous killing fields by murdering or starving to death 1.7 million of the country's 8 million inhabitants. Coming over on the plane, I'd read Ben Kiernan's *The Pol Pot Regime*, which provides the historic context of the Khmer Rouge revolution and how an ideological preoccupation with racist and totalitarian policies led a group of intellectuals to impose genocide on their own country.

Frank and I then visited S-21 Prison, the torture center where the Khmer Rouge processed and killed some 20,000 victims. A sign behind a wire fence on Building C hinted at what took place there: "The braid of barbed wires prevents the desperate victims from committing suicide." We passed a gallows area where prisoners were hung with their arms tied behind their backs.

The Khmer Rouge kept clear records and photographed every victim before he or she was imprisoned and killed. We saw a number of torture mechanisms for breaking thumbs and tearing out fingernails. Our guide, Kim Ky, had lost most of her family, including her parents, in this very place.

After the tour, Frank commented, "I can't imagine how someone would be able to relive this personal horror day in and day out."

• • •

I had mixed feelings about visiting Hagar's program in Vietnam. On one hand, I was excited to learn about a new country and how Hagar was making a difference. On the other hand, this was easily where I could have been forty-two years earlier—as a U.S. soldier in the middle of a war. I'd soon learn that Vietnam was becoming an economic success but that, unfortunately, women and children were bearing the brunt of the country's rapid growth. According to UNICEF and Vietnam's Ministry of Justice, some 400,000 women and children have been trafficked internationally since 1990, and stigma and discrimination challenge the successful reintegration of trafficking of victims in Vietnam.

Due in part to cultural taboos and Communist attitudes, the needs of Vietnamese women from exploitative and abusive backgrounds had not been addressed. Violence was often seen as the fault of the woman, with communities reluctant to intervene. Hagar Vietnam was launched in Hanoi in 2009, in response to the growing magnitude of violence and human trafficking and the acute lack of services available for victims. The first counselors and social workers in Vietnam graduated in 2007. So Hagar introduced a collaborative approach instead of starting its own social enterprises as the organization had done in Cambodia. Hagar would work alongside the Center for Women and Development in order to elevate the quality of residential care. I saw about fifteen girls at the facility I visited, and approximately thirty women were participating in the Career Development program. Hagar also formed a partnership with Joma Bakery Café, which is the main vehicle for job training and placement.

I had an opportunity to interact, along with the Hagar Australia board chair, Richard Frazier, with a group of new clients: five girls, a woman, and her son. One of the girls, Hong, was seriously deformed with a humpback. Her eyes were partially crossed, and she was legally blind. She had buck teeth and stood barely four feet tall.

We were given name tags and asked to form a circle as we participated in some icebreaking activities. We introduced ourselves and were able to ask one question of one of the participants. I learned that Hong had been kept in the corner of a small hovel in the rural north of Vietnam, not far from the border with China. She was not allowed to go to school, as her family was embarrassed by her deformities. Some Vietnamese officials learned of Hong's plight, brought her out of her isolated and deprived life, and handed her over to Hagar.

I asked Hong, "So what do you hope to get out of this training and support from Hagar?"

Hong replied in a very simple but clear manner: "I expect to become everything that I should and can be as a human being." In effect, to reach her true potential.

I thought, *What does it take for someone abused, despised, and isolated all those years to be able to aspire to reach her potential?* I could only be inspired by her strength and gumption to face her challenges head-on and strive for a better life.

Then the group paired up and was given some basic materials to design Christmas decorations that Richard and I would judge. Hong and her young friend Channa were given some paper cups, a string of lights, and a few crayons. An hour later, Hong and Channa held the string of cups and lights above their heads. I was pleased to see that they had by far the most attractive decoration. Every cup had a distinct design and color. I walked away amazed at the potential and strength these young girls demonstrated.

Diep was another survivor I came to admire. She was born in a rural village about 200 kilometers from the border of China. Her parents were poor rice farmers, and everyone in the town knew they had very little to eat. Diep was never allowed to attend school. She simply worked the land with her parents every day.

When Diep was still very young, she moved in with her boyfriend. Her family did not support her desire to marry him, so they never wed. She had two children with her boyfriend, but she was forced to give her daughter up for adoption because the family was so poor. There was a lot of stress in the family, and Diep believed it changed her boyfriend. He began to drink heavily and abuse her severely. After many years of this torment, she left him and returned to her family, leaving her son behind with relatives.

Diep found herself desperate and alone as an outcast in her own community, so she began looking for work in other villages. She was tricked by a false promise of employment near the border of China, and she was forced, once over the border, to marry a Chinese man. Diep became a prisoner to her new husband. In the course of a year, she left the house only once. When she finally escaped and returned to Vietnam, she realized that her life in her own country was almost as desperate as the life she had lived in China. She had nothing: no job, no family, and no idea how to make her life better.

When Diep was referred to Hagar, she was given a second chance on life. She knew there would be lots of hard work ahead but wanted to find a way to support herself and her children. One day at a time, she had begun the long process of healing and reflection. She had already begun Hagar's Career Development program, and she had set personal career and education goals.

• • •

Toward the end of my week in Vietnam, I checked out some of the many cultural and historic sights. Sightseeing can be a challenge in Hanoi, where the roads are jammed with motorbikes. When the bikes are parked, the rows can be blocks long. Electrical wires filled the space above the street. From the balcony of my hotel, I could see a Catholic church that was empty during the day. I assumed it was a museum, but on Sunday afternoon it was packed with worshippers, and at the evening service believers sat in plastic chairs set up outside the entrance. Despite the impact of Communism, Christians were still active.

In the Museum of Ethnology, which represents the culture of the fifty-four ethnic groups in Vietnam, is a home altar of carved dark wood that includes candles, incense, and gold-covered items. The altar is part of Vietnamese folk religion which is not an organized system but a set of local traditions devoted to "spirits" or "gods" which can be kinship tutelary deities and the ancestral gods of a specific family.

Outside the museum are many styles of indigenous homes, including the Ede longhouse. Each afternoon a small pond area in the back is the center of the traditional water puppet shows. The puppeteers are in the water behind curtains, and their traditional puppets appear from under the water.

The National Museum of History, packed with artifacts from many of these ethnic groups, is housed in a stately home with yellow walls and reddish-colored tiles. One of the special exhibits, on the betel and areca culture, reminded me of Sierra Leone, where men and women chew the betel nut with a white powder. One proverb reflects the Vietnamese spirit: "A quid of betel nut is the prelude to all conversation," meaning that, in sharing the pleasures of exchanging and chewing betel, people gain closeness and friendly, warm relationships. This can most often be seen at traditional ceremonies like weddings and funerals. The habit of chewing betel was common among court circles as well as ordinary folk.

Since our Arizona senator, John McCain, had been a resident of the notorious Hanoi Hilton, Frank and I had to see the Hòa Lò Prison, translated by locals as "hellhole." The prison was used by the French to torture the locals, so it's been in business for a long time. As we entered, we passed a central park with a stone wall etched with images of prisoners in chains, several with their hands tied over their heads, being hung from the ceiling. There was an exhibit of American prisoners, including McCain, playing basketball and celebrating Thanksgiving. This revisionist history was not McCain's reality. He and his fellow POWs were constantly abused and tortured. McCain showed both his mental and physical toughness.

WASHINGTON, D.C., APRIL 2013

We each have a responsibility to make this horrific and all-too-common crime a lot less common. And our work with victims is the key that will open the door to real change—not just on behalf of the more than 44,000 survivors who have been identified in the past year, but also for the more than twenty million victims of trafficking who have not. As Secretary of State, I've seen with my own two eyes countless individual acts of courage and commitment. I've seen how victims of this crime can become survivors and how survivors can become voices of conscience and conviction in the cause.

— SECRETARY OF STATE JOHN F. KERRY,
TRAFFICKING IN PERSONS REPORT 2014

I never was able to visit our program in Afghanistan, but I got to spend time with the country director when Hagar's CEO asked me to organize a series of visits with several key partners in Washington, D.C., for both her and the country director for Cambodia.

Our first and most important visit was the Office to Monitor and Combat Trafficking in Persons, at the State Department, as it was our key funder in Afghanistan and often invited our field staff to participate in important international conferences on human trafficking. The TIP Office put together the best source of information on the subject, as well the annual *Trafficking in Persons Report,* which rates all countries around the world based on their efforts to comply with the "minimum standards for the elimination of trafficking" found in anti-trafficking law.

Jane Pearson was our most important advocate, although, as a senior adviser, she had to remain neutral. Jane had monitored human trafficking throughout the U.S. and had traveled the world, witnessing the devastating impact of trafficking on women, girls, and boys.

Our star staffer in these meetings was our Afghanistan country director, Bronwyn Graham, whose level of caring and compassion was second to none. She was a doctor from New Zealand and, since 2003, had various local churches and donors who supported her and her family in Afghanistan, a difficult and dangerous place to work, let alone live.

Most of Hagar's staff members were women, which was especially challenging in a Muslim society where Sharia law is practiced. Even the local staff were often abused by their husbands or family and had to seek refuge with Bronwyn in the Hagar office. She told us harrowing stories about staff being followed and threatened by locals, including the police.

I tried to visit the Afghanistan program in Kabul three times, but each time violence broke out and the trip had to be canceled. I had been looking forward to staying at the central headquarters of CURE International, which sends trained surgeons around the world to provide life-changing operations. CURE had accepted the invitation from the Afghan Ministry of Public Health to take over a Kabul hospital, which offered care for 8,000 patients a year and a training program for doctors and nurses. But in April 2014, three CURE physicians, including an American, were killed by an Afghan security guard. The American's wife forgave the gunman and commented on her husband's "love for the Afghan people" and "desire to be the hands and feet of Christ." I still throw up a prayer of protection for the Hagar staff in Afghanistan during my morning devotional.

In Afghanistan men, women, and children were subjected to forced labor and sex trafficking. Internal trafficking was more prevalent than international trafficking. The majority of victims were children, subjected to forced labor in carpet-making and brick kiln factories or as domestic servants. Some were coerced to beg or smuggle drugs, and many were exploited sexually.

Some families knowingly sold their children into prostitution. Boys became *bacha bazi*, dancing boys used for social and sexual entertainment by wealthy and influential men, including government officials and security forces. The conclusion of the 2014 *Trafficking in Persons Report* for the government on dealing with these abuses does not bode well for the future: "Despite extensive international support of the government's anti-trafficking programming, the level of understanding of human trafficking among Afghan government officials remained very low."

During our downtime, Bronwyn shared the stories of a few survivors.

Anisa was a well-spoken 20-year-old Iranian girl who fell in love with an Afghan carpenter. She could never have dreamed that her love story would lead her into so much trouble. After eloping with her husband to Afghanistan to escape family feuding over their relationship, she faced threats and incredible challenges. Anisa's uncle was highly placed in the Iranian government and had many connections, which he repeatedly used to track down Anisa and her husband. Strong class tensions that have been present for many years exist between Iranian and Afghan cultures, and discrimination against Afghans continues to permeate Iranian culture. It brought great shame to Anisa's family that she wed an Afghan man and helped to explain why the family went through such incredible measures to have them separated.

In mid 2013, Anisa came to Hagar's Transitional Care Centre. Hagar staff would continue to hope with Anisa, all the while making sure she is safe, enjoys her human rights to education and legal aid, as well as individualized psychosocial care. Anisa remained strong in hope that one day she would be able to enjoy a safe and normal life with her husband.

This series of meetings would not generate any short-term income, making it an expensive week, but they did solidify important program partnerships. I met most of the key field staff in Phnom Penh, Hanoi, and Singapore, and brought several of them to D.C. I felt ready to begin developing the fund-raising plan and infrastructure necessary to generate the income to vastly increase the number of lives Hagar could impact around the world.

Nine

The First Ninety Days

The President of the United States gets 100 days to prove himself;
you get 90. The actions you take during your first three months
in a new job will largely determine whether you succeed or fail.

—MICHAEL WATKINS, *THE FIRST 90 DAYS:*
CRITICAL SUCCESS STRATEGIES FOR NEW LEADERS AT ALL LEVELS

Now that you know what I learned about human trafficking and how Hagar International functions, here's how I got the position and what I did to raise the money the organization needed. After all those years of working on so many levels of international NGOs, I'd finally have an opportunity to run an entire operation.

My former boss from MAP International, Michael Nyenhuis, called me. "While at an international conference, I met a friend from Tear Fund, Murray Ellis, who told me about a position I wouldn't have time for, although I'd love to do it. But I think you'd be perfect. Hagar International is looking for a CEO for their operation in the U.S. Have you heard of them?" he asked.

"No. What do they do?" I asked.

"They work with survivors of human trafficking," Michael told me. "Check out their website and connect with Murray."

I called Murray Ellis, who was in Australia, and it ended up that he was a friend of Hagar's key decision maker, Toliman Painter. So I applied, met with the board chair, Jeff Jefferson, and got the position, which was exciting for many reasons—not the least of which was being able to assist the most vulnerable women and children around the world.

I flew out to Maryland for the interview. Jeff had been the CFO for the U.S. Department of Education. He had spent over twenty-five years in the Army, where he served as a commander, with a tour in the Pentagon before retiring as a highly ranked officer. *This will be interesting*, I thought, given that I'd been a conscientious objector during the Vietnam War. But I didn't bring that up during the interview, as it didn't have anything to do with Hagar's mission. And Jeff seemed to be a sincere, down-to-earth guy, and this seemed to be an opportunity to go after.

The board offered me the position, and I felt I was up to the challenge. I called Ligia from the airport in Baltimore to let her know I'd accepted the job. I analyzed the situation at Hagar and began recruiting some savvy mentors to help me move into this leadership role and begin putting together a fundraising machine.

My first choice was my former boss and CEO at World Neighbors, Bill Brackett, who had both business and international NGO acumen. Bill reminded me to focus on the mission vision and values, to connect to the clients and overseas staff, to keep a journal, to interview board members and call them monthly, and, finally, to make a large, unannounced gift (I did—large for me, at least). Bill would be a patient and insightful sounding board throughout my time at Hagar.

Since my focus was to raise money, I connected with one of the best fundraisers and marketing experts for international NGOs: Atul Tandon, head fundraiser for the largest Christian NGO, World Vision, as well as for United Way Worldwide. He'd made a presentation on trends in fundraising at the Hagar board retreat the previous year and had the total confidence of both Toliman and Jeff. He would eventually help me develop a capacity building strategy (a plan to strengthen an organization's infrastructure, including staffing, in order to promote future growth) for Hagar, once it became clear we didn't have the resources necessary to meet the board's expectations.

Since Michael Nyenhuis, my former boss at MAP International, had helped find this position, I went back to him. He had by this time become the CEO of Americares. Michael reminded me to meet the staff at the US Headquarters in Wisconsin before going abroad to see the programs—which I did—and to take notes and be sure they knew I was listening to them.

"Whatever changes you make, have it come from what they've said and what comes out of their experience," he said. "Forget about what we did at MAP."

He suggested that I read *Leaving Microsoft to Change the World*, by John Wood, which helped me see the development process from a young entrepreneurial perspective. Wood represented a millennial version of the extreme do-gooder who left a successful career in the Silicon Valley to promote education for girls in developing countries. After leaving Microsoft, he surrounded himself with talented and passionate people, an important lesson for me as I geared up at Hagar.

Finally, I connected with my friend Ray Buchanan, the founder and president of another international NGO, Stop Hunger Now, who advised, "Set the tone. Listening is good, but you need to know who you are. Wave the flag, and let everyone know that you're leading from the heart. This is a long-term commitment to change the world, not just a job." And so I'd become one of Hagar's biggest advocates and fans.

Bill, Michael and Ray emphasized the importance of a small board and connecting with them regularly. The challenge would be the realization that I didn't have the right type of people on the board in the first place to accomplish its own mandate. But I'd connected with experts on managing international not-for-profits, read the books they recommended, and was ready to get to the work of building a viable fundraising machine for Hagar in the U.S.

Mark D. Walker

Managing Expectations

A man who wants to lead the orchestra
must turn his back on the crowd.

—MAX LUCADO

In an effort to get staff and leadership on the same page, I did a needs assessment and began revising the initial strategic plan, which had been completed the previous year, at the board retreat. I spent a week at the Hagar office, in Eau Claire, Wisconsin, with the three office staff members and interviewed the board members. I visited several key donors and interacted with a number of professionals to come up with the revised plan I was to submit to the board. The plan's theme would be reflected in Henri Nouwen's *The Spirituality of Fundraising*: "As a form of ministry, fundraising is as spiritual as giving a sermon, entering a time of prayer, visiting the sick, or feeding the hungry." More specifically, we'd need to produce a sustainable income stream and a communications plan, strengthen the board, and establish a strong foundation for continued income growth.

June Tyler was the executive director. She had launched Hagar USA's office in Eau Claire some four years earlier and had increased revenues by fifty percent, up to $1.5 million. She did an admirable job accessing funds from a number of churches and Christian foundations. June basically did everything and knew where everything was. She would obviously be my go-to person, though she was doing many of the things a CEO should be doing, with no clear road map or guidance from the board on how to transition to a new role.

Karolyn Crawling was a part-time accountant who seemed to have the accounts under control and knew how to complete the reports the international office requested. Karolyn was a self-avowed soccer mom, so the part-time status fit her family needs. We also had a part-time marketing/volunteer coordinator, who had started as an intern out of college.

Based on the expectations for growth, some additional staff would be a must, so we hired an administrative support person, Stephanie Watts, who had previously worked at a bank but wanted to enter the ministry and looked like a quick learner. During orientation I mentioned that eventually she'd probably be able to visit the program in Cambodia, and she looked concerned, so I asked, "Is that a problem? I'm a firm believer that you're always more effective if you've seen the work first-hand."

"Well, that could be," stammered Stephanie. "I've never flown in a plane before, and that's a pretty long trip, isn't it?"

I tried to hide my surprise but offered, "Maybe you could take a plane for vacation this summer and you can work up to the visit to Phnom Penh?"

We were in Eau Claire and had a limited-to-nonexistent expense budget for growth, so I was happy to have Stephanie on board, and she did an excellent job, although she never would make it to Cambodia.

Eau Claire, at the confluence of the Eau Claire and Chippewa Rivers, was a lumber-producing center. The river valley was covered with trees, with walking and cycling paths, which I used each afternoon to consider what I'd learned that day. Each morning I'd head out on Barstow Street, which crosses over the Eau Claire River on my way to the office. When I left Eau Claire, after a week, I wondered how it would be for June and Karolyn to take my lead after so many years of doing things between themselves. Normally, virtual management isn't a problem, but this small office, with a small, tightly knit team of ladies in a relatively small town in Wisconsin, could prove a challenge.

• • •

Two months later, my first Hagar board retreat would be held at the offices of one of our key funders, First Fruit, outside Newport Beach, California. I'd obtained funds from First Fruit for several of the groups I'd worked with, as its founder, Peter Ochs, was committed to international Christian service. We gave each board member a questionnaire, soliciting his or her expectations for our three days together so we could periodically check in to see how we were doing. We started the retreat with a field update on Afghanistan from the country director, Bronwyn Graham, on a Skype call, and Toliman provided the Hagar International overview.

Rick Dunham, our key presenter, provided an overview on trends in philanthropy and the biblical basis of fundraising, and we discussed plans for an end-of-year campaign and the board's role in the fundraising process. Dunham and Company, the group I was expected to work with—his firm had already done some branding work for Hagar International—was one of the better-known consulting firms that specialize in faith-based nonprofit groups. Rick brought more than thirty-five years' experience, and was an excellent presenter and acknowledged leader in his field of direct marketing, although, in the end, his services were too expensive for a small operation like Hagar USA.

Engaging Hagar Donors

Every time we approach people for money, we must
be sure that we are inviting them into this vision of
fruitfulness and into a vision that is fruitful.

—HENRI J. M. NOUWEN, *A SPIRITUALITY OF FUNDRAISING*

Hagar's major-donor critical mass was located mostly in Northern and Southern California, but I also identified some supporters in the Birmingham, Alabama, area who were particularly interesting. I set up a dinner with Elizabeth Lindquist and her husband, Peter, in Birmingham. They'd met at Wheaton College, a Christian university in Illinois. My underlying interest was based on Elizabeth's relationship to one of the key donors in Christendom, Hugh McClellan, who was a relative. The large gifts Hagar USA received from the family members and the foundations they were board members of were generous, and also added credibility with other Christian-based foundations.

Elizabeth's niece, Frances, was the other dinner guest. Frances had invited Elizabeth and Peter, along with her dad, to participate in a tour of the Hagar program in Cambodia several years before, making all of them true believers. Elizabeth and Peter had two small children, so I knew they wouldn't be going abroad again for a while, and they weren't really interested in joining our board, so I tried to recruit Frances who was in her early 20's at the time. We needed some youth on our board and for young people to identify with Hagar's cause. Frances was focused on her nursing studies, but I put her on our list of potential future board members. In the end, I asked her to review our Capacity Building proposal in case she or her father could identify a foundation donor. I asked Peter and Elizabeth to help us with a $50,000 match for our end-of-year campaign, which they did, so the visit was most productive and would lead to other funding opportunities down the line.

The First Seven Months

There are systematic methods that leaders can employ to both lessen the likelihood of failure and reach the breakeven point faster.

—MICHAEL WATKINS, THE FIRST 90 DAYS

Help us to let go of the present so that we may embrace a better future.

—RICHARD KRIEGBAUM, LEADERSHIP PRAYERS

Seven months after the initial board meeting, and following the end-of-year campaign, I was still nervous about how far apart the board's income growth expectations were and what the consultants were saying. I commissioned an analysis of the actual value of our active donor base of 1,000 donors. Based on projected income growth, Hagar's donor base could generate approximately $650,000 to $1.2 million in 2017. So much for the board's pipe dream income increase to $5 or $10 million a year. At this point, I realized I was in trouble. But the mission was

Mark D. Walker

important, and this was philanthropy: if just one or two donors got really
excited about where we were going, they could change everything.

We organized an end-of-year campaign with Dunham and Company
that included a strategy to expand Hagar's donor base. The campaign
included a $20,000 match, mostly funded by the board, and overall the
income grew 118 percent, to almost $1.6 million, and the donor base in-
creased 147 percent, but even these levels of growth would not meet the
desired growth projections. Also, the effort to acquire new donors was a
disaster. The plan to introduce Hagar and request funding on Christian
radio proved very expensive: it cost $25,000 to generate $8,000 in income and less than a dozen new donors. Normally, this would mean
you'd have to continue testing with different scripts and prospect lists,
but we'd already run out of funding for donor acquisition.

The Eau Claire office was where most of the support work was getting done, and its staff members were doing it, but, as the end-of-year
campaign unfolded, the viability of the office and its new staffing config-
uration was unclear. When I took over as CEO, June, the executive director, was making about as much as the new CEO. So the only two full-time
staff members were both making executive-level salaries. I realized that I
needed to close the office and hire virtual staff because they met the organization's needs—and not just because they lived in Eau Claire. June
had accomplished a lot, but in order for the organization to really grow,
it would need a different level of professionalism and skill sets.

With these delicate human relations, staffing, and office location issues looming, I approached the human relations executive search firm
Alton-Keebler for help. I'd met Sissy Alton and Margo Keebler when I
was at Food for the Hungry, when they helped with some team development activities, and again at MAP International. Sissy had worked for
many years in the HR department of Mercy Corps and knew the international NGO industry inside and out. Her positive disposition was always
helpful, especially when staffing issues got complicated and murky.

After the end-of-year campaign, June called to inform me that she'd
decided to take on a new position in Minneapolis so she could be closer

to her son. "I'll be leaving Hagar in a month," she said. "I've enjoyed working with you and will miss all my friends at Hagar, but this is good timing for me to move on."

Initially, I was disappointed because we were just figuring out the new virtual office model we'd need to move forward. Since June had worked so closely with Karolyn for many years, I wasn't surprised when, two months later, Karolyn announced that she was leaving to take a position that would help her meet her family's needs.

During this restructuring process, the marketing/volunteer coordinator left to pursue her education. During her exit interview, she shared that June's desire to control the work site had been unacceptable, which shows how much you can miss when you're not actually in the office. Finally, in May, the last staff person, Stephanie, whom we'd hired to manage the office, also left, giving only one day's notice.

By this time Alton-Keebler had developed a solid staffing program, focusing on using virtual staff, which would allow us to hire the most qualified staff possible. The firm also developed a benefits program, a CEO evaluation process, salary surveys, and a staff growth plan, over fifty percent of which was underwritten by several donors who funded their work when smaller groups couldn't pay the going rate, all of which might have come too late.

I brought on a part-time chief financial officer with whom I'd worked for a number of years at Food for the Hungry. Gary Gable was a serious accountant type who had his own firm. He immediately began developing the monitoring and reporting systems we needed. He managed closing the Eau Claire office and—with help from Karolyn, who helped pack everything up—sent the contents of the office back to Scottsdale in more than forty boxes, which were still in storage a year later. Gary and I would often have coffee at a Starbucks in Scottsdale to discuss cash flow issues and the types of reports I needed to make good executive decisions for Hagar—and what the heck to do with the forty boxes.

• • •

Within seven months of June's departure, we had set up a virtual office and an entirely new staff. We also identified an excellent shared office opportunity with Partners in Action in the Scottsdale Airpark, which would provide the necessary basic office space and shared services. It would also provide storage space so that the contents of the forty-plus boxes could be sorted out.

When I first met the Partners in Action executive director, Jerry Bowman, it was like déjà vu. I looked around and asked him, "Why do I feel like I've been here before?"

"Well," he said, "this used to be Food for the Hungry's office years ago."

"Oh, so that's it—the same office I went to each day for six years, just ten minutes from my home. Well, you've definitely fixed it up because I didn't recognize it at first."

I felt that I'd come full circle and that we were on track to make some headway in a fundraising plan that would generate additional cash for future growth.

Dark Clouds on The Horizon

The overriding goal in a transition is to build momentum by creating virtuous cycles that build credibility, and by avoiding getting caught in vicious cycles that damage credibility.

—MICHAEL WATKINS, *THE FIRST 90 DAYS*

Despite all the positive developments, the disastrous results of our initial list-acquisition program made it clear that the original growth projections were unrealistic and, along with the closure of the Eau Claire office and the staff departures, represented bad omens for the beginning of 2013. Over the next eight months, we'd begin developing our major-gift program, board development, and the use of smaller, more-focused fundraising partners. We made progress, but I noticed signs of deterioration of the board's confidence in the new direction we were taking.

Different Latitudes

August 2013

Board development would be an important part of any capacity building effort, as large donors always look at your board members to determine if they should take you seriously. We did a board analysis to define what type of members to look for and recruited two new members: Frank Thomas, a Christian businessman from Scottsdale who attended the same Bible study group I did, and Molly Morgan, a two-star general who specialized in strategic marketing. Unfortunately, due to a lack of relationship building with potential leadership, Molly—like our chairman, Jeff Jefferson—would be recruited online, with no prior involvement with Hagar. Although Frank didn't have any pre-Hagar experience either, I was able to take him with me to see the programs in Cambodia and Vietnam, and he hosted an event in his home in September 2013 that Toliman participated in.

Although this was positive, five very capable women declined invitations to join Hagar's board. One was a former board member at a top CPA firm who had done a pro bono audit of a Hagar social responsibility program in Phnom Penh years before, but she had seen some things at Hagar USA over the past few years that did not impress her (although she never told me what), so for as long as I tried to engage her with Hagar, she would never commit. Another candidate was a donor and a vice president at one of the largest credit card marketing firms in the country. She had a degree in theology and did research on human trafficking, but once again, she didn't commit. Some of this unwillingness to step up was due to being too busy, but it was largely the result of a lack of personal contact and engagement with Hagar and a lack of confidence in its future. Also, a board member who personified the characteristics of a dynamic leader—not the CEO—should have been leading the board recruitment process.

At the August board meeting, at the Department of Education in Washington D.C. I caught another glimpse of Hagar's murky future. New board member Molly was asked to review and present our strategic plan, but when the board chair distributed the materials, I realized that he had included the plan he'd developed a year before I started, not the fundraising strategy we'd agreed upon at my initial board retreat.

Molly had experience in Afghanistan, where Hagar had a major program. She would be designated as the new board vice-chair and the chair's replacement in a year. This was exciting, but she'd only recently learned about Hagar and hadn't received any formal board training. Her presentation was fairly basic and didn't relate to what we'd discussed or learned over the previous year. The slide that surprised me the most was a Pew Research Center survey stating that the military posed the greatest "perceived contribution" to society's well-being. I thought, *Obviously, I didn't participate in that survey.* And what relevance did this have to Hagar USA's strategic plan? But the board chair was a retired lieutenant colonel, and the vice-chair was a soon-to-be-retired two-star general, so I didn't say anything.

Afterward, we met in Jeff's dining room for a final meeting on my evaluation and the fundraising program. Four board members attended, and the big question to me was, "How sure are you that we're going to meet our income projections? Fifty percent? Ninety percent?" I tried to explain that we didn't have the monitoring mechanisms or the previous track record to make such predictions, but that our new CFO was developing a more effective dashboard reporting system that would allow us to better project our performance, and that we were developing a solid end-of-year campaign to maximize our income. Wrong answer. I really needed to say, "Eighty-five to ninety percent, no problem." After all, I was the only fundraiser at the table, so a board member might dispute my income projections, but it would allow us to move on until the end-of-year campaign had ended and we knew the results. But I was thinking as a confident fundraiser who had a good team and would be successful in the long term, when I needed to be focused on reassuring the board and gaining their confidence.

By hiring a qualified CFO, as well as a group to analyze the value of our donor base, we'd be able to predict our income more accurately in the future, but not yet. Here's what one seasoned fundraiser and founder of Sea Change Strategies said about these predictions: "A fundraising program is analogous to a small business. You do everything right, but the outcome is never certain, and it's devilishly hard to predict. If you want certainty, stick with death and taxes."

With 20/20 hindsight, certain comments or impressions took on new meaning. I remembered asking about previous leadership when I was being interviewed for the position. I was told that another CEO had been hired in Dallas, but he left soon afterward due to "ego problems." Also, soon after I started, the facilitator of a board retreat told me that the executive director, June, had been against the decision to hire a CEO and the need to begin focusing on major gifts. Finally, I should have appreciated the consequences of the board's unwillingness to deal with the contradictions between a director and a newly hired CEO having many of the same responsibilities and virtually the same salary.

As the key international executive and decision maker, Toliman would always be a challenge to deal with. He warned me when we first met that, though he was a U.S. citizen, he wasn't "your typical American," having been brought up as a missionary kid in Kenya and having spent much of his professional career in Thailand, the last fourteen years with World Vision. Even though we disagreed on a number of issues, I could usually see his Asian mind-set, with its aversion to any type of direct conflict, kick in. He never confronted me about our disagreements and would get nervous when I'd present him with a different idea, like promoting a major-gifts approach to raising funds, instead of what he called a retail donor, or direct mail, program.

One afternoon I was listening to National Public Radio, when I heard an interview with Toliman. My first thought was, *Why wasn't Hagar USA informed that our international executive was being interviewed on one of the largest media outlets in the country?* Then I realized that the interview focused on social responsibility activities that Toliman was involved with in Cambodia and that had nothing to do with Hagar, and, much to my surprise, the interview ended without even mentioning his leadership role at Hagar. When I saw him, a few weeks later, and asked about the interview, he said, "Sometimes it's better not to mix the two."

That didn't make much sense to me. I had just participated in the Justice Conference in Philadelphia, where International Justice Mission's CEO and founder, Gary Haugen, was the keynote speaker. He brought the audience of some 2,500 to tears about the injustices that his organization dealt with and reportedly was a dynamo with its donors. So I checked out Toliman's LinkedIn profile, and, sure enough, his role at Hagar International was only a footnote. The primary jobs he'd listed were his positions as founding chair of a low-income mortgage bank in Cambodia and owner of the largest organic farm in the country. I learned that his farm covered a large piece of land and his wife managed it when he was away, but it seemed to be a major operation. In Toliman's LinkedIn profile, our organization was listed as Hagar Social Enterprise Group, which is the social responsibility part of the operation. As time went on, I realized that he was more of an entrepreneur and didn't have much fundraising experience at all. It also became clear to me that Hagar USA was just one of many things Toliman was trying to manage, so I couldn't expect the level and type of support we would need.

All these omens reminded me of a party I attended in Phnom Penh on my first trip to the program director's home. Sarah Bearup was a dynamic leader who was able to balance her family and program responsibilities with the utmost efficiency. She had witnessed the cruelty of sexual abuse first-hand in her home country of Australia, which made her a strong advocate for the abused.

All the key program staff and a few board members were at Sarah's home for a scrumptious dinner and lots of beer and wine. As the evening wore on, I sat down by a table filled with empty glasses and bottles to chat with one of the program staff and noticed that Toliman took a picture of us. When I mentioned it to him, as we were leaving later that night, he said, "Oh, I e-mailed the photos to Jeff. I thought he should know what you're up to."

I found this rather strange, as it would be open to misinterpretation at best. Jeff, the board chair, cc'd me on his relatively quick response to

Toliman: "With all those glasses and bottles on the table, I'm assuming that Mark wasn't the only one drinking?"

This was what many staff referred to as a "Toliman moment," which usually defies a rational explanation other than the fact that he was setting me up and wasn't going to be a big fan of mine.

September 2013

Toliman made a visit to Scottsdale and participated in an event that board member Frank Thomas and his wife, Carol, organized in their home. In attendance was a relatively small group of donors, as well as several representatives from partner organizations and our church, Scottsdale Bible Church. Although Toliman was personable enough, it was clear he wouldn't bring anyone to tears nor inspire any breakthrough giving.

While in town, Toliman stayed at our home. When he arrived, Ligia gave him a hug, which was traditional for greeting guests in our home, but Toliman seemed cool and distant. We offered him Ligia's desk and computer in our office, but he preferred to spend most of his time alone in the guest bedroom. As usual, Ligia was watching out for his every need. She'd ask him what type of rice he liked and how he preferred she cook it. Would he like to try some Guatemalan black beans? Did he mind our dogs around, or should we leave them outside? But Toliman was quiet, awkward, and self-absorbed.

We sat in the living room to review our marketing plan and discuss some of the challenges facing Hagar USA. By the end of his visit, I thought we were more in sync. When I dropped him off at the airport, he gave me what he called a Latino hug and said, "I'm glad we could spend some time together. I feel more confident in what you're doing here, Mark."

October 2013

A month after his visit, I asked Toliman to provide a vision for Hagar's future growth, as there was no strategic plan for the organization to guide me in developing a Capacity Building strategy to fund future growth.

Toliman referred to the five-page document as his ramblings, but they proved quite clear. For the first time, I realized what was driving the desire for immediate growth and wished that I had been handed this plan when I was hired, a year and a half earlier.

Hagar International had developed a regional approach to Southeast Asia as the victimology of its clients was often regional in nature and impacted by regional economic and political changes. Some 30 percent of girls in Hagar Cambodia's programs were of Vietnamese origin, according to Toliman, who went on to state, "In Hagar's case, our clients are often out of community, migrating, trafficked, refugees, minorities, and highly vulnerable to significant economic and political changes. In this type of situation, Hanoi and Singapore can be more connected than Hanoi and Ho Chi Minh."

But this process would necessitate scaling up quickly because in international NGOs, according to Toliman, there's a "missing middle": either you stay small or grow big like a Save the Children or World Vision. Hagar would need to grow ten times to compete and afford the needed infrastructure, and the only way to accomplish that was to promote retail donor development (direct marketing) and government funding. Although the plan made sense and Hagar International hired a consulting firm to do some rebranding—a good first step—nobody seemed to have figured out what it would actually cost to reach this level of growth, nor what revenue model would work.

All of this would remind me of the fundraising analysis Atul Tandon had done for us when I first joined Hagar. He had indicated that Hagar would need an additional $1.2 million to acquire the 10,000 new donors the board (basically Toliman) wanted us to recruit. Atul had also pointed out that rallying the board around a new vision of expansion would take a minimum of three years, and that building a larger donor base would easily be a three- to five-year process. But the real problem would be my belief that only through major gifts would Hagar be able to access the considerable resources we'd need to grow quickly, while Toliman was set on a retail donor model despite a lack of the necessary funding and of professional fundraisers on the international level. Toliman had recruited marketers to fill this role in Phnom Penh, but they were working on a mostly volunteer basis and they had no formal fundraising training, which made it difficult to develop a strategy everyone could get behind.

The Call
DECEMBER 2013

O, woe is me, to have seen what I have seen, see what I see!

—WILLIAM SHAKESPEARE, *HAMLET*

Two months after his Scottsdale visit, Toliman sent an ominous message to the U.S. board saying that he thought we wouldn't meet our income projections—news to me, since we were exceeding our projections and previous year's giving—which meant that his salary, and that of key staff in Phnom Penh, would be jeopardized. Wow, what a confidence builder. And talk about making the organization's cash flow limitations a personal issue.

We moved ahead with our second end-of-year campaign, which was going out to our donors in early December 2013. Typically about sixty percent of our income would come in the last few months of the year. I got a call from Jeff, who started the conversation with, "Mark, the board has decided to make a leadership change."

"What?"

"We've decided to make a leadership change, and today is your last day with Hagar."

"Why?" I asked.

"We have an at-will contract, which means I don't need to say why."

I thought, *Are you serious? We're sending out our most important end-of-year appeal to our key donors tomorrow under my signature, and you're sacking me?*

"Mark, are you still there?" Jeff asked.

Are you crazy? Why wouldn't you wait until after the mailing to find out if we actually met our income goals?

"Mark, are you on the line?"

What are these people thinking? Don't they realize they'll probably take a $150,000-plus income hit from major donors for this?

"Mark, have I lost you?"

"No, Jeff," I said, and I forget what happened after that, but that was my last day as the Hagar USA CEO. I was stunned and initially thought, *What do I tell Ligia?* That evening, I told her I had some bad news. She took it in stride. "Well, it's Hagar's loss, and I still have my job, so we'll manage, don't worry."

Postscript

The next day it occurred to me, *Wait, Jeff never asked for an exit report. How can that be?* Well, it could be, so I spent the next few weeks writing my own report, and I shared it with some key staff and a few board members. I couldn't imagine the next CEO being hired with no clue what he or she was getting into, as had been my case.

A few days later, I asked Frank Thomas, whom I'd recruited to the board, about the dynamics of the board's decision. He said that Jeff and Toliman had called the last board meeting, not so much to discuss the decision to fire me as to announce it, and since Frank had been on the board for only a few months, he didn't see any point in objecting. Not one of the US staff or consultants—not even those I'd hired and had a fifteen- or twenty-year relationship with—nor anyone from the board ever provided an explanation, nor did anyone make an effort to contact me.

I did reconnect with a few staff members after receiving a large check from a foundation for Hagar at my home address, just to be sure they were announcing the "leadership change" to their key foundations and individual donors in a timely manner. Not even the staff of Alton-Keebler, with whom I'd worked so closely to develop a new staffing plan and direction, gave me a heads-up of the pending change (although it's possible they weren't told either). They never bothered to connect after I'd been let go—not a peep. They actually acted as the search firm to find my replacement and recommended a personal friend, whom Sissy

Alton had introduced to me at her home a year or so earlier. He'd take over on an interim basis and would be one of the candidates for the CEO position, although he was not selected.

Three months later, Hagar USA had a new CEO, Correy Gilbert, who did contact me after interviewing board members and staff, and said he appreciated that he's "standing on the shoulders" of the past leadership and wanted to connect. Much to my surprise, he was never given a copy of the strategic plan or the capacity building strategy, and had not seen my exit report, all of which he asked me to send. I responded to some questions, and he answered mine, but after thirty minutes, he said, "Mark, I need to share something I feel deep in my heart and soul. I need to apologize for the way Hagar treated you."

"Wow," I said. "That's a surprise but a very much appreciated gesture, Correy. I do have one question. What was the official reason the board and staff gave you for my departure? I'll admit I've been concerned about my reputation as a professional and what might be being said internally."

"Basically, I've been told it was 'bad chemistry,'" said Correy.

"No way," I said. "Just 'chemistry'?"

"That's right."

It was an eye-opener, although, under the circumstances, what else could they have said?

About this time, I learned that International CEO, Toliman, had been working on a merger of Hagar USA with another, similar NGO in the U.S., which would have provided the expanded donor base and income Hagar was unable to afford. I'd met representatives of this group at the Justice Conference and was impressed with their branding and marketing capability. I'd discussed such a merger with Toliman, but he never responded and had never let me know about his plans. Even the U.S. board wouldn't find out until the entire report was completed.

Several months after I left, Toliman presented the board with a 180-page document on how the merger would take place—a process that would dissolve Hagar USA as a brand and would merge its board with the other organizations. Not only had *I* been in the dark about the possible merger—possibly because my position would have been eliminated)—but evidently the board wasn't even involved in developing a plan that would have represented the most important change in Hagar USA's history.

As if this situation was not bizarre enough, Toliman and the international board chair designated Hagar's other affiliates (the other five fundraising country offices) to make the decision on whether to accept the merger, as opposed to the Hagar International and USA boards, which were the appropriate governing bodies. When no consensus could be reached and the merger didn't take place, Toliman decided to leave. When I learned of this chain of events, I realized that a lot more than a "leadership change" was going on.

These poorly orchestrated events had a devastating impact on Hagar USA's bottom line. The Hagar affiliate that should have been showing the lead in fundraising had to be bailed out by the international entity, and it's fundraising has suffered ever since.

As for the board, the two-star general/vice-chair was gone several months after her strategic plan presentation, leaving only four board members. Within two years, only two of the board members I worked with remained. By 2016, most of the members I had worked with would be gone and replaced by new ones recruited by the new CEO, but Hagar USA would struggle to simply cover his salary.

• • •

When I left Hagar, a number of the overseas staff and a few of my mentors did contact me, which was nice, and I've stayed in touch with several of them.

From Rafaela Herrera, former country director of Hagar Vietnam:

Your report was fantastic—very thorough yet concise. I think you did a remarkable job. By the way, I heard that the proposals for HVN (Hagar

Vietnam) didn't bring in the amounts we asked for and that funds went to H-Myanmar. Darn it. Poor HVN. It will continue to have problems. I still don't understand why they would let you go since you were finally beginning to bring in revenues. Any suspicions?

On a brighter note, meeting and working with you was a wonderful and positive experience.

Take good care, Marco, and may God bless your future endeavors.

Abrazos,

Rafaela

From Michael Hoag, executive director of Hagar Singapore:

Thank you for reconnecting and sharing this report with me. Your report is very helpful and constructive. I must say I was very shocked when I first knew of your departure. No one explained what happened. But I thank God for His grace over you during this period and also leading you to this new company.

I really appreciate your taking the time and effort to put together this report for us. Thank you for your grace towards Hagar. Personally, I want to thank you for always sharing and extending help to me. If you do come through Singapore again, do give me a buzz, will love to go for a nice sushi dinner with you again. :)

Blessings always,

Michael

From Don King, executive director of Hagar New Zealand:

Thank you for your helpful and candid report where you identify many of the common issues we live with.

I was surprised by your exit, and there are obviously a number of frustrations and unrealistic expectations that you experienced.

I wish you all the best in your consulting role, which, hopefully, will have fewer headaches for you in 2014. Thanks for the report again & the offer of assistance, which I will avail myself if the need arises.

Blessings to you for the future year ahead.

Kind regards,

Don

From Logan Cooper, marketing director for Hagar International and Hagar USA:

Thanks for this. I see you have a new role? Will be nice to work with local staff in an actual office with talented staff, I bet!

Great insight in this report, and I am really sorry for how it turned out.

I, like you, was very surprised by the decision, and timing . . . particularly with the end of year appeals and major donor letters about to go out.

In hindsight, it was also an impossible task for you with June continuing in her role . . . I agree though that the direction needs to be marketing and fundraising staff that know the US market well.

I hope you enjoy the next adventure and enjoyed our time working together. The results in their end were pretty good!

Have a great year, Mark, and much love to your family.

Bless you,

Logan

From Rory Starks, new-business VP at Masterworks and former executive VP at Food for the Hungry:

I looked the document over and think you did a very thorough job of outlining the issues. It's always sad to see a ministry with such great potential (and doing such good work) get killed by cultural barriers that could be eliminated if everyone could see them clearly. Well, you did your best

and that's all any of us can do with what God places before us. Onward and upward!
   Rory

My time with Hagar was a revelation, not only because of the gruesome nature of human trafficking, but also as a reminder of the complexity of international NGOs and all the factors that go into managing such agencies. Also, I was reminded that Christian-based organizations can be unprofessional and less than compassionate and transparent in the way they treat their staff.

My tenure at Hagar would represent my last full-time position with an international NGO, but I could say, when problems or obstacles with international NGOs came up, "Been there, done that." Consulting opportunities would open with a number of organizations I was most interested in—including the National Peace Corps Association—and I would have a lot more time to spend with our beautiful grandchildren and three children, all of whom lived within forty-five minutes of our home. But the story would not end here.

Ten

Philanthropy: Ripples in the Pond

Sometimes our concern for the poor may carry
with it a prejudice against the rich.

—Henri J. M. Nouwen, *The Spirituality of Fundraising*

W hen I left Sierra Leone and Plan International, in 1985, and became regional director for CARE International in Denver, little did I realize that I'd go from being an advocate for the poor to becoming an advocate for the rich. I would also become aware that, just as the poor suffered due to a lack of resources, many of the largest donors would suffer due to an abundance of wealth. These individuals would be approached constantly by different groups trying to convince them to share some of that wealth with their cause. The challenge was to separate our ministry from the competition and turn it into one of the top groups a donor supported.

An Advocate for Wealthy Givers

Each of us will one day be judged by our standard of
life, —not by our standard of living; by our measure

Different Latitudes

of giving, —not by our measure of wealth; by our
simple goodness, —not by our seeming greatness.

— WILLIAM ARTHUR WARD

I met Ruth Newhouse when I was a regional director with MAP International. Ruth and her husband, Bob, who lived in the small mountain community of Bishop, California, had been supporters of MAP for many years. Ruth's father owned a large Los Angeles–area orange grove, which was the basis of their estate. The Newhouses didn't have children, and when Bob died, Ruth decided to move to a retirement community outside San Diego.

Whenever I met with Ruth, I'd bring MAP's CEO or one of the overseas staff from Kenya or Côte d'Ivoire, so they could share their stories about the impact of MAP's work, often at a gathering of her friends at the retirement home. When I was in town, Ruth would put me and my colleagues up at the facility's guesthouse. She also had friends in the Phoenix area, so she occasionally visited Ligia and me at our home in Scottsdale. We'd sit out on our back porch with a cup of coffee, allowing Ruth to rest after the long drive, and she would chat about her new car and what she'd be doing while in our area.

Ruth couldn't travel abroad to see our programs because of her weak knees, but in May 2000 we made sure she was able to attend one of our Vision Weekends, when we brought our key overseas staff and donors together on Saint Simons Island, near our headquarters in Brunswick, Georgia. Ligia agreed to pick her up at the airport in Phoenix and accompany her for the remainder of the trip to Brunswick, allowing her to relax, shop, and get to know some of our board members, overseas staff, and friends. We were also able to recognize her support in a low-key, appropriate manner.

As Ruth reorganized her estate to meet her retirement needs, she also wanted to benefit the several charities she supported by working with the National Christian Foundation staff and Greg Sperry, who once worked with some the same MAP donors as I did. Greg was a very competent lawyer who specialized in wealth management. Because of her interest in education, I asked Ruth to consider a major gift to enhance our staff training and educational activities abroad. Eventually, she'd restructure several trusts and provide MAP with one of its largest gifts from an individual ($1.4 million).

As a professional fundraiser, I love these sorts of campaigns. They allow me to ask for that special, once-in-a-lifetime gift and often offer naming opportunities and other donor incentives that aren't normally available to international development organizations (although Ruth never expressed interest in such naming opportunities).

Even after I left MAP, Ruth and I stayed in touch. She loved dogs, although she didn't have one at the time, so we'd send her pictures of our Airedales with a note saying "bowwow." About ten years after I left the organization, I learned that Ruth had been diagnosed with Parkinson's disease. She died a few years later. I recalled a comment she once made, when I told her what an incredible impact her gifts had on the ministry. She replied, "I've always felt part of the MAP family, and I have to admit I've gotten more from this partnership than I've given." It was the greatest compliment and benchmark for success a fundraiser could ask for.

• • •

Major-gift and campaign fundraising would become one of my specialties over the years. Each organization has a different definition of a major gift, but for the groups I worked with, it was $10,000 and over. I appreciated that individuals could have a major impact on an organization and have their own lives transformed through the process. Their lives would have so much more meaning than if they'd used the resources on frivolous items. This method of fundraising would be the most cost-effective: I could generate ten to twenty times more from major gifts than the cost to the charitable group.

Lifelong Partnerships and Long-Term Value

Fundraising must always aim to create new, lasting relationships.

—Henri J. M. Nouwen, *The Spirituality of Fundraising*

Roy and Louise Waszok were longtime supporters of MAP International, and I'd soon learn their involvement went back to the organization's founder, Ray Knighton, through his cousin, Esther, who'd been a missionary in Africa. They visited MAP's small office, which had just opened in Wheaton, Illinois, and had given faithfully to the organization ever since.

The Waszoks were born in the Chicago area and had spent most of their lives there, Louise as a secretary and Roy as an architect involved in engineering the city's first subway system. Their first date was to the Chicago World's Fair, and they were married in 1933. Roy's engineering firm was sold to another company, and the stock appreciated considerably. Instead of suffering capital gains taxes, he set up a trust with the help of Greg Sperry, from the National Christian Foundation. The Waszoks didn't have children, and MAP was one of their favorite charities.

Roy and Louise were well into their eighties when I met them. I'd occasionally visit them when I was in Tempe, Arizona—they had moved to a retirement home there—and we'd have a meal at the home's cafeteria. I once asked Roy what had motivated them to include MAP in their trust.

"The resources aren't ours anyway," he said. "We're giving them back to the Lord, where they belong."

Louise said she felt "euphoric" when she learned that Roy had decided to make part of their gift while they were still alive to enjoy it (which made two of us).

I asked the Waszoks to allow us to share their story in the new *Knighton Circle* newsletter, which we'd established for long-term donors, and they agreed, not because of the recognition, but for the opportunity to share how happy they were to make such a special gift to MAP. After their deaths, MAP International was the recipient of the final payout of their estate, which amounted to over $500,000.

• • •

MAP cofounder Beth Knighton introduced me to another elder donor who loved the organization, but had been forgotten because we hadn't received a gift from her in a long time. Ruth Hinton lived in a retirement community by Lake Washington, outside Seattle. She was in her eighties when I showed up to thank her for her past support of more than $430,000 over the years. She was actually from back East and had lived on Saint Simons Island, near MAP's headquarters, for part of the year. Ruth and her husband, Ken, knew the Knightons well and helped pack the Travel Packs in the warehouse with essential meds to be sent abroad to various short-term missions.

Eventually, I'd bring the MAP CEOs—first Paul Thompson and then Michael Nyenhuis—to thank her for her more than thirty years of support. On one of my visits I met her nephew Richard Hinton, who shared the concerns of his other siblings that Ruth and Ken had perhaps given too much of their estate to MAP. What was the relationship there? Was MAP taking advantage of them? This began a long-term process of getting to know Richard and keeping him in the loop on everything we would do with Ruth. I explained what MAP does and how Ruth and Ken had volunteered for so many years at our headquarters. I think that Richard eventually began to appreciate how his aunt's life had, in fact, been enriched through her support of MAP. I also provided materials and answered questions from some of the other nephews, and eventually, some of them became donors. We gave Ruth and her nephews copies of the founder's book, *Serving the Servants*, and highlighted her profile, and that of her late husband, in our *Legacy* newsletter. When Ruth passed away, five years after I met her, one of our local donors represented MAP at the funeral. The organization would receive an additional $400,000 from her estate.

• • •

One pleasant surprise was the critical mass of donor support I discovered in Oklahoma City, where I'd spend six years with World Neighbors. The MAP founders made a presentation at the Christian Medical & Dental Associations there, and, evidently, all the right people were in attendance, including two of our earliest supporters, Jack and Jodie Hough. Jack was a respected otologist who had set up his own research clinic, which provided low-cost solutions to many with hearing problems for more than forty years. Jack served on the MAP board and introduced a number of key programs, including an award to the most impactful staffer in the organization. Beth, MAP's cofounder, once said of the Houghs, "Not only have they given of their time and talent, but they have led many fellow Oklahomans to support MAP."

Jack Humphreys and his wife, Bonnie, were friends of the Houghs and MAP. Jack was an avid retailer and eventually a very savvy investor who was very generous to MAP. He told me that he was one of the first retailers to include hair products for African Americans in many Oklahoma stores. I always brought our CEO to their home and was able to meet and get to know several of their children, who would eventually take over the philanthropic decision-making.

A committed Christian, Jack Humphreys told me that his initial contact with MAP showed the hand of God orchestrating his connection with the organization. In 1962 he had gone on a mission trip to the highlands of Guatemala, where "we were overwhelmed by the sickness and disease that we saw everywhere. A missionary nurse told us that a lack of medical supplies and pharmaceuticals kept them from curing these unfortunate conditions."

The situation weighed heavily on his heart as he flew back to the States to attend a Christian businessmen's convention in Houston. When he went to breakfast the next morning, a waitress asked if he would mind sharing a table with another person. That person turned out to be MAP's founder Ray Knighton. Jack and Bonnie would make sizable gifts to MAP, with a seven-figure gift after both had passed away.

The Philanthropic Quest

Because the needs of the world seem incalculable, it's
hard to see that the capabilities of the world are too.

—JAMES GREGORY LORD, FOUNDER OF
THE PHILANTHROPIC QUEST

You can tell whether a man is clever by his answers. You
can tell whether a man is wise by his questions.

—NAGUIB MAHFOUZ, NOBEL LAUREATE

Since 1994, I'd utilized a new paradigm for raising funds, centered on a concept of philanthropy that transforms the donor as well as the recipient organization. I'd bring together the key potential leaders of an organization, especially in philanthropy, and ask a series of questions, the "appreciative inquiry," to help them identify what's most important about the organization, how they relate to its mission, and what they can do to help the group's leadership exceed their expectations to make a difference. Jim Lord was the cofounder of the approach and my mentor over the years to apply it to the different ministries I'd work with. Jim had spent five years with Ketchum, the premier PR and campaign consulting firm of the time and in 1983 wrote *The Raising of Money*, which challenged the conventional wisdom by asserting that "organizations have no needs," insisting that a successful program of philanthropy is built on strengths, accomplishments, and potentials of the organizations and its donors, rather than on problems and deficiencies. The aim would not only advance the organization but create the kind of society we want.

I hired Jim in 1994 to organize a series of workshops at Food for the Hungry to take donors, staff, and board members through the Quest. Jim started the appreciative inquiry process by posing questions to both staff and donors: *How is the world changing around us? What is the worth of FH? Can you remember a time when you felt you were most engaged, most excited, most gratified in any dimension of FH? What kind of world do you want? How are you going to get there?*

As the participants shared their stories about their most transformational experience related to giving, they realized how important philanthropy was in their lives and how much they had in common with everyone in the room. I shared the story of my trip to Ignacio, Colorado, with a church youth group—my first experience helping an underdeveloped community. Others shared how their parents' or grandparents' giving traditions impacted them, and several shared how mission trips changed their worldview and desire to seriously help others.

As a result of this process, donors were given a higher status at FH, as were their interests. This greater appreciation resulted in staff taking more initiative and responding quicker to donor requests for information. This change in attitude affected staff all the way up to the executive level. The FH execs made themselves available to make donor visits when the opportunity arose, as opposed to when their schedule allowed. The Quest initiative culminated a year later with the formation of a President's Advisory Council at a local resort in Scottsdale, where several board members and key donors gathered to listen to FH's Executive Director as well as the international program Director Randy Hoag's vision for the future.

A few years after introducing the Quest at Food for the Hungry, major-gift donations increased twenty percent over the previous year, and deferred gifts—donations made through wills and trusts—doubled, to $420,000. Over the years, I'd use the Philanthropic Quest approach with over a dozen organizations, leading to both organizational and philanthropic transformation.

Dialogue on Inherited Wealth

We must claim the confidence to go to a wealthy person knowing
that he or she is just as poor and in need of love as we are.

—Henri J. M. Nouwen, *A Spirituality of Fundraising*

The poor are shunned even by their neighbors,
but the rich have many friends.

—Proverbs 14:20

As a professional fundraiser with limited financial wherewithal, I'd have to admit my limitations in dealing with certain challenges facing major donors, so I'd often link them up with another well-to-do donor with whom to discuss and resolve problems. At an FH advisory council meeting, I asked Howard Anderson, who'd inherited his fortune from his father's home savings bank in Orange County, California, if he would share with Bill Williams some of his experiences on the challenges of inherited wealth. Bill's grandfather, the founder of a giant international chemical company in Philadelphia, and his father had set up a foundation and had also set up a trust for each of Bill's children.

"I'd be happy to," said Howard, and thus started a most interesting dialogue.

Howard shared the following with Bill:

"What impacted me the most when my father announced that I'd be leading his foundation and managing much of his estate was how to find career vocations without the personal need to earn or raise any income. Also, I'd have to deal with peer issues and secrecy surrounding all aspects of inherited wealth, not to mention international and external pressures to have social significance in a society mesmerized by power and money. Fortunately, I was brought up a Christian, which helped me sort through much of this, but also I've had to deal with pressures and misunderstanding in a conservative culture that does not understand any role for the wealthy other than that of a business entrepreneur."

Howard followed up with Bill by sending him a number of references and information from John Sedgwick's *Rich Kids*:

> *Conservatives have always liked money. Many of them have also developed a special affection for those who have it that goes beyond ideology. But there is one group of wealthy people that conservatives have rarely understood, and, partly as a consequence, few of this group have ever supported conservatives in the last two generations. These are the trust-fund babies, sometimes referred to less politely as "rich kids." In order to qualify under this heading... you need to have not arrived at this position through your own efforts and talents.*

Howard pointed out that rich kids are very isolated. "We do not form a community. Our upbringing has not generally specifically trained us to handle money. If anything, we have a tendency to a mental block when it comes to anyone even saying the words *trust, stock, bond*, etc. "

As Sedgwick puts it:

> *For all its undeniable glory, the money involves hazards that all rich kids have to face. It is like some magic sword; it gives the holder rare powers, but only the mightiest warriors can keep from being nicked themselves by the blade... For rich kids, however, their sword is presented to them whether they can handle it or not.*

The personal relationships with the execs and field staff—seeing the power of their giving and how it transforms the lives of so many desperate people in far-off places—have their own value to this special type of donor.

I have no doubt that Bill learned a good deal from Howard's insights on inherited wealth and was able to deal more effectively with his own children. I'd help facilitate both men's relationship with FH's CEO as well as promote their contact with the programs and staff they supported in the field so they could see the power of their giving and how it transformed the lives of so many people. Howard would visit FH's program in Kenya, and Bill and his children would make several visits to Nicaragua and Guatemala.

Ripples in The Pond

Asking people for money is giving them the opportunity
to put their resources at the disposal of the Kingdom.

—Henri J. M. Nouwen, *The Spirituality of Fundraising*

One of the mystical aspects of fundraising is that you really never know how your efforts might impact a donor, or when they'll take what you've told them to heart. A fundraiser's best efforts to engage and motivate a donor might not generate a special gift until the fundraiser has left, and often it will benefit an entirely different organization. This was the case with my friends since high school, Dave and Patty Thyfault. I knew they had big hearts and could see that Dave's real estate and investment businesses would eventually pay off big time, so I told him, "You know, Dave, I've been working with some folks who set up their own foundation, and they've already defined how to meet the needs of their children and now can focus on how to utilize their resources to help others—a win-win situation."

"I know," said Dave nonchalantly. "We set up our trust years ago. Our tax adviser has us dialed in on most of the opportunities to reduce our tax liability."

That didn't stop me from sharing some of the suffering I'd witnessed while visiting programs with MAP International, and Dave and Patty did come through with a few nice gifts, but they never met my expectations, nor their potential, based on the growth and success of Dave's real estate business.

After I left MAP, we discussed their involvement with Woody's Haven of Hope a group in Denver helping the homeless that resonated more with them since it related to a lack of what they had built their business on—housing. I started asking questions like, "To what extent is the organization meeting the needs of the growing number of homeless? Has it considered asking its volunteers to help generate the resources necessary to expand its facility? You and Patty have done a great job giving them clothing and the other things Woody's Place requested, but you could probably have an even greater impact."

Six years after I left MAP, I asked Dave for an update on Woody's Place's campaign to share with my friends at André House of Hospitality in Phoenix, which also helps the homeless. I received the following update from Dave on their support of a $2 million expansion effort Woody's Place had organized:

If you scroll down further [on Woody's Place's website], you will see they offer to sell naming rights to various services and portions of the building. Patty and I sprung for $50K for the vision clinic because that is something we can relate to [Dave has some vision problems and can't drive at night]. Further down, you can see the scoop on the Lou Holtz banquet, which is next Saturday. We took the lead sponsorship of that too (cost=$10K). In addition, we were lead sponsors for the golf tournament in the summer (cost=$5K). Then there are other trips with food and clothes throughout the year.

I share the amount of our donations with you to illustrate something you said years ago, to the effect of "You never know what somebody can do unless you ask." At the time, you lent great importance to touching base with your then current donors because they might be willing to do even more if anybody bothered to tell them there was a need. This stuck with me.

In our world, we were always relatively generous, but until the last few years, our resources were fairly modest. Then the real estate market in Denver exploded. Out of the blue, we had new cash flow, new values to our properties and more money than we will probably ever need. So, in a case like that what does one do?

Fortunately, over the years you inspired us to rethink our own charitable giving and we found a place that suits us well. It seems wholly appropriate for people who derive their success from homes to uplift those without homes in whatever ways we can. Of course, I'm sure you inspired other people too. They just don't know you like we do, so they would be less inclined to let you know the impact you've had on them. The bottom line is we probably would have never had the inspiration to help God's children to the extent we now do, were it not for knowing you and Ligia, and for that, we are grateful. So is Father Woody's and hundreds of homeless people.

• • •

When all is said and done, here's how easy it is:
The Right Person
asks
The Right Prospect
for
The Right Amount
in
The Right Way
at
The Right Time
for
The Right Cause
with
The Right Follow-up.
And you . . . you are the right person.

—JEROLD PANAS, *ASKING*

Journey to Become A Professional Fundraiser

Blessed are the money raisers, for in heaven they
shall stand at the right hand of the martyrs.

—DWIGHT L. MOODY

Different Latitudes

A fundraiser stood at the heavenly gate,
His face was scarred and old.
He stood before the man of fate
For admission to the fold.
"What have you done," Saint Peter said,
"To gain admission here?"
"I've been a fundraiser, sir,
"For many and many a year."
The pearly gates swung open wide,
Saint Peter rang the bell.
"Come in and choose your harp," he sighed,
"You've had your share of hell!"

—Jerold Panas, *Asking*

After my crash course in fundraising and setting up the new office for CARE International, in 1986, I recognized the complexity of philanthropy and realized I'd need help from like-minded professionals, so I joined the National Society of Fund Raising Executives, with a chapter in Oklahoma City that had about eighty members. I was told that I needed to be certified, which shows you have at least five years of fundraising experience, passed a test, and fulfilled robust criteria—which I accomplished in 1990. I'd formally entered one of the fastest-growing professions in the country. The organization would change its name to the Association of Fundraising Professionals in 2001 and would inspire global change and supported efforts that generated over $1 trillion by 2016. I'd be one of nearly 30,000 individual and organizational members, who would raise over $100 billion annually.

• • •

When I arrived in Phoenix, in 1993, I joined the board of NSFRE and after more than fifteen years of active involvement, I became the president of the Greater Arizona chapter of the AFP (new name, same group). We had almost 300 members. I focused on diversity and tried to engage the Hispanic community—representing forty percent of the Phoenix population—by expanding the available resources for their community. We invited several community leaders to join the AFP and tried to recruit young fundraisers to our mentor program and board, but progress was slow.

I managed to recruit J.P. Dahdah, who is Guatemalan, as a speaker and advocate for promoting philanthropy in the Hispanic community. I'd met J.P. at the Phoenix Committee on Foreign Relations, of which my son, then a law student in Arizona State University's Barrett honors program, was an honorary member. When John heard J.P. mention Guatemala, John said to him, "I was born in Guatemala." So, thanks to my son, I met J.P. and helped him realize his dream of setting up a foundation to support groups helping poor Guatemalans. I have been a board member of the foundation J.P. founded called Advance Guatemala, which provides funds for community development programs, ever since.

The next year, Andy Carey, executive director of the U.S. Mexico Border Philanthropy Partnership, discussed the challenges and opportunities of promoting cross-border activities between Mexico and the U.S. Andy presented some of the cultural considerations in involving the Hispanic community and provided valuable resources. Almost sixty people attended his presentation, most of them Hispanic non-members, which was our target audience. We also recruited several young Hispanic professionals to our mentor program. Throughout this process, we developed a list of Hispanic leaders and professionals whom we would invite to all the events that related to their interests and needs. Our AFP chapter's program has received the national organization's Friends of Diversity award for three years running.

We sent a member of the Hispanic community, Guille Sastre, executive director of a neighborhood group supporting the Salvadoran community, to attend the Hemispheric Congress on Fundraising in Mexico

City. Guille was the recipient of a scholarship and appreciated the opportunity, which was a great example of the synergy that should exist between the Hispanic communities in Phoenix and their Latin American counterparts.

Here's what Guille had to say:

Impressive, the Congress was fabulous! This is my first time and I came very happy to have the opportunity of sharing goals, triumphs, and above all the learning and opportunity of new possibilities. To know so many people with unique circumstances, but all with a vision in common to be part of a transformation for a better world, to inject energy and to offer a special place to be supported. After having participated in the Congress, I feel more capable to continue strengthening Creciendo Unidos in the area of fundraising. Thanks so much for this opportunity.

My second focus as an AFP chapter president was a cross-border initiative promoting philanthropic exchanges. Our effort to partner with an AFP chapter south of the border began in 2007, when the Guadalajara chapter was just forming. Our chapter provided scholarships to the Hemispheric Congress on Fundraising for members of the Guadalajara chapter, as well as books for its library and two presentations at its National Philanthropy Day event. Now the Guadalajara chapter has more than twenty-five members, with the momentum to assure growth in the future.

When I arrived at the Guadalajara Airport in 2008 for a speaking engagement, my counterpart at the local AFP chapter, Marcela García Bátiz, picked me up, and we headed for the historic downtown. With big bluish-green eyes, brown hair, and a smile that never stops, Marcela was a little powerhouse.

After some sightseeing and a few beers, Marcela and I went out for a simple dinner with a few other speakers. I savored the city's signature *torta ahogada,* or "drowned sandwich," a dense roll stuffed with pork and drenched in a spicy salsa. I also checked out a bowl of *pozole,* hominy soup made with chicken. I stuck with the white *pozole*, as I'd already had more than my share of "spicy hot."

The next day, Marcela and her crew took us to a spectacular venue, the not-yet-totally-completed Jalisco Public Library at the University of Guadalajara. The all-wood stage was very classy, with two flags behind the speaker's stand and flowers everywhere. As I looked out into the audience of about 150, I was overwhelmed by the Orozco murals, which covered the entire auditorium, even the center of the chapel-like ceiling. It was awe-inspiring. José Clemente Orozco and Diego Rivera are my favorite mural-ists, and I always visit any art gallery or museum where their art is shown. Their murals are like a historical and cultural kaleidoscope of Mexico. I stood on stage for a few minutes looking out at the murals, totally mesmer-ized, taking in this special and inspiring moment . . . until I realized that everyone was looking at me and I thought, *Oh, that's right. I'm the speaker.*

My presentation focused on fundraising in the U.S. and Mexico, with an emphasis on the impact culture has on giving and how the exchange of experiences and best practices will help professionals on both sides of the border increase their giving.

The U.S. Consulate had set up a number of press interviews, and the next day, an article titled "Promoting Professionalization" was published in the local newspaper. The entire production had been perfectly organized. Just before I left, Marcela and the board hosted a lunch where they pre-sented a "certificate of participation as well as the bilingual edition of the *Guía del Tequila,* which explains everything you need to know about tequila. Marcela's kind words after my presentation made all the effort worth it:

> *On behalf of all the members of the AFP West Mexico Chapter, I am writ-ing to express our gratefulness for the support your chapter provides ours, through Mark Walker's presence and lecture during Philanthropy Day 2008. The speakers were brilliant. Their speeches generated hope and gave us excellent ideas for our work next year.*

• • •

Different Latitudes

Rose Sandoval was my other contact at the Guadalajara event. She was the AFP coordinator for Latin America located in Mexico City and the editor of AFP's Spanish-language newsletter, *Te Informa*. Here's the English version of part of Rose's interview with me for the newsletter:

What do you believe is the greatest challenge facing fundraisers at this time in Latin America?

To develop individual giving to its true potential. Historically, most of the funds in Latin America are generated from fees-for-service, as well as corporate giving and some foundation giving, but individual giving has been limited in size and scope. Few really large, strategic lead gifts have been developed. With the naming of Carlos Slim as the wealthiest man in the world, and his foundation giving in excess of $70 million U.S., the perception of the importance and level of individual giving will be changing.

What would you like to do that you have not accomplished?

As a Board member and President-elect of the Greater Arizona Chapter of AFP, I have actively tried to develop an effective partnership with the Hispanic community in Phoenix to explore the areas of commonality that exist between philanthropy in the Hispanic community and philanthropy as it has developed over the years in Latin America. Although our chapter has sponsored several successful events and we've received the Friends of Diversity award, we have not been able to identify and recruit a significant number of Hispanics to our group or to our board, nor have any of the Hispanic-owned foundations or businesses been willing to underwrite the effort, making this a vision I'll need to continue working on.

If you could invite three people to dine, who would they be and where would you take them to dine?

Jim Lord has been my mentor in developing the use of the "Philanthropic Quest," a paradigm shift in promoting organizational development that leads to breakthrough fundraising. Over the years, I've used this approach with over twenty organizations. Mal Warwick is a fellow Returned Peace Corps Volunteer in Latin America and one of the world's great fundraising minds. I met Mal at the Hemispheric Congress on Fundraising, where we were presenters. Mal is a consultant, author, and public speaker who has taught fundraising on six continents and trained many new fundraisers. I'd also invite my daughter Nicolle, who participated in our chapter's mentorship program, which is one of the best in the U.S., and which was instrumental in her being named the Director of Development at IRC (International Rescue Committee) in Phoenix, Arizona. Since my wife and three children were born in Guatemala, the venue would be at the Santo Domingo del Cerro, above the gorgeous colonial town of Antigua Guatemala, a great place to pass along some real wisdom on philanthropy and fundraising to the next generation.

• • •

The most important result of my Guadalajara visit was a request from the local AFP chapter for help in developing a mentoring program. The need for new, young professional fundraisers was crucial, as the chapter's president was often asked for candidates to set up a new development department. Naturally, I was thrilled to learn that the Guadalajara chapter's need would allow us to share a program we'd developed over more than fifteen years, making it one of the best in the AFP world. Since the U.S. Consulate staff attended this event (they had also covered my travel expenses), Ana Luisa Ramírez, the Guadalajara AFP president Elect, and I cornered them to discuss their ongoing support for our cross-border initiative.

Within two years, AFP Greater Arizona had developed a curriculum for a mentor program, which we sent to our counterparts in Guadalajara to have translated. Past president, and my successor, Anne White, went to Guadalajara to present the mentoring program to some twenty trainers in a conference center. The training allowed the initiative to spread to all the chapters in Mexico and continue to develop young professional fundraising leadership.

Hemispheric Congress on Fundraising

The problem of our age is the proper administration of wealth, so that the ties of brotherhood may still bind together the rich and poor in a harmonious relationship.

—ANDREW CARNEGIE, *THE GOSPEL OF WEALTH*

Bill Gates confessed in the commencement speech to the 2007 Harvard graduating class that, "We don't read much about these deaths (preventable deaths of children under five each day around the world). The media covers what's new – and millions of people dying is nothing new. So it stays in the background, where it's easier to ignore. But even when we do see it or read about it, it's difficult to keep our eyes on the problem. It's hard to look at suffering if the situation is so complex that we don't know how to help. And so we look away. If we can really see a problem, which is the first step, we come to the second step: cutting through the complexity to find a solution."

Matthew Bishop and Michael Green, authors of *Philanthrocapitalism: How Giving Can Save the World*, call this kind of thinking "the spirit of philanthrocapitalism."

• • •

In January 2007, my interest in global philanthropy led me to the Hemispheric Congress on Fundraising–Latin America, in Mexico City. More than 400 nonprofit executives and fundraising professionals from twenty-one countries attended the event.

As part of organizing the task force, I made two presentations in Spanish. Approximately seventy attended my presentation "Best Practices," during which I recruited three professionals who offered personal stories of a time or event related to their involvement in fundraising that they were especially proud of. Many other participants felt confident enough to share their own success stories, and a good deal of momentum was generated. I invited the directors of Operation Smile from Ecuador and Colombia and of Casa de la Amistad from Mexico, which provided a nice cross-cultural mix of experiences.

From 2010 to 2013 Carlos Slim was designated the wealthiest man in the world—imagine a Mexican wealthier than Bill Gates! Many of us at the Congress thought this marked a new growth opportunity to enhance the importance of individual giving in Mexico and Latin America. Slim is mentioned several times in the book *Philanthrocapitalism*. In his book *Giving: How Each of Us Can Change the World,* Bill Clinton asks, "Will giving make you happier?" and then lists a diverse group, including Carlos Slim, who, he concludes, "seemed happy." Clinton continues, "Who's happier? The uniters or the dividers? The builders or the breakers? The givers or the takers?"

But as I discussed this with my Mexican counterparts at the Hemispheric Congress, they told me that Slim was less than enthusiastic about the power of philanthropy, and did what he did because of pressure from heavy hitters like Clinton and Gates. In reality, he still felt his role was to generate more jobs, and the giving his foundation did was narrowly based on Slim's preferences. He certainly never provided the inspirational philanthropy many of us hoped for.

The highlight of my first Hemispheric Congress was meeting Milton Murray, a pioneer in the field of fundraising. He shared story after story from his long, illustrious career, including that of the three students who raised money to build an auditorium for their school in Mexicali. The students, with Milton's help, won a matching grant from the Ford Foundation, which was one of the first grants the foundation gave for a project outside the U.S. Milton worked for two decades to get a postage stamp honoring philanthropy. In 1998 the Postal Service issued the stamp, "Giving & Sharing: An American Tradition," featuring a bee with flowers. His life was profiled in the book *The Makings of a Philanthropic Fundraiser: The Instructive Example of Milton Murray,* written by Ronald Alan Knott and published in 1992, the same year Milton retired. I met him many years after he'd retired, but he was still an active advocate of everything philanthropic—a real prince in our profession and an extreme do-gooder of philanthropy.

• • •

The board of AFP Greater Arizona normally nominates the next president, but as someone who would have to work closely with the president for a year, I rejected its nomination and chose Anne White. With more than thirty-five years' experience, Anne had a track record with some of the top charities in the state. She was the development director of Special Olympics and several groups in New York City, and she brought a directness not often found in these parts. I always enjoyed her New York-New Jersey accent, which I'd also had at one point, until my family moved out West. Anne's speech was peppered with "I'm just saying . . ." She also received the highest designation as a trainer for AFP and was the ideal board member to lead our chapter's mentoring program with the Guadalajara chapter.

After nominating Anne as our next chapter president, I also nominated my daughter Nicolle to the board. As the fundraising manager at the International Rescue Committee, she took after her old man: a world traveler and staunch advocate for human rights. She would make me proud, becoming a solid member of the AFP board and, eventually, its treasurer. The next generation of international fundraisers was on its way.

Eleven

THE WORLD OF OVERSEAS DONOR TOURS

*I have found out that there ain't no surer way to find out
whether you like people or hate them than to travel with them.*

—MARK TWAIN, *TOM SAWYER ABROAD*

Dominican Republic, 1996

B.B. Lane, board chair of Food for the Hungry, and his wife, Minnie,
were visiting headquarters to attend a board meeting.

"Mark," B.B. said after taking me aside, "I'd like your help passing
on some of our values on giving to international ministries to our grandkids. Could you organize an overseas trip for our daughter, Lucy her
husband, Ted, and their four kids? That would mean a lot to us."

That was music to my ears, as multigenerational giving is the name
of the game.

B.B. was one of our largest donors, and his leadership had been crucial. When the board was considering having its funds "doubled" by the
Foundation for New Era Philanthropy in the late 1980s, the stoic, pragmatic B.B. said, "Anytime I'm told I can make over 15 percent profit on
anything, I look under the table to see what else is going on." The board
turned down the foundation, which ended up being a Ponzi scheme that
swindled 1,100 donors—mostly Christian religious organizations—out

of $135 million. MAP International lost over $100,000, and many other groups lost much more, but B.B.'s business sense prevented Food for the Hungry from going down that path. Now, that's valuable leadership.

B.B. and Minnie had made their fortune manufacturing furniture and cedar chests in Virginia. Minnie's family also owned a furniture company, so they represented a sizable enterprise in the industry. Their daughter, Lucy Corrly, was the spitting image of her mother—tall, lanky, energetic, not afraid to express her opinion. There was never a dull moment with Lucy in the room. Her husband, Ted, was a middle-aged, amiable businessman who had set up his own customized furniture company. They had four children: a teenager, an eight-year-old, and two younger siblings.

The Dominican Republic (DR) seemed a good site for the visit, as FH had a well-established program with an excellent country director, Luis Sena, who knew how to handle volunteers and donors. The DR, with its spectacular beaches, is the second-most-visited Caribbean country. Santo Domingo is a UNESCO World Heritage site with the oldest street, cathedral, and university in the hemisphere.

Our initial gathering was with Dr. Bennet, FH's CEO, and a few local staff members. Luis described the devastation of Hurricane George, which had hit six months earlier and was one of the most destructive in the country's history. He explained that George wreaked $1 billion of damage and killed over 380 people, with 7,000 people being evacuated to shelters in Santo Domingo. Homes were blown to pieces, roads and bridges were destroyed, and water systems were polluted. Later that evening, we had a beachside chat with Dr. Bennet, who provided us with an overview of the challenges they faced, along with his vision and new strategies for the future. Nothing like sitting down around a fire with the CEO to share how everyone is feeling and what they hope to learn over the next week.

The next morning, we piled into a small van and headed up-country to see George's devastation first-hand. As we drove along, we were struck by how the winds had broken all the trees of one forest in half, as if they were matchsticks. We arrived at the community of Constanza, where much of the population had been forced to build their simple homes of wood and sheet metal in the riverbed because nobody owned the land, which made them the most vulnerable during a disaster. Predictably, the flood washed away everything.

Lucy and the three girls were brought to tears when they entered one schoolhouse where hundreds of families were staying in hot, filthy conditions, with only a few latrines for everyone. Sheets divided the spaces where families lived. Some families had lost friends and relatives.

The next day, we headed for the border with Haiti, which represents one of the poorest parts of the DR. Haiti had been a French colony with a strong African influence and a propensity for voodoo, while the DR was Spanish-speaking, with a more vibrant economy.

Food for the Hungry's DR program was team-based, which meant that its U.S. volunteers came from several churches and stayed a week working with the community to build latrines and the school. The team members all had stories about getting shaken up on the way up-country in an old rickety van over horrendous roads, and were impressed that the locals could deal with the hot tropical sun that they wilted in. The volunteers gained respect for the community's leaders and the FH field staff, who had to use the same roads and rickety transportation. I would learn that the donor team returned to their churches and raised $35,000 for a new vehicle, proving that there's nothing like hands-on experience to bring about a real appreciation of how others live.

After our weeklong visit to the island, I gathered the family together in a garden inside the hotel for a debriefing, including some of my "appreciative inquiry" questions to help them reflect on what they'd learned and what they were going to do about it. My questions included, What was the most important thing you learned on this trip? How did the children in Constanza play? Which local food did you enjoy the most? What do you think you'll remember the most about this visit after you've returned home? How did you feel about the families who lost their homes in the hurricane? Which FH program or activity did you like the most?

Ted used his video camera to film each family member's story. The children expressed an appreciation for the local culture and beauty of the island, but also an appreciation of how blessed they were in comparison with the majority of the children they met on the trip. The Corrlys spent some time with Luis Sena and his wife, and established a great friendship. Luis requested support for some of the wells in the affected areas. When the Corrlys went back home, the children made presentations at their church, including the video footage, and they mobilized resources from the church and Ted's father, who gave a first-time appreciated-stock gift. Ted's giving and that of those around him went from $250 a year to $32,000. Ted would soon become a board member and, eventually, the chairman of the board, and who knows what the impact would be on their children. I felt confident that I'd fulfilled my promise to B.B.

GUATEMALA AND NICARAGUA, 1997

I identified Bill Williams, an inactive child sponsor with Food for the Hungry, who just happened to be the grandson of the founder of one of the largest chemical companies in the world. His father had formed the William Penn Foundation in Philadelphia, which gave away over $45 million a year. Bill and his wife, Jennifer, had five children, whom they homeschooled in the Pocono Mountains of Pennsylvania. Bill was already supporting several missionary groups and orphanages in Nicaragua. What surprised me was that all the William Penn Foundation's giving went to programs in the Philadelphia area, despite the fact that the company whose profits had led to its formation had strong international roots, with some 17,000 employees in over 20 countries.

On my first visit to the Williamses' home, I shared an article with Bill from the *Chronicle of Philanthropy*, which ran a story on the William Penn Foundation gifting over $600,000 for the construction of a canoe ramp on the river that passes through Philly. I argued that these funds would have far more impact helping programs that met the basic needs of women and children in Central America. I offered to take Bill to Central

America to give him a better appreciation of the realities of the developing world, to emphasize his responsibility to make a difference through giving (his grandfather had given each grandchild a $5 million trust), and to help him develop a strategy to convince the foundation board to begin funding international programs.

In March I took Bill and two of his daughters, fifteen-year-old Sara and eight-year-old Emily, to Guatemala. My associate, John Scola, also invited John and Jeanette Tornquist from Illinois, who were generous and committed supporters.

We took two small planes from Guatemala City up to Santa Maria Nebaj, in the Ixil Triangle of the Department of Quiche. The area was the center of a thirteen-year period of violence, with the local population caught between leftist guerrillas and right-wing death squads a subject we'll address later in the book. Some 15,000 had been killed and thousands displaced. This was not an area for the faint of heart, but FH's programs were excellent and we were all impressed by the dedication of the staff who coordinated our visit. At no point did we feel that we might be in danger.

When we arrived, a Hunger Corps volunteer, Jodi Johnson, provided an overview. The Hunger Corps was like a Christian Peace Corps, organized by FH. Volunteers made a two-year commitment. After this session it had clouded over and I realized the two planes would not be returning due to inclement weather, so we had to commandeer a small bus to get us over to Cobán, a full day on one of the most horrendous roads in the country from Nebaj through Uspantan and eventually our destination Coban. We were all shaken up and in a daze when we finally disembarked.

After a quick orientation in Cobán, the provincial capital of Alta Verapaz, from Patricia Cuba, the country director, we headed out in Land Cruisers for the community of Chiguorran, where FH helped a local school program. The classes were taught in the Maya language of Poqomchi'. During recess, little Emily distributed balloons and played with the students, who were all about her age. Then she and the Tornquists showed the children how to blow bubbles. They were all laughing and having a good time together—the language barrier didn't seem to be an issue.

FH pairs up a U.S. sponsor who pays about $21 a month to provide support, such as education and food, to a child in a program country like Guatemala. The Williamses' encounter with the child they sponsored, Carmela, was the highlight of the trip. We hiked out twenty minutes from the vehicle to Carmela's home, which was traditional for the area, with a thatch-roofed kitchen in the back and a wood plank dwelling in the front. Firewood was piled up on the front porch. Several coffee and fruit trees, such as bananas, surrounded the home. The animals—some chickens and a few piglets—were kept behind the kitchen area. The home had a cement floor and several spaces separated by sheets.

A tiny girl with brown eyes and black hair, Carmela wore a simple white blouse and a blue skirt, with plastic sandals on her feet. She was shorter than Emily's shoulder, although she was probably the same age. I took a picture of Bill with the two girls, and another with Carmela and her brother and father. I didn't see any windows at all in their house, which would explain why it seemed so dark inside, even during the day.

Carmela's father showed us around, and then we all sat on the front porch. Bill and the girls asked questions about how they lived: What do you grow? Why doesn't the kitchen have a chimney? Where will Carmela go after she graduates from the local school? What do you eat for dinner? Carmela and her father responded to these questions and asked a few of their own before I had to bring the Williamses back to Cobán.

• • •

Since Bill was planning to visit one of the orphanages he supported in Nicaragua the following year, I offered to organize a visit for him and his seven-year-old son, Jonathan, to see some of FH's work there. I worked closely with my friend from the Hunger Corps in Guatemala,

Ken Ekstrom, who was now the coordinator for Central America, based in Managua, Nicaragua's capital city. Ken had small boys of his own, so he developed a schedule that took into consideration the attention span of a child. We also had backup systems: friends of Bill's could take care of the children if they got bored visiting programs.

Ken started us off at one of the schools where many of FH's sponsored children studied. Jane Jennings, a Hunger Corps volunteer at the school, put Bill and me to work as an "expert panel" to explain the U.S. educational system, which allowed us to interact with the students. As a teacher himself, Bill had learned the skill of listening to students and did an excellent job responding to their many questions. Then Ken took us over to meet the principal, who wanted to thank Bill and Food for the Hungry for providing additional staff, books, and activities for the students. Although FH promotes child sponsorship, most of their support funds other projects that benefit the entire community. These projects are important as community leaders and a mobilized community hold the key to continued development after the international NGO departs.

Living in one of the poorest countries in Latin America, Nicaraguans had never had it easy. The U.S. occupied the country from 1912 to 1933, and by 1937 dictator Anastasio Somoza had come to power. Then the country was hit by several horrendous earthquakes. When we visited, much of Managua was still vacant lots where buildings had fallen down during the earthquake of 1992. The Communist Sandinistas further damaged the economy by alienating the local and international business communities. Anything that was from the U.S. was evil. Inflation got out of hand. As in Cuba, medical professionals and teachers were underpaid at best, and the hospitals didn't have any medicines.

I was looking for street signs in order to take Bill and the kids to the FH office, but there were none, so I rolled down the car window, and a lady told us, "Yes, I know their office. Just go two blocks more and turn right at the big cottonwood tree, then another four blocks and a right at the red house where the widow Martínez lives." So much for street signs.

Four months after we returned from the trip, I set up a visit with FH's CEO, Dr. Bennet, to visit with the Williamses at their home in the Poconos. Dr. Bennet wasn't that interested in visiting donors, which was one of my challenges. After we arrived and had a chance to get acquainted, the CEO launched into a story about his recent trip to North Korea and how horrendous the situation was there, with hundreds of thousands starving due to a drought and the brutal circumstances under Communist control.

He ended with, "So, Mr. Williams, we'd like you to consider helping us with a $25,000 gift to meet this crisis in North Korea." I almost fell out of my chair, since we'd been focusing on the needs in Central America, where the Williamses' expressed interests were, and I'd taken them on two site visits with their children! Well, what do I know: within a week, a check for $25,000 arrived for North Korea disaster relief—over and above what they gave for Nicaragua.

Over the years, I stayed in touch with the Williamses, even after I'd moved to MAP International. Bill had utilized the MAP essential meds contained in their Travel Packs, so he was familiar with the organization. About ten years after our visit to Nicaragua, MAP received a $25,000 gift out of the blue for a hurricane relief effort in Nicaragua from Bill's son, Jonathan, whom I'd first met as a small boy. Since all the children had their own trusts, Jonathan, who was now a young man, was making his own gifting decisions. His father had taught him well, and he had a heart for helping the less fortunate in times of need, strengthening the legacy of philanthropy in this special family.

Bangkok and Nepal, 1992

Area Representative Tom Arens met our group of ten at the small and unimpressive airport in Kathmandu, Nepal. Tom was a former Peace Corps volunteer, with more than twenty-five years' experience in the area, most of it with World Neighbors. He'd eventually retire after more than thirty-five years with the organization, another example of the committed staff that made World Neighbors the premier village-based NGO.

Different Latitudes

Once we purchased our hiking licenses, which were necessary for all tourists in Nepal, we were ready to embark on our journey to the hinterlands with our World Neighbors staff.

We threw our luggage on top of one of two tan Land Rovers and headed northeast of Kathmandu on the only road that leads to China. In Kathmandu we met the World Neighbors staff at a health center. As is typical of World Neighbors outposts, the Kathmandu program worked with local partners that were independent, indigenous-run operations. Here, the program focus was reproductive health and agroforestry.

Nepal is a poor, isolated kingdom nestled north of India in the Himalayas. As we climbed up the mountains, the basically Hindu population gave way to the Buddhists at about 6,000 feet. That's when the special temples and prayer wheels became prevalent. We visited a few temples to see the red and yellow lacquered gods with fierce-looking monkey-like heads glaring at us. Below were endless brownish foothills that reached to the horizon, where the snowcapped Himalayas emerged.

Since all of World Neighbors' villagers worked in the hills, hiking was the main mode of transportation, with the aid of about six Sherpa helpers. Fortunately, we were there during the dry season. Tom said that during the wet season, roads were impractical because of the difficult terrain so walking and small boats on the river were the key forms of transportation. Also, he told us, the trees swayed toward you as you passed from the weight of leeches jumping off to feed on you.

On our second day in Nepal, we were hiking up the side of the Himalayas when Harvey Milken, one of our donors, passed out. I thought, *Not again!* (thinking of the donor who fainted upon arrival at the high altitude airport in La Paz, Bolivia) *We're in the middle of nowhere. No roads within a day's hike.* We had screened the participants for such challenging visits, and Harvey was an avid hiker. Okay, he was eighty, but he seemed to be in good health. I turned to his wife, Emma, to see if she had an idea what was going on, and she nonchalantly said, "Well, he does have a heart condition, you know."

I was incredulous, and said, "Of course I didn't know, or we wouldn't be here in this precarious situation!"

Obviously, we had to get Harvey down the mountain, and fast, but how? Tom recommended we put Harvey into one of the cone-shaped baskets the Sherpas used to carry our luggage. *No way!* I thought. But within ten minutes, the six-foot-three Harvey was in the basket, and the Sherpa was heading down the mountain. Harvey, in the basket, looked twice as big as the Sherpa, but the Sherpa seemed to take it all in stride.

We were halfway up the mountain and could see the terraced hills below. They looked close by, but they weren't. Harvey was taken down to one of our host medical centers to recuperate from pushing his heart too hard. Four days later, he'd climb to the other side of the mountain to meet us on our return, just to prove that he could do it. You can't anticipate craziness sometimes, but we didn't have any fatalities among our twelve hikers, which included donors, staff, and Sherpas, so I was a happy tour guide.

We stayed in medical centers and an occasional sparse lodge during the next week. The Sherpas carried nearly everything. After a week, we were all very tired of dal, a lentil-based sauce with cumin, coriander, turmeric, and other spices. In my most culturally sensitive manner, I suggested a vegetable soup with some cheese as a change of pace. We got a lentil and potato greens soup with the same spices, which, although it might have contained some cheese, tasted basically the same. It wasn't like we could go down the street to the next restaurant.

After a grueling day of hiking, we stopped for tea at the home of one of the local World Neighbors promoters. We entered a small village with two-story dwellings on the right and a drop-off down the mountain on the left. The lower level of the house was lined with small children gawking at the strange-looking foreigners. We were shown into the living area, an open room with small windows and shelves lined with dishes, pots, and spices. Our promoter was a short, well-tanned guy with brown hair and a mustache. He wore a dirty shirt with a suit coat and khakis.

We all sat cross-legged in a circle on a grass mat and watched the promoter's wife prepare the tea. She dumped in a clump of cream, so what we got was a nasty concoction of salt and cream overwhelming the tea, but it was hot, our hosts were generous, and all of us were pleased to be off our feet and grateful for their hospitality.

The promoter's home was spotlessly clean. When I looked in the backyard, I realized that the promoters practiced what they preached by adapting the appropriate technologies that World Neighbors promoted, including a greenhouse for vegetables. They used leftover agricultural and food waste to produce bio-gas, a mixture of gases produced by the breakdown of organic matter in the absence of oxygen. I noticed a strange odor and found out that biogas is primarily methane, carbon dioxide, and hydrogen sulfide and it's all used as fuel for cook stoves. I also saw a variety of fruit for the market, and nitrogen-fixing bushes to maintain the soil. We looked into the village still, which included a few clay pots, a metal pot, and a bucket on a floor strewn with straw. I have no idea what brew they were working on, but we had to move on before I could sample it.

As we left the village, five smiling kids waved to us from some stone steps. A small girl on the bottom step, with beautiful brown eyes and hair, wore a maroon dress over long pants (it was cold at that altitude). Another cutie wore a bluish dress with flowers, a blue sweater, and flip-flops. One of the boys had a ball cap on his head. By the look of these confident, tranquil-looking kids, Nepal would have some good days ahead.

In the end, no mega-gifts came out of this trip. Certainly, I would be better prepared to tell World Neighbors' story to donors as a result of this first-hand experience, but these were older donors who didn't have the capacity to provide large cash gifts. But every member of the tour had World Neighbors in his or her estate plan, which would bode well for the organization down the line.

Guatemala, 1998

On the way to the Food for the Hungry office in Cobán in Alta Verapaz we stepped out of our van and headed down the hill to visit some Maya caves. The deeper we went down the well-worn steps carved out of the hill, the darker it got until we reached the bottom ceremonial area where candles and copal were burning, exuding a strong smell of incense.

I had warned everyone not to shout or cause any commotion, as this was a religious area for the Maya. Caves were often described as entries into the watery Maya underworld. For the Maya, life and death occur at middle zones between this world and the underworld. Caves, then, are associated with both life and death: when something emerges from the underworld, that something lives, and when something descends into the underworld it dies. Caves are seen as birthplaces where humans and group ancestors were born (and lived).

As I was organizing this visit—for Steve Tanninbaum and his two sons, John Jr. and Jesse—it occurred to me that my sixteen-year-old son, John (Henry), hadn't returned to his birthplace since he was a small child, so I brought him along. I took a picture of him on the side of the mountain, looking down at the valley, to San Jerónimo, where he'd spent many memorable weekends with his grandfather, riding horses at his ranch. John's blond hair and blue eyes and his button nose reminded me of photos I'd seen of Ricardo when he was young.

Using the FH donor base, I'd tracked Steve Tanninbaum from Louisiana, where he was a physician and had made some sizable gifts, to a small town outside Kansas City, which put him in my territory. Realizing his potential for future large gifts and possible leadership, I visited him and his family when I was in the area visiting donors. His wife was a registered nurse. John Jr. was fifteen; Jesse, twelve. Their Christian beliefs tied the family together and were their major motivation for giving to FH.

After an orientation at the FH office in Cobán, we headed to the small village where the Tanninbaums' sponsored child lived. There we met Maria, a small eight-year-old, who wore an orange blouse and a green Maya skirt. Her mother was a small woman with black hair, wearing a white *huipil*, an intricately woven blouse, along with a traditional black and gold skirt and plastic sandals. Maria's father was away for the day, harvesting coffee at a plantation.

Maria was one of eight children, who ranged from four to twelve years old. Their home was fronted by a small store, where the family sold staples, fruit juices, and candies. They had a concrete floor and rooms separated by sheets. Their kitchen was in the back and had a fuel efficient woodstove with a chimney, which were among the appropriate technologies MAP promoters introduced, as it reduced the amount of smoke getting into everyone's lungs. Maria's grandmother was cooking corn tortillas over the *comal*, a sheet of metal that distributed the heat evenly. With a spot of salt, a tortilla was a great mid-morning snack.

Behind the home was a traditional steam bath, made of adobe-like material and painted white. The entrance was so small that only Jesse could easily fit in. He found a wood floor with a fire pit in the middle; rocks were heated in the fire pit and water thrown over them to produce steam.

After saying good-bye to Maria and her family, we headed down the road and came across some men carrying bundles of firewood, connected by ropes to a headband to evenly distribute the heavy weight between their backs and necks. The boys were intrigued and asked to try it. John Jr. and Jesse were barely able to pick up one bundle. My son was able to manage it but could walk only a few steps before putting his load back down. I asked the two men carrying the wood how long they walked from the mountain where they cut it to their homes. "Three hours," they told us. The boys looked at one another in amazement. Such long treks were necessary because households had cut all the trees close to home.

Our next visit was with a group of farmers the FH staff was training to enhance their production of corn and beans and to diversify by growing other types of vegetables. The farmers proudly showed us their model vegetable garden, and John Jr. and my son tried their hands at cleaning out the weeds with one of the traditional hoes. They got a lot done but were ready to move on after about fifteen minutes. The farmers also showed us how they processed hemp fiber into rope. The hemp plants looked similar to magueys, used to produce tequila. They cut the large spiny leaves, dried them, and pulled them apart to get to the fiber.

Different Latitudes

We hiked to another village, where assistant director Arturo Cuba was mentoring a group of a dozen pastors. Only four of the pastors were literate, which was fairly common in the highlands of Guatemala, so Arturo used stories and graphics to make his points. Unlike some Evangelical training, his program didn't focus only on one's personal relationship to Christ, but also included issues of how Christianity relates to, and works in, the community, as well as what biblical precepts help drive sound integrated community development.

Small kids piled into an FH pickup were arriving at the local hospital for checkups the same time we did. The boys carried colorful woven cotton bags filled with whatever they'd need for the day. The girls wore blue *huipiles*, with traditional blue plaid skirts. They were all sponsored by FH donors, and the first stop would be to have their teeth checked. Since Steve Tanninbaum was a physician, we got a tour of the operating room, which was sparse but clean. Most children in the villages MAP worked in did not get annual checkups, nor were there equipped clinics where they could go even if they wanted to, so the FH-sponsored children were given a distinct advantage.

Since coffee was one of the key crops in the country and influenced the economy considerably, we visited the Finca Santa Margarita, which was built by a German family, the Dieseldorffs, over 110 years ago. My son, John, was too young to have visited the plantation in his mother's family, so I thought this would be the next best thing.

A German colony was established in the area during the middle of the nineteenth century, due to some generous concessions of land from the Guatemalan government. The Germans formed a tight community that British archaeologist Alfred Maudslay described:

There is a larger proportion of foreigners in Coban than in any other town in the Republic: they are almost exclusively Germans engaged in coffee-planting, and some few of them in cattle-ranching and other industries; although complaints of isolation and of housekeeping and labour troubles are not unheard of amongst them, they seemed to me to be fortunate from a business point of view in the high reputation that the Vera Paz coffee holds in the market . . .

All of this explains why Maya women with blue eyes are not that rare as intermingling among the Germans and Mayas was common. Some of the German plantation owners would send their clothes to be cleaned on a railroad they'd built to Lake Izabal and then on a boat down the Río Dulce to the Caribbean and ships bound for Germany.

Our trip would help solidify the relationship between FH and the Tanninbaums, who continued to be major donors, and John would soon become a board member. I was able to spend some quality time with my son and to reintroduce him to his native country. The trip was just part of what might have impacted the boys as they matured, but John Jr. became a physician, like his dad, and Jesse entered the law. My son, John, also became a lawyer and, after a few years, a judge. I like to think that exposure to those making a difference in the lives of so many can only help in the child-rearing process.

Amazon Basin in Ecuador, 1999

This tour group included three board members. The donors included former Ambassador Edwin Corr, a couple from Seattle, and another couple from Louisiana. One of our first activities in Quito, the Ecuadoran capital, was to meet with the recipient of three Travel Packs of essential medications the board members had brought. Ben Cross, a young doctor, had studied and worked in Ecuador for years. He was building a new medical center in the south of the country and never had enough meds. His father lived in Southern California and was a strong MAP supporter, so I volunteered us to bring the meds down to Ben personally. This was one of those great opportunities where a board member like Ed could hand the meds directly to the doctor who would be using them.

Byron Morales, the MAP International country director, and his wife, Laura, were a dynamic team, developing programs with a focus on education and preventive healthcare. They provided our initial orientation. Laura had been a teacher for many years, and Byron was involved in program development in several other countries, including Mexico.

The next day, we piled into the van and headed for El Coca, a six-hour drive down to the Napo River. From Quito east of the Andes the hills fall away to tropical lowlands. Some of the beautiful wilderness remains unspoiled. Before getting into our motorized canoes, we had to check in with the U.S. naval base and get a permit. The river was almost a mile wide in some parts and filled with branches and entire trees from a previous night's storm. Things got exciting as we flew by huge logs and fallen trees barreling down the river. The pilots pulled the engine out of the water just as the trees and trash overtook us.

After four hours on the Napo, we reached the Yachana Eco Lodge, the operating center of the program. Douglas McMeekin from Tennessee was the founder of the lodge and of the indigenous group MAP partnered with, FUNEDESIN (Foundation for Integrated Education and Development). Each room had its own porch and hammock overlooking the river—as well as some rather immense insects. Douglas informed us that mosquitoes weren't a problem because the bats ate them.

When we arrived at the lodge's guest center, I heard someone on their shortwave radio. Douglas told us it was Juanita Lopez, one of twenty-five health promoters who worked with FUNEDESIN. Juanita was talking with the FUNEDESIN physician from her clinic. All the promoters were connected to the clinic and lodge by radio to assure a quick response in an emergency. She was describing a patient's symptoms, which included a high temperature and chills. The doctor correctly diagnosed the problem as malaria, so we set out with Dr. Javier Remato to pick up Juanita, who would lead us to the patient.

In the Napo River valley, the river ruled. People swam in the water, washed in it, drank it. All the homes were on stilts because when the river overflowed, everything flooded. One of the greatest causes of death for small children was snake bites. We saw many gigantic semi-aquatic rodents called capybaras, as well as beautiful parrots and macaws, which the locals often shot and ate. Word had not gotten out that the wildlife could attract tourists, who could, in turn, generate much-needed income. Douglas told me that the future of the Amazon Basin was in the hands of the small farmers, most of whom had no more than three years of education. In the end they would determine if the local animals would survive or be killed off.

The only transportation was the river. After an hour's canoe trip, we found Juanita waiting for us. Most of the promoters were men; Juanita was an exception to the rule. Like most local women, she had a large family: she and her husband had seven children. Her husband was in the field, harvesting coffee, when we arrived. Juanita had only four years of education, which was typical for the area, but she could read and write.

Different Latitudes

After another half hour on foot, we reached the patient's home, which was built on stilts. We climbed up a log ladder placed against the entrance. The patient, Miguel, had been lying in his bedroom for six days. His family had visited the local shaman before contacting Juanita.

Juanita told us of one little girl who almost died from a snake bite because her parents took her to see the shaman and left her there for six hours before they realized he wasn't going to cure her. The FUNEDESIN doctor administered anti-venom, but it wasn't enough after such a long delay. She had to be airlifted to Quito, at great expense, for a skin graft, which saved the girl's foot—and life.

Dr. Remato and Juanita went to work immediately on Miguel, asking questions and taking his temperature. Once his diagnosis was confirmed, the doctor explained the proper dosage and use of medications to Miguel's wife and Juanita. Juanita would make a follow-up visit in a few days to ensure that he was improving. For his visit, Dr. Remato would charge a minimal amount that Miguel's family could pay off over time. FUNEDESIN was flexible on the payment plan, which could include chickens or coffee to be consumed at the lodge.

On the way back to the river, we stopped at Juanita's home, which was also on stilts. She had a small home garden to supplement her family's diet. Next to her home was the village *botiquín*, or mini-pharmacy, which included basic drugs, vitamins, and antibiotics provided by MAP. The radio she used was on the wall of the *botiquín* and ran on a solar battery, the only available source of electricity unless someone owned a generator. The radio was encased in a Plexiglas tool kit to protect it from the intense and never-ending heat and humidity.

Douglas McMeekin had worked in the Amazon jungle for more than ten years, helping the petroleum companies come to terms with the indigenous groups. He had established several local industries at the lodge, such as jelly and honey preparation, which provided much-needed income to support the program. Students also spent several weeks at the lodge, receiving college credit for courses offered on environment and tropical wildlife, as well as local cultures. Douglas had also set up a successful travel agency, which handled many of the details for upcoming donor visits. In his own way, he had become an extreme do-gooder with an entrepreneurial bent.

• • •

After four days in the Amazon jungle, we flew back to Quito and headed north to the Hacienda Pinsaqui, in the foothills of the Imbabura volcano, on the far side of Lago San Pablo and just north of the famous market, Otavalo. Once the mainstay of a booming agrarian society, the restored estates of Ecuador were again contributing to economic growth in the Andean region known as the Avenue of the Volcanoes. The hacienda's claim that "Bolívar slept here" was no idle boast. It hosted the great liberator on his trips back and forth to Bogotá, and was the site of the signing of the Treaty of Pinsaqui. As we entered the incredible gates, which included two large white columns and a massive tree dripping with purple bougainvillea, we saw the resident peacock spreading his iridescent train. The rooms were filled with colonial antiques and handcrafted furniture. You felt like you were being drawn back centuries.

The hacienda took its name from a people who had predated the Inca. Built as a textile workshop in the late 1700s, Pinsaqui counted over 1,000 indigenous weavers laboring at its looms. Extensively damaged by an earthquake in 1867, the hacienda of one of the workshop owners had been faithfully restored. The onetime storerooms had once again become outsize living and dining rooms with massive fireplaces. We spent more than a few hours in the sunken bar, which had a quaint fireplace and numerous trophies attesting to the hacienda's equine tradition. Lest anyone doubt the high esteem in which the hacienda held its horses, some of the photos showed the owner escorting his favorite steed into a room dominated by an ornate chandelier.

When we returned to Quito, we visited Laura and Byron Morales's favorite project, a school in one of the marginal parts of the city, where families barely made a living. Unfortunately, MAP International was unable to support the entire school, so it was looking at a major budget deficit. The parents were asked to pay a monthly stipend, but it didn't come close to covering the staff salaries and services provided.

That evening at the hotel the three board members called a meeting. Ed Corr got right to the point: "We have this shortfall on the school program, which is so important to this community. What are we going to do about it?"

Since the board members were running the fundraising show, I backed off and let them go to it. Thanks to an impassioned plea from Ed's wife, Susanne, the next morning Ed announced that they'd made a commitment over the next few years of $35,000. Several $5,000 annual pledges were made. This was especially encouraging to the Morales's, who had worked so hard to make the school viable.

Guatemala, 1997

Just as B.B. Lane asked us to help him pass along his values of Christian philanthropy to his grandchildren, Merrill Ewert made a similar request: "Mark, I'd like your help to empower my executive staff to appreciate the work Food for the Hungry does, and also to teach them to appreciate the power of philanthropy." He named two executives with "lots of potential": Dan Manternach, president of Professional Farmers of America, and Merlyn Vandekrol, a high-ranking executive in one of Merrill's businesses.

"No problem," I told Merrill, "I know just the place."

It was the perfect excuse to organize a tour to my beloved Guatemala, the Land of Eternal Spring.

Merrill sponsored several FH children, but I soon realized that he had a lot more potential. He was an international business journalist, publishing entrepreneur, and the author of eight books. He'd founded or built several businesses that had a global reach, including Ewert/Dow Jones Commodity News, FutureSource, *Futures* magazine, and Professional Farmers of America. He was also one of the founders of

Pinnacle Forum, a Christian ministry aimed at influencing Western culture. Merrill spoke from a wealth of personal and global business and ministry experience on visionary leadership, cultural change, spiritual fitness, and spirituality in the workplace.

I planned to take the executives to visit programs in the Cobán area, just north of where I'd met Ligia in San Jerónimo. But when Ligia reviewed my initial itinerary, she laid down the law. "You can't just show them the poverty and problems of Guatemala," she said. "You need to show them the incredible natural beauty, cultural diversity, and ancient history all around us."

What could I say, other than, "*Tienes razón*"—"You're right"—one of the reasons were still married after forty-four years and counting. And of course she was, as has happened way too often over the years.

So we started our visit in Antigua, the former colonial capital of Central America and my favorite city there. The colonial atmosphere makes it feel like you're in the 1700s. I took the group to my favorite restaurant, La Posada de Don Rodrigo, located in one of the renovated colonial homes. From a colonial arch just beyond the restaurant, you could get a great view of the yellow church, La Merced. The dining area looked out on a gorgeous garden with several colors of bougainvillea. A marimba band played, and the specialties included several types of tender beef, cheese, black beans, plantains, grilled shrimp in garlic butter, and shish kebab. For dessert there was flan and several different types of fruit, including *nísperos*, which looked like little apricots. We had strong cups of real coffee grown right on the slopes of the nearby volcano.

The next day, we wound our way up the green mountains for over four hours to Cobán, where FH country director Patricia and her husband, Arturo Cuba, the assistant director, would talk about the programs there. That afternoon, we stopped at a school, where the majority of the students were sponsored children. About twenty-five kids swarmed our van to ask about the purpose of our visit. Ernie Davis, our guide for the day, explained that we were from Food for the Hungry and wanted to see how they were doing. The kids wore rubber boots in the constant rain during the rainy season. Several of the girls wore traditional, bright-colored *huipiles*. A few of the older children asked to know more about which country we were from.

Most of the people in the rural areas we visited were Q'eqchi'. In the 1870s and '80s, many were forced to escape when President Justo Rufino Barrios rallied Ladino and *mestizo* populations against the Q'eqchi', making their land available to European coffee farmers who used the locals as forced labor. That is why, when traveling down the Río Dulce, in the jungle area, you hear Q'eqchi' spoken, by descendants of those displaced from their farmlands.

After a quick visit at the school, we hiked down a ravine, to the home of one of the children Merrill sponsored. The mother, Maria, invited us in. She wore a traditional hand-embroidered *huipile* with rows of geometric and floral designs in bright colors. She was a small woman—no more than five feet tall—with dark skin and black hair pulled back. I spotted the family's Maya/Catholic altar, which had items from both traditions. A large wooden cross was on a table, propped against the wall; corn husks and dried ears of corn hung from the cross and leaned against its base. This mixture of symbolism was quite common.

After saying good-bye to Maria and her daughter Sarah, we hiked up the Biotopo del Quetzal, just outside Cobán, a protected tropical cloud forest filled with an incredible variety of flora and fauna, like jaguars and the famous quetzal, Guatemala's national bird. This resplendent bird is emerald green with a red chest and long feathers trailing behind it. In ancient Maya culture, the quetzal's tail feathers were used as currency and are now found on the modern Guatemalan currency called quetzales. The bird reportedly cannot survive in captivity, making it a symbol of freedom. Like many species in the jungles of Guatemala, the quetzal is in danger of extinction.

The incredible green canopy of the forest shaded us from the sun and was often engulfed in a thick mist in the early morning. Hundreds of varieties of orchids were attached to many of the trees. At the top, we made a brief rest stop. Dan and Merlyn waited for me to catch my breath before we continued on in a slow, soft drizzle the locals call *chipi-chipi*.

Shortly after we returned home to the U.S., I spoke at the Professional Farmers of America national convention in San Antonio, Texas, about FH's programs in Guatemala. I was nervous in front of hundreds of members of the farmers' association but settled down when I began describing the needs and opportunities to give in Guatemala. The audience was forgiving and generous: 100 of them became new child sponsors. I'm sure many continued after Merrill sold the company. As was the case with other donors, I felt I'd kept my promise to Merrill and that his young executives would become even more compassionate leaders, which I believe they did.

• • •

Nobody gained more from these donor tours than I did, and I've led a dozen of them all over the world. These trips energized and motivated me to raise even more funds for programs I saw first-hand and also provided stories on the impact programs had on the lives of those we served. I could tell the story of how a child's health had been radically improved by the introduction of clean water and a feeding program at school, or how a social enterprise provided gainful employment for human trafficking survivors and the resources they'd need to start a new life.

For my part, it was the best benefit package. Salary levels would never be my key motivator for working for international not-for-profits, and Ligia understood that from the get-go. But involvement with these groups offered the greatest opportunity to see the world and share my appreciation for the cultural and natural wonders that each program country offered. The local staff were always more than happy to help me get there on a tight budget. Consequently, I was able to visit the ruins of Tikal and Copán, to see up close the natural beauty of Lake Titicaca and the jungles of the Amazon Basin, to visit the Himalayas of Nepal and the haciendas of Ecuador, to marvel at the wildlife on the plains of Kenya, to experience the exotic cultures and cuisines of Cambodia and Vietnam. None of it would have been possible without these field trips.

The donor tours also offered me opportunities to meet innumerable extreme do-gooders, including the field staff who dedicated their lives to changing the world, who managed to bring up their own families under challenging circumstances while making a difference in the lives of so many.

As for the donors themselves—people who took the time to learn how others live and then used their resources to support the programs that served them—they'd become the organization's best supporters, diplomats, and leaders, bar none. Those donors who brought their children found that, when they returned home, their children were more mature, better grounded, and less apt to be overwhelmed by the MTV world around them. The young man who sent a $25,000 check for a disaster relief effort for the country he visited ten years earlier beautifully reflected the ongoing impact of these cross-cultural experiences.

Twelve

*Man has affinity for his fellow man, regardless of
race, creed, or politics, and the greater the variety, the
more the zest. All that friendliness needs is a sporting
chance; it will take care of itself in any company.*

— Paul P. Harris, founder of Rotary,
"A Road I Have Travelled," *The Rotarian*, February 1934

I n February 2003, I finally got my group of fourteen Rotarians up to the highest navigable lake in the world, Titicaca. We were all in a daze from altitude sickness, so we stopped at a restaurant for a drink. I looked at the television and thought, *Oh, shit. What are all those troops and tanks doing in La Paz? Isn't that the same road we just came out of?* This was all I needed. I'd gotten these folks all the way up here, and now we couldn't get out! I knew enough about La Paz to realize that the highway goes through the working community of El Alto, and when the inhabitants got pissed off about something which negatively impacts their community and stage a protest, the troops moved in right away, and all hell broke loose. It's not like you can take another route—there isn't one. This was the end of the line: no airport, just a slow canoe across the majestic lake to the other side, which is Peru. Now what?

I glanced around at the tour members in the room, looking for help, and spotted Ed Corr, a MAP International board member and friend from the many tours we had shared. A stocky, middle-aged academic type, Ed taught at the International Programs Center of the University of Oklahoma, but he was also a college wrestling champ and a former Marine. He'd had a long career in the Foreign Service. He was a former ambassador to Bolivia, El Salvador, and Peru, and an antiterrorism expert. He would know what to do.

I worked my way across the room, weaving through the crowd, who had no idea of the trouble we were in, and pulled Ed aside. I whispered to him my concern that we were trapped at Lake Titicaca unless we figured out an escape route of some sort. "Ed, could you call the ambassador to find out what the hell is going on?"

He stepped outside to make the call. When he came back in, he shook his head and looked concerned. "David said under no circumstances return to La Paz with a busload of gringos," he told me. "He said we had to wait it out."

I nodded but knew we couldn't wait. I had to get this group to La Paz in a couple of days for their departure. We got through to our tour company in La Paz, and, as luck would have it, it also had an office in Lima. Saved! I called my contact. "So, Alvaro," I said, "looks like we're stuck up here for the duration, and our plane departs from La Paz in a few days. What would our plan B look like?"

Alvaro simply said, "Give me a few hours. We might have to divert the group through Peru."

The next day, we skipped across Lake Titicaca on a hydroplane and landed in Puno, Peru. We spent the night and the following day boarded a plane for Arequipa, one of my favorite communities, with its Spanish buildings and many interesting churches built of sillar, a pearly-white volcanic material. Arequipa sits in a beautiful valley at the base of the perfect cone of a snowcapped volcano, El Misti. We changed planes and within a few hours were in Lima.

Alvaro's counterpart, Lidia, picked us up at the airport and took us to the city center and the Plaza Mayor, where we checked out the Cathedral of Lima and colonial buildings. We saw the official guards goose-stepping in front of the government house. We visited the oldest residence in Peru, the Casa de Aliaga. The family still lived there, and it was a veritable museum, filled with pictures of famous family ancestors and centuries-old artifacts and furniture. At the end of our two days in Peru, we boarded a plane and headed back home.

I was pleased that most of the tour participants assumed that the last leg of the trip to Peru was part of our original travel plans, as the changes had been seamless. Ed Corr and I acted like nothing unusual had happened. Although my more than twenty-five years as a Rotarian weren't always this exciting, they included innumerable opportunities for travel and fellowship around the world.

• • •

I joined Rotary International in 1981, when I was a director for Plan International in Bogotá, Colombia, and I continued as a member when I was in Freetown, Sierra Leone. I've "made up" (attended a weekly meeting of another club) in several clubs in Latin America, Africa, and Asia. I've attended three international conferences, one of which was in Scotland.

I joined a downtown club in Bogotá that had about twenty members, and like most clubs in Latin America, their members represented some of the key business and government leaders—and they were all male. We had weekly dinners, which were obligatory unless one had a good excuse. I figured this would be a good place to stay in touch with what was happening in the country, as well as an opportunity to meet some well-positioned professionals who could open doors when necessary. As

I became better acquainted with the members, I was able to share some of the challenges I faced managing the three Plan programs, especially when I ran into some very complex legal and, eventually, security issues.

Dr. Ricardo Flores was by far my favorite Rotarian. Handsome and distinguished-looking, Ricardo was the senior doctor at one of the hospitals Plan clients used in the three slum communities. He was always upbeat and had time to meet the needs of his many very needy patients.

Ligia and I invited him for dinner so we could introduce him to some basic Guatemalan cuisine, like black beans and beef piled with onions. At the designated time of seven, we were ready—table set and the food hot—but no Ricardo. By nine, we decided that he'd forgotten the invitation. Just as I climbed into bed, at ten o'clock, I heard knocking on the door. It was Ricardo, with a big smile, as always.

"Ricardo, *cómo estás?*" I asked. "*Qué pasa?* We thought you'd forgotten."

"No, Mark," he said. "How could I forget your generous offer to experience some of your wife's excellent cooking?"

By then, Ligia had come down, and, as one would expect from a good Latina hostess, she acted like nothing out of the ordinary had happened. It never occurred to Ricardo to apologize for being three hours late, nor did we bring it up. We just heated up the food, sat down to a delightful dinner, and chatted well into the wee hours of the next day. Ricardo would become my greatest Rotarian confidant over the years we lived in Bogotá.

• • •

Rotary is the largest international service club in the world. A lawyer in Chicago, Paul Harris, started the first club over 110 years ago, and at this time more than 1.2 million Rotarians are in 34,823 clubs, divided into some 537 districts around the world. Latin America has almost 99,000 clubs alone, which allowed me to "make up" when I was there.

I joined the downtown club in Denver, then the North Oklahoma City Rotary, and in 1996 through 1997, I was the president of the Rotary Club of Scottsdale North, in Arizona. The Youth Exchange program had the greatest impact on our family, as all three of our children would go to either Germany or France as part of the exchange program. Ligia and I hosted two students over the years and were trainers for the outgoing students and their families.

Bolivia, 1997

Over the years, I have led U.S. Rotarians to visit fellow Rotarians and programs in Guatemala, Honduras, Kenya, and Uganda, but Bolivia would be the country where this partnership would have the greatest impact on me.

One Bolivian program I visited was in Potosí, the highest city of its size in the world. Potosí was founded by the Spaniards in 1545 after they found the locals working in the mines they called Cerro Rico, where immense amounts of silver would be extracted over the years, much of it sent to Panama City on its way to Spain. Like many mining towns, Potosí watched its future rise and fall with the value of the ores.

John Harbison was my key U.S.-based Rotary partner. As the past president of the Grand Island Rotary Club, near Niagara Falls, and chairman of the club district's World Community Service program, John had a real passion to serve. He had developed and led visits to Haiti to promote a vitamin enhancement program for children. John was definitely an extreme do-gooder brand of Rotarian. We'd work together over the years on a number of Rotary initiatives in Bolivia. For this program he challenged the Rotary Clubs I worked with to raise $5,000 so his club could raise $10,000 for a total of $15,000 which was doubled by a Rotary Matching Grant. On this particular trip to Potosí, John was brought down by altitude sickness, which causes difficulty breathing, lethargy, and a desire to sleep, which he did for a day and a half.

Our adventure began at the airport in Sucre, where we were met by the district governor, Rotarians from Potosí, and staff from Food for the Hungry. An exhilarating drive over twisting gravel roads—which drop off into eternity if you miss a turn—took us over the Khari Khari range. We drove into the rural program area with several Rotarians and Buck Deines, the FH country director. Buck was a former Peace Corps volunteer from Oregon who, like me, had served in Guatemala. He loved travel and community development work. We often wore our matching Indiana Jones hats and downed a few of Bolivia's best (i.e., beers).

After visiting the program's experimental and training center, one of the local Aymara leaders pulled out a long, ruler like stick and used a large organizational chart on the wall to explain the program's objectives and structure. We saw that the local farmers learned how to analyze the results of the experiments and pass the knowledge on to other farmers through an extensive training program.

We also visited an irrigation canal that the farmers were building. About twenty Aymara in white shirts and pants and bowler hats were clearing away the rubble from blasting holes for the canal. At the end of the visit, one of the farmers' leaders, a short, stout woman, made a presentation to our group in Aymara and presented each Rotarian a traditional hat and scarf as a token of their appreciation. My hat was way too small for my giant gringo head, but I didn't complain when laughter broke out when I put it on. No doubt these leaders, most of whom were women, had endured extremely harsh conditions to feed their families and appreciated the high-altitude greenhouses my fellow Rotarians had made possible. We were all moved that these two groups, from very different parts of the world, could come together to celebrate the success of a program and share the mutual respect that resulted from our time together. I felt honored to be part of the effort, and the bowler hat and scarf still hang at the entrance to my office.

The next day we visited the renovations of the Germán Busch School in the slums of Potosí. The local Rotary club was involved in the design and construction of the new bathrooms, which, according to one parent, were "the only such facilities in the neighborhood, and it is providing inspiration for other parents to think about flush toilets in their own homes." The improved conditions were instrumental in school attendance increasing fivefold, from 60 to 300 children. The partnership between Rotary and the community proved to be a catalyst for the local government to change its posture of benign neglect and take a more active role in helping make this program a center of community activity.

Back in Potosí that evening, the local Rotarians invited us to their meeting, which included lots of good music and food. One of the specialties of Bolivian cuisine is a potato soup, which is black because the potatoes are freeze-dried so they can be used for the remainder of the year. The Bolivians also have lots of good beer because of a strong German influence. *Chicha* is a local brew created by women who chew and spit out the corn, which is later fermented. This "spit in the drink" process was a bit much for me, even though I pride myself in trying everything at least once.

We also made the initial contact with Rotarians in Cochabamba, which would result in a $300,000-plus Health, Hunger and Humanity Grant from the Rotary Foundation to combat the scourge of Chagas' disease. The Food for the Hungry Country Director Buck Deines would leverage this with a U.S. Aid grant (the U.S. governments overseas development entity) for a total of $500,000. The disease is caused by a small insect known by disparate names like the kissing bug and the assassin bug, which falls out of thatched ceilings and burrows into its victim, eventually incapacitating the person. Chagas' disease exceeds malaria as the major killer in the country.

COCHABAMBA, BOLIVIA, 2003

I was working with MAP International when I got involved with Rotary's Water Resources Task Force. My job was to increase awareness that every fifteen seconds a child dies from acute diarrhea, which is totally preventable. In February of that year, I converged on Cochabamba with a group of twelve Rotarians from Oklahoma and Arizona. We would meet with Gastón Pol, the former district governor, among other local Rotarians, and the leaders of the MAP training center, Jose Miguel De Angulo and Luz Stella Losado, to see the work first-hand.

Former District Governor Gastón Pol was also my favorite overseas partner. He must have been in his seventies and was a former banker who became the leader of an agricultural bank. A graduate of Pepperdine, in Malibu, California, he spoke perfect English. He was always on top of all the details and seemed to deal with possible glitches before they surfaced. He'd held almost every Rotary position and, as a program evaluator, he analyzed the impact of Rotary programs in Bolivia and several other Latin American countries. Gastón was another Rotary extreme do-gooder.

The Rotarians flew into La Paz, and in order to recuperate from the high altitude, we all sipped coca tea before flying on to our destination. Cochabamba, Bolivia's fourth largest city, is set in a bowl of rolling hills at a comfortable altitude of 6,000 feet. Its parks and plazas are a riot of color, from the striking purple bougainvillea to the subtler tones of jasmine, magnolia, and jacaranda. Cochabamba was founded in 1574, and during colonial times, it was the "breadbasket of Bolivia." Its fertile foothills provide much of the country's fruit and coca. Unlike in the U.S., coca is quite legal in Bolivia. For centuries the plant has had a special place among the indigenous population. One of the coca co-operative leaders, Evo Morales, would go on to become the president of the country. The documentary film *Cocalero* describes the incredible circumstances that led to his rise to power.

Jose Miguel and his wife, Luz Stella, had been developing the integrated, community-based program in Cochabamba since 1988 and had been with MAP International for more than twenty-five years. They were from Colombia and had a modest home at the Community Center where they raised their five children. Jose was a medical doctor with a degree in public health from Johns Hopkins and a degree in theology from Eastern Baptist Theological Seminary. He came from a well-to-do family who owned their own businesses, but obviously Jose had taken a different direction. Luz had a degree in health and education from Maastricht University in the Netherlands. Both were totally qualified for the challenging work they'd embarked on, and both were strong Christians, which was reflected in everything they did and how they interacted with others, whether the poorest peasant in the highlands or the wealthiest donor from MAP. I always felt honored raising awareness and funding for their lifelong work, which benefited so many. They were great examples of extreme do-gooders.

The FH program staff and local Rotarians reported that 3,000 families in 300 communities were beneficiaries of the health training program. The program also introduced clean water by drilling a well and building a holding tank. The host Cochabamba Rotarians provided all the technical support and had made twenty-five site visits in the participating communities.

COCHABAMBA, BOLIVIA, 2004

Having survived that rather unnerving internal uprising at Lake Titicaca the year before, I returned at the same time of year in 2004 with fourteen more Rotarians and their spouses from Arizona, Oklahoma, and Texas, including former Ambassador Ed Corr. We were met at the airport by the Cochabamba Rotarians, including Gastón Pol. The next day, Saturday, the local Rotarians organized a fellowship picnic with the visiting Rotarians and their families. A band played, and most of us got up and danced on what was a perfect sunny afternoon. The fare included *choclo*, or white corn with giant kernels, and local drinks, including beer. Despite the language challenges, everyone seemed to have a great time together.

We spent several days at MAP's Community Center in Chilimarca, outside Cochabamba. Above the entrance are the words, *It is good to live helping one another,* in Spanish, Quechua, and Aymara.

As we entered the part of the Community Center which focused on the needs of children who were victims of sexual abuse, we found a large piece of paper hung up on the wall with impressions of each child's hands, representing his or her uniqueness, along with quotes from the children on their rights not to be hit or abused in any way. Both parents and children participated in this display, which must have been a great consciousness-raising activity.

The Rotarians spent time in the playground with some of the kids, who radiated enthusiasm at having all this attention from visitors. We also attended an orientation on the educational programs in the new, octagonal classrooms. The rooms were filled with light, there were happy paintings on the wall, and the tile floors were spotlessly clean. This contrasted with so many classrooms I'd seen in marginal areas of Latin America— classrooms that often lacked windows and bathrooms and had falling-apart desks, dirt floors, and leaky roofs (if any at all).

Later that day, we joined thirty-five of the community health coordinators who were attending their second of many training sessions as part of MAP's Total Health Village program, which empowers villagers to work on water, sanitation, economic security, and conflict resolution, among other things. The participants represented all ages, and there were equal numbers of men and women. We sat around in a circle, and, for the first time, the health workers were urged to ask the Rotarians questions, as opposed to the normal process where the donors ask all the questions. The questions included, what's Rotary? Why would you spend your time to come from so far away to help us? Do you represent any U.S. government entities? Would you ever return? All were insightful and challenging questions that we tried our best, in broken Spanish, to answer.

After a full-day planning session with local Rotarians, we flew to the La Paz airport and waited eight hours because ice had formed on the incoming plane. We finally boarded the first of several small planes that would take us down—way down—to the tropical Amazon Basin region outside Rurrenabaque. After a good night's rest, we piled into large motorized canoes and headed up the massive Beni and Tuichi Rivers to the Chalalán Ecolodge, which is part of the Madidi National Park. The park includes rain forests—and rain it did! The Tuichi River was powerful, like most key rivers in the Amazon Basin, so I was pleased we were all provided with life jackets, since you never knew when your canoe might hit a tree coming down the other way. At the halfway point, everyone started pointing at the capybaras —giant rodents that look like guinea pigs—on the side of the river.

When we got to the lodge, I put on my swimsuit and jumped into Chalalán Lake, next to our camp, but noticed I was the only one swimming despite the oppressive heat. I also felt something nipping at my legs and feet—a *lot* of somethings. Come to find out, the lake had small piranhas in it. That evening, we took out three canoes, and as the sun set beyond the jungle, about a hundred small squirrel and capuchin monkeys came jumping from tree to tree, swooping in perfect unison before our very eyes—what a sight! The park has been cited by *National Geographic* as one of the world's most extensive biodiversity preserves in the world.

The next day, we split into three groups for a trek through the pristine rain forest, where we saw macaws and even a few boa constrictors. I remember crossing a bridge made out of mahogany, or some type of hardwood that was very dark brown in the middle—a reminder of the wealth these forests represent to loggers and drug companies (so many of our medicines' ingredients come from the rain forest), all of which makes these preserves so important.

My group of six, which included a local guide as well as my favorite tour partner, Ed Corr, all had our walking sticks, broad-brimmed hats, and serious hiking shoes. We were ready for a long, adventurous trek. The guide seemed to know every plant and animal we saw along the way and answered all our questions without referring to Google. When we returned, we visited stalls selling items—like rings and bracelets made out of nuts—produced by the lodge staff. The staff own the facility and make a living by maintaining the rain forest.

A small group of us went on a night trek with a guide, Nicolás, who pointed toward a small stream and whispered, "See those two eyes? That's an eight-foot caiman. He came to greet us!" Fortunately, we were high above, on a steep bank, far from those staring eyes.

We finished our jungle experience with a dance with the staff and a few glasses of their very potent "tiger milk," which, although we never understood what it was made of, packed a punch. After a couple of glasses of this concoction, nobody felt any pain. After saying my good nights, I weaved my way back to my tent.

Our departure would be delayed several days by torrential rains, but we finally boarded a propeller plane and headed back to La Paz, where we visited the "witch market," which sold a number of strange relics, including llama fetuses, to ward off evil. At five in the morning, we flew to Sucre, where we refueled and headed back home. The larger jets can't fuel up at the La Paz airport due to the altitude, so they fly down to Sucre, which is at the lower altitudes of Bolivia, and from there back home.

Over the years, I'd bring more Rotarians to Bolivia than to any other country because the needs there were so great and the local clubs so active and in tune with those in difficult circumstances. As a bonus, Bolivia offered incredible sights visitors would never forget: the breathtaking mines in Potosí, 13,000 feet up; Titicaca, the highest lake in the world; the lush jungle; and the massive Beni River and its wildlife.

My work with Rotary International in Bolivia would be recognized with the Service Above Self Award, Rotary's most prestigious award. To be one of 123 recipients in 1998 from over 1.3 million Rotarians, was one of my proudest moments.

Guatemala, 2011–2012

In early March 1977, a young Guatemalan cardiologist, Dr. Federico Alfaro, experienced one of those moments in the life of a physician that can only be described as transformative. A previously active and athletic nineteen-year-old named Paolo from the nearby village of Jalapa came to Dr. Alfaro with a complete heart block—a serious ailment, but not necessarily fatal. The doctor knew that what Paolo needed was a pacemaker, an implantable device that would regulate the electrical impulses of his heart and allow him to pursue a normal, active life. But Paolo was poor, without the resources to pay for any sort of care, certainly not the thousand dollars or more that it would take for a pacemaker. Dr. Alfaro searched frantically for financial assistance to save Paolo's life, to no avail. In the end, all he could do was watch helplessly, along with Paolo's family and friends, as the young man died several days later.

As sad as it was, Paolo's tragic death was to give hope to many thousands of others in similar circumstances in the years to come. Within just a few months, Dr. Alfaro, with the assistance of the Asunción Rotary Club in Guatemala City, managed to establish a program to provide pacemakers for the needy. He called it a pacemaker bank, a term that was used by Heartbeat International for many years but has since been changed to Heart Center.

Dr. Alfaro's friend and former medical school instructor, Dr. Henry McIntosh, made a fortuitous visit to Guatemala City in 1984. Dr. McIntosh found Dr. Alfaro's story about Paolo's heart block compelling, and knew that his death would not have occurred in the United States, where almost anyone, no matter how poor, would have been afforded a pacemaker. Something had to be done, and soon they would access over 400 pacemakers to distribute.

As a VP and senior counsel for Carlton & Company, which is based in Boston, I interviewed Rotarians in Mexico, Guatemala, Honduras, and Trinidad and Tobago for a fundraising study. The Rotarians provided pacemakers for the many folks who didn't have insurance or the resources necessary to obtain these lifesaving devices. This seemed a compelling partnership, since cardiovascular disease was the leading cause of death worldwide. According to the World Health Organization, it killed more than seventeen million people in 2004. Of those deaths, more than twelve million were from heart attacks and strokes, which have risk factors that are eighty percent behavioral. Those deaths were mostly preventable.

Dr. Alfaro was one of those rare professionals who decided to take the road less traveled. A graduate of Duke who studied at the Texas A&M College of Medicine, he is one of only three or four heart surgeons of his time who returned to Guatemala to develop his practice. He's now a world-renowned heart surgeon and the dean of the Francisco Marroquín University School of Medicine in Guatemala City. A Rotarian for over twenty years, he's now in his sixties. I visited with him and his fellow Rotarians several times over a two-year period to develop a global fundraising campaign for Heartbeat International (HBI).

Dr. Alfaro was always available to call a board meeting or to meet with the press to announce when the next batch of pacemakers came in. I always felt he was a kindred spirit, despite the age and level of professional fame that separated us. He was undoubtedly an excellent example

Mark D. Walker

of an extreme do-gooder, and I felt privileged to help him reach his vision of meeting the cardiovascular needs of the poorest Guatemalans. During my two visits to Guatemala in support of the Rotary based HBI program, my cohort Peter Nagle, president of Carlton & Company, and I were able to identify some major donor opportunities for HBI Guatemala based on Federico's contacts and the high regard with which he was held in the professional community. Up to this point, HBI Guatemala had depended on a few special events run by the local Rotarians to underwrite its work, plus the support of several corporate partners like BIOTRONIK, which provided the pacemakers. The Rotarians managed the distribution of the pacemakers and took care of all the necessary paperwork with the local hospitals. Unfortunately, the HBI leadership wasn't ready to embark on the extensive campaign we recommended, so many of the funding opportunities we identified would probably not be taken advantage of.

Scotland, France, Switzerland, and Germany, 1992–1993, 1996–1997, 1999–2000

Travel is fatal to prejudice, bigotry and narrow-mindedness, and many of our people need it sorely on these accounts. Broad, wholesome, charitable views of men and things cannot be acquired by vegetating in one little corner of the earth all one's lifetime.

—MARK TWAIN, *THE INNOCENTS ABROAD*

All three of our children participated in Rotary's Youth Exchange program. They already spoke Spanish, as they were born in Guatemala and studied there for a number of years, but they also studied either German or French in order to take advantage of the opportunity to spend a year studying in the language of their host country. The Youth Exchange program is a fabulous opportunity for 8,000 or so students a year to share their own culture and embrace a new one and help promote global understanding—very similar to one of the basic goals of the Peace Corps.

270

Different Latitudes

The key to being a successful exchange student is a willingness to learn a new language and culture. Exchange students are encouraged to share their own culture and embrace a new one in order to foster global understanding—and to learn a great deal about themselves and their home country in the process. Students are typically juniors or seniors in high school who are flexible, open to cultural differences, and willing to be ambassadors for their own country.

It's a very competitive process, although, as a lifelong Rotarian, I knew the ins and outs and had the local contacts necessary to identify the host Rotary clubs. Our oldest daughter, Michelle, was hosted by my club, the Rotary Club of North Oklahoma City. Our other daughter, Nicolle, and our son, John, were hosted by my Scottsdale Rotary Club. Ligia and I were already active in the program before our children were eligible because we were trainers. Our job was to provide inbound and outbound exchange students with the basics of cross-cultural communication and the rules of the road, such as you can't drink alcohol or drive, in order to keep the insurance costs down (though in Europe the no drinking part was not that realistic).

Ligia and I paid for just the kids' airfare and insurance, and all students were hosted by an entire club, not just one family. This meant they changed families every three to four months and so experienced different personalities and lifestyles over the course of the year. They studied some serious subjects, like chemistry and literature, in the host country's language, so it was a full-immersion program.

• • •

As our oldest child, Michelle was often our guinea pig for new projects. I'd already been a Rotarian for eleven years when she was old enough to apply for the exchange program, and I always assumed she'd want to participate. The North Oklahoma City Rotary Club sent Michelle to Düsseldorf, Germany, the international financial center of the country and very close to the Netherlands. She changed families every three months and wrote us that the exchange students categorized their hosts as a Mercedes-Benz family (conservative) or a BMW family (liberal), which was a unique way to see people.

One of her host families organized a trip with Hungarian Rotarians, and Michelle was taken hunting with a falcon and for a ride in a glider. She turned eighteen when she was in Germany, so she was considered an adult and given a great deal of independence. At the end of her year, she traveled through a number of European countries. Her German was excellent.

What I didn't realize, until twenty-six years later, was that, as she put it to me one day:

I was a little travel-weary by then, not to mention I had to move families every three months. I felt like I wanted to head home and just start my life after high school. Then we moved yet again from Oklahoma to Arizona, so I had to start over again. It was a hard time for me personally, as I struggled to connect with people. I had no friends to start college with, and though I spoke four languages, I really did not care to talk to anyone.

It dawned on me: We had taken her to Colombia, then Sierra Leone, from there to Guatemala, then to Denver, and then to Oklahoma City. And when she was returning home after her year abroad, we had to change her airline ticket from Oklahoma City to Phoenix. No presentations to the Rotary club that had supported her, no closure with her high school friends who had graduated when she was away. This was probably the experience of many of the children of the extreme do-gooders I'd met. Of course it had passed right over my head, as I was focused on taking on a new, senior-level position with an international NGO in a new city, planning for a conference in some far-off place, and purchasing our first home.

• • •

Different Latitudes

I n 1997 I stopped in Glasgow, Scotland, for the Rotary International Convention on my way to France to visit my second daughter, Nicolle, who was completing her exchange year. I wanted to attend this convention since my great-grandparents on my mother's side were from Paisley, which is now part of Glasgow. Glasgow is the industrial center of Scotland, not to mention the source of its best whiskey, and yet I'd never been there.

More than 23,000 Rotarians from all over the world converged on Paisley (which seemed like a lot until more than 40,000 attended the convention in Osaka, Japan, a few years later). The Rotary International president, Luis Vicente Giay, was Argentinean, and his theme for the year was "Build the Future with Action and Vision." A stadium was the venue for the opening ceremonies, which highlighted Scottish dancing and music, including bagpipes.

The convention halls were crammed with Rotarians from 100-plus countries, dressed in every imaginable form of clothing, including turbans and multicolored gowns. The exhibits showed off some of the more successful World Community Service projects, overseas development programs promoted between a local club and a club abroad. One of these projects was PolioPlus, which, at more than $400 million, was the largest privately funded international development program ever. By 2016, Rotary International would raise $1.3 billion to protect two billion children worldwide.

As the president of Scottsdale North Rotary, I was able to get together with a few other members of our club to imbibe some world-renowned whiskey. We also went out to dinner together and found some tasty salmon, rich pâté, and the inevitable haggis, which is basically sheep innards mixed with oatmeal and stuffed into a stomach lining. As someone with good Scottish lineage, I had to try it, but concluded that it's an acquired taste.

From Glasgow I headed to one of the most beautiful cities in the world, Paris, to visit Nicolle. When I arrived in Angers, south of Paris, she and her host father, Jean Pierre, and his family, took me to one of

Nicolle's first host families, where I would stay. Their home was a 400-year-old converted schoolhouse. I stayed in the attic, which had been totally renovated, with its own bathroom. When I looked out the back window, I saw nothing but beautiful fields and fruit trees.

We hiked all around Angers. At an impressive castle on the Loire River, Nicolle told me about her many adventures over the previous year. She'd learned to ski at Chamonix, in the French Alps. Another family took her to the island of Noirmoutier, where she learned to make crêpes from the grandmother. One of her favorite Rotarians was Alan Sanders, a judge of the Rhône wine region who could identify the type and year of wine while blindfolded. Alan, an Australian married to a Frenchwoman, was also my favorite as he took us wine tasting. We went to a few off-the-beaten-path vineyards owned by his friends. I loved the variety of wines, although it took a while to get used to the proper tasting technique, which included spitting the wine out.

After saying good-bye to Alan and Nicolle's host parents, we hopped on the train for Paris, where we spent three days at the three-star Hôtel Britannique, which had small but lovely rooms not far from the Seine. Nicolle seemed to really know her way around, and when she asked two policemen for directions, they thought she was French. She had been around Paris with one of her host families, who had taken her to where the entertainer Josephine Baker used to perform and to the Lapin Agile, which was frequented by Picasso.

After several days Nicolle left me at de Gaulle Airport and headed back to Angers to attend a rock concert with her friends. A month later, she returned, safe and sound, to Scottsdale.

Nicolle made lifelong friends of several of her host families as well as fellow exchange students including an Aussie and a Finn. When I asked her what was the most important part of the exchange program, Nicolle said, "The experience forces you to step beyond your comfort zone and strengthens your character." Like her father, she would go on to pursue a career with international NGOs, and she has used her excellent French many times with refugees from French-speaking countries.

• • •

My son, John, went to Germany with his high school friend Kurt Stancl. Both had studied German for five years with a German-speaking teacher, so they were able to hit the ground running. John went to Leer, a town in northwest Germany, not far from the North Sea, with the Netherlands to the west.

Toward the end of John's exchange year, in June 2000, he met his parents and his uncle Paul at Frankfurt Airport, and we all boarded a train north, to Berlin. He'd organized the entire two-week trip through Germany, down to Paris, and over the Pyrenees, to Madrid, without a hitch. We stayed with two of Ligia's best friends: Maria Rene Jacobstahl in Hamburg, the same friend who had lent us her VW Bug to drive through Mexico on our honeymoon, and Esther Cabrera, who lived in an apartment in the middle of Madrid.

We had time to learn about John's exchange year on the train north. Like Nicolle, he had learned to ski in the Alps: for John, it was the

Austrian Alps, in Mayrhofen. Both John and Kurt participated in a youth exchange international camp in Bavaria, where they discussed juvenile crime in Europe as well as learning about southern Germany.

We stopped in Munich on our way north and checked out the famous beer gardens of Bavaria. John ordered us all beers in giant steins, and the servers thought he was German until they heard us speak, which wasn't easy with the blare of the oompah bands.

We worked our way up to Wiesbaden and Cologne on the Rhine River. We took a ferry down the Rhine and enjoyed the magical trip past old castles shrouded with clouds and hills hatched with endless rows of grapevines. On the trip back, we stopped off at one of the towns known for its fine wine to do some tasting. Wine tasting in Germany is different than in France. To begin with, they let you drink the wine! Johnnie and I tried about eight rosés and whites, including lots of Rieslings. Some were dry and fruity, while others were too sweet for my palate.

When my brother, Paul, saw John sipping the wine, he scolded me, then turned around and left. I guess he thought I was a bad influence, but John had probably consumed more liquor that year than all his classmates in the States combined. Good wine and beer are staples in Germany and are common at most dinners, so I couldn't imagine visiting the Rhine without checking out its most famous export. Sometimes our American sensibilities and worldview prohibit us from experiencing things the same way most locals would. I tried to explain all of this to my brother, but he wasn't buying it.

One of the most important experiences of John's exchange was a month long vocational internship with an architectural firm in Bremen. He had been convinced he wanted to be an architect until he found out that computer software had taken the place of drafting and design work. Consequently, he returned home more mature and more focused and would become an honors student and a law school graduate.

Both Nicolle and John, as well as his friend Kurt, were supported by the Scottsdale Rotary Club. When I first joined this club, I was told that its members weren't interested in the exchange program because the members were too "old" and their children had all graduated from college and started their careers. I began inviting Nicolle, John, and Kurt to our weekly meetings and events to share their stories and photos about their host clubs in Europe, as well as what they'd learned during their exchange years. After a few months, several club members stepped forward to host inbound students, which allowed our club to send several more students from Scottsdale to other clubs overseas. I also recruited a new member, Max Rumbaugh, to take the lead for this program, and over the years Scottsdale Rotary has hosted several students each year, and Max went on to become club president. Nothing like the energy and vision of young people to get a club enthusiastic and active in promoting cross-cultural understanding.

Thirteen

Guate mala Guate Peor

*This book relates the dreams and nightmares of a
land pulled apart by the Army, raped by businessmen,
lied to by politicians, despised by doctors.*

—Writer Eduardo Galeano, on *Rigoberta:
The Granddaughter of the Mayas* by Rigoberta
Menchú, with Dante Liano and Gianni Minà

There's a Spanish saying, "Salir de Guatemala y entrar en
Guatepeor"—a play on words that means to go from bad (*mala*) to
worse (*peor*).

After all the places I've traveled, one mystery I grapple with is why the inhabitants of such incredibly spectacular places are still so poor, and why
so little has changed since I was a Peace Corps volunteer forty-four years
ago. The answer, of course, differs from country to country; I'll focus on
the one I'm most familiar with: Guatemala.

Almost half of Guatemalan children suffer from chronic malnutrition, one of the highest rates in the world, according to Elisabeth
Malkin's article "Next Test for Guatemala's Protest Movement: Improving

Citizens' Lives," in the September 15, 2015, issue of the *New York Times*. The birth rate is high, at more than three children per woman, and is even higher among rural and indigenous populations. This, plus a lack of economic opportunity, political instability, and natural disasters, has increased emigration to the U.S., including many of the 50,000 children who streamed up from Central America in 2014. Guatemala City itself seems more prosperous, well organized, and clean, and it is now the largest city in Central America, but sources have told the New York Times that "a raft of statistics illustrate that its stubborn inequalities persist."

"You can only explain that (unaccompanied children fleeing north to the U.S.) when you have a state that doesn't work," said Frank La Rue, a longtime human rights activist in Guatemala and a former United Nations official told the New York Times. "You have sixty percent of the population in poverty, and it affects an entire nation."

Another explanation might be that the government collects the lowest taxes in the world and spends the least on health, education, and infrastructure, according to the World Bank.

"Five or six percent of the population leads this country in every aspect," said Valerie Julliand, the representative for the United Nations Development Program in Guatemala to the Times, referring to the mostly white urban elite. But, she added, "The real face of this country are those of young indigenous women."

According to a secondary source to the Times, "To hear the powerful business community tell it—new rich and old—the solutions to Guatemala's problems would fall into place if corruption were removed and tax evasion were curbed," but the problem goes deeper than that, and over the years, I've been looking for some answers.

Many of the country's problems are based on poor land distribution. About 2 percent of the population owned 73 percent of the land after the armed conflict in 1996—a situation that by 2014 had worsened, with only 3.2 percent of the population owning 84 percent of the land. Most Guatemalans, especially the Maya population, have such small, unproductive plots that they're forced to head to the South Coast to harvest coffee or go to the capital city looking for a job—or, in growing numbers, leave for Mexico en route to the United States. This helped explain the two farmers I saw heading down to the South Coast when I first arrived in Ixchiguán. They were carrying heavy racks of pottery through the mist at 10,000 feet to supplement their meager farming income.

Even the relatively modest coffee plantation of Ligia's family, San Francisco Miramar, hired 300 coffee pickers from the highlands' indigenous population for part of the year, while fifty permanent workers lived in simple homes on the plantation. The profit in a good year was $25,000 to $75,000, while the cost could be $70,000, depending on the value of the coffee. The entire system was based on a steady source of cheap labor from the highlands and the value of coffee on the international market at any given time.

The weekends I spent at San Francisco Miramar offered a bird's-eye view of the plantation system. Many of the farmers from villages I'd worked with would spend three to four months at the plantation to supplement their income. They made one dollar a day for arduous work under the hot tropical sun. They wore their long-sleeved traditional clothing, which was far more comfortable in the cool highlands than in the heat of the coast. An entire family would harvest coffee for more than twelve hours a day. They lived on a simple concrete platform with a metal roof. No walls separated families. They slept on straw mats, or *petates*. At least there were latrines at San Francisco Miramar, which provided more basic services than many other plantations did.

Many other rural poor were forced into the capital city to look for work. When I first arrived in Guatemala, in the early 1970s, I visited La Limonada, one of the largest slums in Guatemala City, and was amazed at how many of the inhabitants lived off the garbage at the landfill. Small children trawled through the trash looking for something edible or for bottles to resell. Every morning, I'd look out the window of our second-floor apartment as the trash collector passed by the street below. A small white horse pulled a large yellow trailer on two wheels, and a man stood on a tire pulling out cardboard, bottles, and anything of value—a mobile trash-sorting machine. Many of the slums near the city dumps were larger than ever when I returned more than forty years later, as was the number of partially employed Guatemalans selling candies and pencils.

As an American, I was perplexed—appalled—by the obvious role the U.S. government had in maintaining the skewed political and economic infrastructure of injustice in Guatemala. In the early 1950s, the U.S.-based United Fruit Company, or La Frutera, exacerbated the poor distribution of land, as the company owned over a half million acres of the country's richest land and left eighty-five percent of it uncultivated. La Frutera employed almost 50,000 workers in Central America (most were Central Americans, except for the management, who were U.S. citizens), including 15,000 on just two of its many plantations in Guatemala. It owned the only railroad and controlled the key port of Puerto Barrios. The interests of United Fruit were considered the same as the interests of the U.S. Secretary of State John Foster Dulles and his brother, Director of the CIA Allen Dulles, were both partners in United Fruit's law firm, Sullivan & Cromwell. This "secret" history is beautifully told in Stephen Kinzer's *The Brothers.*

In 1950 Jacobo Árbenz was elected president of Guatemala and began promoting social reform policies and land reform, which was a problem for the country's largest land owner. United Fruit carried out a propaganda campaign that turned the U.S. government against the new regime. American newspaper headlines included "Red Front Tightens Grip on Guatemala" and "United Fruit Becomes Victim of Guatemala's Awakening." This led to a coup d'état in 1954, and a new president, Carlos Castillo Armas, took dictatorial powers, banning all political parties, torturing and imprisoning political opponents, and reversing the social reforms of the Guatemalan Revolution—in effect, dealing a death-blow to Guatemalan democracy.

> *Simply, I'm a grandchild of the Mayas. Not even a daughter,*
> *because a daughter is closer. To be a grandchild means to have*
> *grandparents, to have history, to have a past; at the same time*
> *it represents having young blood, to be part of a new generation,*

to take a peek at the future. I am a grandchild of the Mayas and
believe that there are things which will change in the future.

—RIGOBERTA MENCHÚ, *RIGOBERTA:*
THE GRANDDAUGHTER OF THE MAYAS

Race has been a little-discussed factor in Latin America, and certainly in Guatemala. Only in recent history has the Maya population been represented in the government and, more importantly, the educational system. When the Nobel Committee awarded its 1992 Peace Prize to Rigoberta Menchú Tum, the daughter of a poor K'iche' family from Uspantán, it created a sea change in Guatemala, and all of Latin America, by acknowledging indigenous groups. But even then, many in the ruling classes of Guatemala were critical of Menchú's books, as well as her involvement in promoting the rights of indigenous people. Without a doubt, Maya groups continued to be marginalized and to suffer inequality, based on a number of metrics. As big as the Guatemalan economy is, the country will not prosper as long as more than half of its population is left behind, and no amount of international aid or good works by NGOs will change this reality.

• • •

I n January 1980, as I was visiting the home of the director of Plan International, in Guatemala City, several blocks away from the Spanish Embassy, I heard a ruckus—people were screaming—but I thought it was just another street protest. Little did I know that a group of Ixil and K'iche' Maya had peacefully occupied the embassy to protest the kidnapping and murder of peasants in Uspantán by elements of the Guatemalan Army. The police broke down the doors, and a fire started, killing thirty-six, including Menchú's father, Vicente.

The Spanish ambassador, Máximo Cajal López, survived by escaping through a window. The only other survivor, demonstrator Gregorio

Yujá Xoná, suffered third-degree burns. He was taken to a hospital, from which he was kidnapped by a band of armed men, probably including the Judicial Police. They dumped his body on the campus of the University of San Carlos as a ghoulish reminder of what can happen to protesters, especially those from the Maya community.

The Guatemalan government claimed that its forces had entered the embassy at the request of the ambassador, and that the protesters, whom they referred to as terrorists, had "sacrificed the hostages and immolated themselves afterward"—claims the Spanish Ambassador denied. Spain terminated diplomatic relations with Guatemala.

The official Guatemalan government response to this "unnatural disaster" was especially bizarre. It claimed that, although 300 police had stormed the embassy, the fire was caused by Molotov cocktails from within the compound. Although the police wouldn't let anyone escape after the fire started, it was the "terrorists" within who were responsible for the deaths—thus blaming the victims for their own demise. Such a story line could be possible only when a government lacks even the minimal level of transparency and accountability.

The vice president during this period, Villagrán "Paco" Kramer (who had presided over our wedding, seven years earlier) didn't buy this story and resigned seven months later. According to Amnesty International, between January and November 1980, "some 3,000 people described by government representatives as 'subversives' and 'criminals' were either shot on the spot in political assassinations or seized and murdered later; at least 364 others seized in this period have not yet been accounted for." Ironically, in 1994 Paco would be elected to Congress and serve as the president of the Committee on Human Rights.

> Silence on the Mountain *is a virtuoso work of reporting*
> *and a masterfully plotted narrative tracing the history*
> *of Guatemala's thirty-six-year internal war, a conflict*
> *that claimed the lives of some 200,000 people, the vast*

majority of whom died (or were "disappeared") at the
hands of the U.S.-backed military government.

—Publisher's description of *Silence on*
the Mountain: Stories of Terror,
Betrayal, and Forgetting in Guatemala,
by Daniel Wilkinson

The day before the twenty-ninth anniversary of the Spanish Embassy Massacre, the Guatemalan government filed 3,350 criminal complaints alleging human rights violations against former soldiers and paramilitaries. Some justice, albeit belated, was dispensed. In 2015, the former SWAT police chief—who had ordered that no one be allowed to get out of the burning building alive—was sentenced to forty years in prison for murder and crimes against humanity. He was sentenced to an additional fifty years for the murder of two students at the funeral for the embassy fire victims. The burning of the Spanish Embassy reflected the government's disregard for the Maya protesters and everyone else in the building, and was another indicator of the brutality of this period.

The violence that Maya groups experienced was made clear by a story from a former Peace Corps volunteer, who lived in the Ixil Triangle, in the central part of the department of Quiché, in the mid-1970s. "My sense was that the disappearances and oppression from paramilitary and death squads were clearly driving people into the conflict and toward support for the guerrilla groups (primarily the EGP, or the Guatemalan Army of the Poor). They were already being forced to begin to choose sides," he told me. "Similarly, my own fear while living in Nebaj was 100 percent due to the death squads/government/military side, who were threatening and disappearing people we knew, and directly and indirectly harassing some of us who were with the Peace Corps. For example, paramilitary men came to my house while I happened to be working out in the *aldeas*. They told my wife that they were looking for me and that I better be careful or I would be among the disappeared."

He shared dark memories of how *judiciales* (death squads) hauled away friends and neighbors in the middle of the night; some never returned. He remembered "the squeaky squeal of one of the wheels of the *judiciales*'vehicles and us lying in bed at night and listening in fear to see if they would stop outside our house." He slept with a machete by his head.

Ironically, the Guatemalan military gladly accepted U.S. financing and training but was deathly afraid of the work that U.S.-based Peace Corps volunteers were doing in some of the most isolated parts of their country.

• • •

Like the accounts of most observers, my analysis of the role of violence during the many years of fighting focused on the military. But my wife's uncle, Tío Coco, told the story about a schoolteacher on the family's coffee plantation who was kidnapped by the guerrillas. Although it was a war, to what extent did the guerrilla groups commit atrocities against the Maya population?

Columbia University anthropologist David Stoll conducted interviews between 1987 and 1992 in and around Santa Maria Nebaj, one of the three towns in the Cuchumatanes mountains that form the points of the Ixil Triangle—one of the regions hardest hit by the violence of the Civil War. I worked farther to the south of Nebaj, but I've led donor tours to the area. According to Stoll's book *Between Two Armies in the Ixil Towns of Guatemala,* the guerrillas—in this case, the Guerilla Army of the Poor (EGP)—were behind several massacres, and their presence was critical to the military's operations in the area. This perspective was confirmed by a former Peace Corps program coordinator in Colombia. As Ed Corr, a former ambassador to three countries in Latin America, told me, "Human rights abuses are committed by nearly all guerrilla groups but, with the exception of Sendero Luminoso (a Communist militant group in Peru), have received very little recognition or condemnation."

In some cases, the simple presence of the guerrillas resulted in brutal reprisals by the military. According to Stoll, "To discourage Ixil farmers from helping the guerrillas, the army burned down all hamlets and homesteads outside the three towns. At first in reaction to guerrilla ambushes, then by plan, army units shot, hacked, or burned to death thousands of unarmed men, women, and children." To a certain extent, the farmers were forced to take sides, but, Stoll writes, the situation led to "the deep-seated neutralism so evident in Ixil campesinos today."

Stoll interviewed a Maya farmer from Pulay, near Nebaj, who summed up the farmers' dilemma: "The guerrillas said they would protect the people but did not fulfill their promise, the moment would arrive and they would run away, so the people protested. [The guerrillas] replied, that's war. The people of Pulay got angry, turned their back [on the guerrillas], and went to town to tell the army. The army did not realize: it thought that all the people were guerrillas."

Many of the guerrilla leaders were in fact Ladinos, and according to Stoll, Maya intellectuals who became politicized in the 1970s were more pro-Indian than pro-Marxism. "They defined the oppression of their people primarily in ethnic rather than class terms, questioned ladino control of the Left, and were reluctant to collaborate with revolutionary groups." As is often the case in Guatemala, what seems to be, oftentimes isn't, and the story of the rural Maya population is the last to be told.

• • •

During my time as a Peace Corps volunteer living outside Ixchiguán, in 1972, I witnessed how pervasive poverty impacted both the Maya community as well as the more Westernized Ladinos. Part of the annual Day of Calapté included the crowning of the Maya Indian queen. The community was predominantly Ladino, while many of those in the surrounding area were Maya, or *indígenas*. The young candidates for queen felt out of place with so few fellow Maya community members attending the celebration. They wore the traditional skirts, but not the colorful *huipiles*, their spectacular ancestral blouses. One of the Maya *indígena* men who escorted the candidates stumbled over a poem he was to read—it was obvious Spanish wasn't his mother tongue (it was Mam, one of twenty-one Mayan languages spoken in Guatemala). By contrast, all the Ladino young people were nicely dressed, in white shirts and dark suit coats, and spoke perfect Spanish.

As the evening proceeded, the harshness of life among both the Maya and Ladino participants became more evident. The look and feel of poverty were pervasive. Many of the men were drunk, and their eyes reflected an almost animal state of unawareness, with tongues hanging partially out as they swayed from side to side. The Ladino master of ceremonies was so drunk, I could hardly understand him. There were many toothless grins on the faces of those lingering to get another drink of *guaro*. People were sockless, their clothes made almost completely from patches. Many were filthy, and the smells mixed with the cheap perfume the queen candidates had doused themselves with. Many of the women were older, with sunken eyes and deeply furrowed faces, their hair in disarray, clothing torn. Some wore blank expressions that made it seem that they didn't fully understand why the group was applauding. There were people with birth defects, like missing limbs and cleft palates, though the disabled were usually hidden at home. The children seemed content to be out, but were dirty, had snotty faces, and got in the way of those making the presentations.

Although many of the Ladinos in my community looked down on the Maya, they all suffered from the isolation and complete abandonment of their government. While racism manifested itself on a number of different levels, it was the overall isolation and poverty of the highlands population—both Maya and Ladino—that eroded everyone's self-image and quality of life.

• • •

D uring a visit to the Cobán area of Alta Verapaz in June 2016, I noticed that, with the introduction of the palm oil industry, large corporations still impact land use and favor profits over the basic needs of the community. All along the road up to the lagoons of Semuc Champey, the hilly terrain and diverse plant life were interrupted by fields of one plant as far as the eye could see. From my time in Sierra Leone, I recognized it as the variety of palm tree that produces oil. Large corporations like Cargill were purchasing the oil through the Guatemalan company REPSA and promoting palm oil plantations throughout Central America. The roads were now better, in order to get the product exported, but at a cost. The situation harkens back to the United Fruit days, when one company would buy up all the land for one crop and displace small farmers, who would be forced to go to the coast to work for a pittance or emigrate north.

REPSA has dumped pesticide-laden waste into the Pasión River, a practice the Guatemalan courts would refer to as ecocide. On September 15, 2015, one of the plaintiffs in a suit against the company, a Maya schoolteacher, was shot dead.

Fighting over the land has been a part of Alta Verapaz's history since the colonial period, when it was known as "the land of war" because Spanish troops had failed three times to subdue the native population. So when I returned home after this latest visit, I wasn't surprised to see in the Guatemalan newspaper *Prensa Libre* that the national police, with the support of the army, were trying to wrest control of the Semuc Champey lagoons from the community. The locals were protesting that CONAP— the government agency responsible for protected areas—had paid them only a third of the proceeds from entrance fees. The community also wanted control over the area to assure that the environment wouldn't be compromised by the influx of visitors. The battle for land use continues, although big corporations, local businesses, and landowners—all with the support of the government—have the upper hand.

• • •

C orruption exacerbates an already difficult situation, and Guatemala has one of the highest rates of corruption in the world—even worse than Sierra Leone's. (Guatemala had a score of 28 on Transparency International's 2015 Corruption Perceptions Index, compared with Sierra Leone's 29, with 0 being highly corrupt.)

After the MAP International CEO and I appeared on TV with Guatemala's First Lady, Evelyn Morataya, in 2001, our cabdriver told us he had seen us with *la Primera Dama de la Corrupción*. Her husband, Alfonso Portillo, would eventually be extradited to the U.S. and charged with laundering $70 million in Guatemalan funds through U.S. bank accounts. He was convicted and sentenced to nearly six years in prison.

The president is among the highest paid per capita, and their salary is a fraction of the wealth politicians can access through their "public service." In 2015 Vice President Roxana Baldetti resigned halfway through her term after the news broke that millions of dollars of government funds had been deposited in overseas banks. A populist protest mobilized by social media asking for Baldetti's resignation generated tens of thousands of RSVPs.

Within several weeks, President Otto Pérez Molina, a former general, was accused of being part of the same customs corruption scheme Baldetti had been involved in. The scheme, called *La Línea*, included kickbacks for all types of imports. Initially, Pérez Molina was defiant, so thousands of protesters took to the streets again, this time to demand the president's resignation. A day of action kicked off on August 27, filled with a diverse and peaceful crowd that included students from public and private universities, the indigenous poor, and the well-to-do. Eventually, the president stepped down and was shown being taken to jail—an unprecedented image, as were pictures of the diversity and relative peacefulness of Guatemalans who collectively said, "Enough."

Corruption makes it impossible to tell where the state ends and the underworld begins, as highlighted by the 1998 assassination of Bishop Juan José Gerardi, two days after publicly presenting a major Catholic Church–sponsored report on human rights abuses. He was beaten to death in his garage by three army officers, including Captain Byron Lima Oliva. I remember the day the bishop's death was announced and how saddened I was that a defender of human rights, especially of the Maya community's, should meet such a brutal end.

According to an August 16, 2016, *New York Times* article by Anthony W. Fontes, "The Demise of a Prison Lord," "Bishop Gerardi's murder is widely believed to have been planned and carried out by a military network extending far beyond Mr. Lima," to high-ranking generals and economic elites with links to organized crime. Incredibly, Lima's power was not curtailed by his eventual conviction and incarceration. While in prison, he managed to take control of the sale of drugs, cell phones, and sex, and taxed restaurants, stores, and other prisoner-run businesses. The guards addressed him as *Mi Capitán*.

Lima's power peaked as Pérez Molina, the general-turned-president, allowed him to direct official prison appointments at every level. The money from these schemes circulated from Lima to accomplices on both sides of the law. But all of this ended when Pérez Molina and much of his administration were thrown out of office and faced criminal charges, at which point Lima's prison profiteering made him a liability and led to his execution-style murder.

Still, according to the *Times* article, his death and the ongoing corruption trials won't change Guatemala's violence or corruption. "These men were just the tip of the iceberg. The real powers-that-be don't expose themselves by becoming president, much less going to prison," so the country's budget continues to be "sucked dry by a parasitical political class."

• • •

Guatemala has also become a major transit country for cocaine and heroin. In 2005, 100 hectares of opium poppies were cultivated, with a potential production of one metric ton of pure heroin. Guatemala's proximity to Mexico makes it a major staging area for drugs, particularly cocaine. Money laundering is a serious problem as well. The brutal violence of the drug traffickers causes tremendous displacement, but the economy is impacted in many other ways as well. In Huehuetenango, where the father-in-law of Ligia's brother lives, the locals are being priced out of their own real estate market because the cartel members are paying for everything in cash, at hundreds of times more than market price.

The recent proliferation of *maras*, or gangs, began with the mass deportations of Los Angeles criminals to Central America, particularly El Salvador, in the mid-1990s. In 2011, the United Nations Office on Drugs and Crime reported that Guatemala had the highest number of gang members in Central America, with 32,000. Like most postwar societies, Guatemala has a very young population, with a higher propensity for violence. Youth transitions in a postwar context often become harder due to lack of funding for public education. The Guatemalan Civil War not only transferred public education funds to military expenditures, but schools and students were specifically targeted by military forces. All too often, young gang members were thrown into the prison system, where they were recruited by organized crime.

According to a *New Yorker* magazine article by David Grann, "A Murder Foretold," "Overwhelmed by drug gangs, grinding poverty, social injustice, and an abundance of guns, it's no wonder that violent crime rates have been sky-high. In 2009, fewer civilians were reported killed in the war zone of Iraq than were shot, stabbed, or beaten to death in Guatemala," and a staggering majority of homicides—ninety-seven percent—go unsolved. The U.S. State Department rates the threat of violent crime in Guatemala as "critical." The Peace Corps moved its office out of Guatemala City and prohibited volunteers from even entering the city due to security concerns.

Consequently, private security has become a booming industry, with an estimated 150,000 private security guards, which contrasts with 30,000 police, according to BBC business reporter Anna-Catherine Brigida. These services were not cheap. The cost for a bodyguard starts at $775 a month—a price that can be afforded only by the wealthy, creating yet another fissure in Guatemalan society. In Brigida's report, Adriana Beltrán, a security expert at the U.S. think tank Washington Office on Latin America, said that private security firms in Guatemala were in demand because people don't believe that the police can protect them.

After so many years of traveling to Guatemala, I understand the basis of its poverty, but don't feel any more effective in bringing about the change necessary. So many of its problems—social injustice, disproportionate allocation of resources, a failed state, racism, the drug trade, the growing impact of gangs—seem beyond one's control. They leave but one alternative: continue the fight to empower local leaders. But promoting a groundswell of local initiatives based on income-generating activities, worthy goal though it is, isn't enough. We also need a better appreciation in the U.S. of our own government's role in maintaining a power structure and economic development model that ignore the needs of so many Guatemalans.

Fourteen

POSTSCRIPT: REFLECTIONS ON A LIFE WELL TRAVELLED

Si yo pudiera vivir mi vida otra vez . . .
haría más viajes,
contemplaría más atardeceres,
subiría más montañas, nadaría más ríos.
Iría a más lugares adonde nunca he ido . . .

If I could live my life again . . .
I'd take more trips,
I'd watch more sunsets,
I'd climb more mountains,
I'd swim more rivers.
I'd go to more places I've never been . . .

—"INSTANTES" ("MOMENTS"), UNATTRIBUTED

Almost forty-five years have passed since I left Colorado for an adventure that has taken me to so many places around the world. It seems like a lifetime. In that lifetime, I went from being barely able to ask where a bathroom was in Spanish to speaking it every day of the week; from being a Peace Corps volunteer without a clue about community development to a manager of development programs in three countries;

from raising a paltry few thousand dollars to build a school in the highlands of Guatemala to raising six- and seven-figure gifts as a certified
executive fundraiser for overseas programs; from bachelorhood to married life with an incredible Guatemalan lady, which led to three children
and six grandchildren, all living within forty five minutes of one another.

That initial desire to see the world and make a difference by helping others turned into a journey around the globe, with many ups and
downs, from Latin America to Africa to Southeast Asia to Europe. My
first gig, with Plan International in Guatemala led to a posting in Bogotá,
Colombia, with challenges and surprises that were then surpassed by
those of Sierra Leone in West Africa. I admired, and was constantly inspired and motivated by, the self-sacrifice and caring of the founders of
the international ministries I represented.

That desire to serve and volunteer through Rotary and my trips
abroad with donors connected me with the most generous and caring,
salt-of-the-earth people, who were interested in, and committed to, making a difference in the lives of those most in need.

*Travel is a state of mind. It has nothing to do with distance
or the exotic. It is almost entirely an inner experience.*

—PAUL THEROUX, *FRESH AIR FIEND: TRAVEL WRITINGS*

The church and my own spiritual walk have been an important part of
my journey overseas. My upbringing in the Presbyterian Church and the
youth group field trip to Ignacio, Colorado, turned my attention to the
needs of those outside my own community. I worked with, and received
funding from, various Evangelical Christian groups for programs I developed after finishing my tour with the Peace Corps. Working mostly with
faith-based organizations, I was painfully aware of the Evangelical community's focus on a personal relationship with Christ while often ignoring the social injustices that limited their members' economic growth
and that would, in turn, limit their spiritual growth.

Different Latitudes

Far from helping, church outreach in local communities often created division and dependency in those communities. I also dealt with many conservative, but very wealthy, donors affiliated with the Evangelical church who were strong advocates of a larger military presence around the world and who felt nothing but disdain for immigrants coming across the border from the south. These donors felt that building ever-taller walls was a viable solution to many of the problems, some of which have been facilitated by our own country's foreign policies.

Of course, since my wife and our children had been born in Guatemala, I brought a different perspective on this and related controversial issues. Over the years, as a professional fundraiser, I walked a tightrope between meeting the needs of the very wealthy while trying to provide resources for those who lacked even the basics. In order to not fall off that tightrope, I followed several rules:

1. Stay focused on the goal: generating income to help meet the needs of those in difficult circumstances overseas.
2. Never, ever discuss politics. Every time I'd visit one particular donor—a banker outside Bakersfield, California—I'd sit down with him to listen to Fox News and its assorted conservative talking heads and just nod and smile at their commentary.
3. Appreciate the beautiful homes, cars, and belongings of the wealthy, but never aspire to obtain them. I never learned how to play golf despite being near some of the best golf courses in the world because of the game's time and cost commitment. And I got around in my aging Nissan and Subaru Forester in a community where Jaguars and BMWs were the norm. I was fortunate enough over the years to stay in palatial homes in exclusive communities but never aimed to live there.

I'd consider a number of well-to-do donors my friends, and they would invite us to their homes and we'd do the same. We're always able to share our thoughts on issues of common concern and interest such as travel and the education and well-being of our children and grandchildren. My life and that of my family have been enriched by these friendships.

It wasn't just politics we differed on but from a religious perspective, I was condemned by conservative Evangelicals, like the mission small plane pilot in Guatemala who went crazy when my Norwegian friend pulled out a beer to celebrate. I was also reproached by a conservative Catholic priest in the highlands of Guatemala who accused my program of stealing his sheep, even though, in our own ways, we were all striving to meet the needs of the often isolated villagers we worked with. But overall, I felt that I was accepted by many sides of the Christian spectrum, and although I didn't agree with their theology or their politics one hundred percent, I never let those differences slow down opportunities to help those in need or inhibit my own spiritual search.

We never forced our children to be Christians but opted for a gentler form of evangelism which made sense since we came from two different church traditions. Ligia and I felt that introducing them to various solid Christians over the years would provide the support they'd need. Our oldest, Michelle, become a teacher and leader in her church. Over the years, I have moved toward a more proactive idea of religion, with a focus on walking the walk: helping those in need improve their quality of physical life, which will open them up to enhancing their spiritual lives.

More recently, I've been drawn to groups like André House in Phoenix, whose motto is "I was hungry, and you gave me food. I was thirsty and you gave me something to drink" (Matthew 25:35). Much of my approach was articulated by Christoph Friedrich Blumhardt, who, in the book *Everyone Belongs to God: Discovering the Hidden Christ*, provides advice based on the reading of Saint Paul's letter, "Therefore, do your utmost to understand the needs of the people and to learn how and where they can best be met." He continues, "The principle of mutual understanding between people, with their different needs and circumstances, is what will put an end to social strife and religious rivalries and jealousies."

I can clearly see God's hand in my life's journey: His protection during my long backpack trip through Latin America, my not being drafted during the Vietnam War, doors opening to influential individuals and extensive resources for the groups I worked with, the food on my family's table, and the grace and forgiveness for many botched projects and broken relationships. But as a true boomer, I must also admit an underlying belief in the fickle finger of fate. I might have ended up doing my Peace Corps service on the rainy jungle island of Borneo and never met Ligia. I have a relatively short list of shoulda, woulda, couldas, as I usually opted for the difficult challenges and opportunities that confronted me over the years. But this forging-ahead-no-matter-what life had its downside too. I regret not having been as supportive a husband and father as I should have been, or as attentive a son to my aging parents and brother to my siblings. I regret not listening enough to the wisdom and needs of those who worked with and around me. I regret never appreciating or thanking those people I was trying to help, like Cole, the gate guard in Freetown, Sierra Leone, who gave us beautiful tables that he had carved by hand.

And yet, despite the incredible suffering, depravity, and violence I've witnessed over the years, I've always come across something that bodes well for the future. For years Ligia refused to go online but now is a regular user of Facebook, which allows her to connect with friends and family all over the world.

One evening I asked her, "So who is Maria in that post about graduating from the University of San Carlos?"

"Maria is the daughter of one of our nannies in Guatemala, La Naiya. Maria's two granddaughters will not only be graduating from college, but both have cell phones and are constantly posting on Facebook in English."

Wow, I thought, *despite all the bad things happening in Guatemala—the corruption, the drug-related violence, the growing level of malnutrition among children—some of the kids of those in the lowest stations of society have managed to pick themselves up and make a go of it, as well as having access to the technology to tell their story.*

• • •

Ligia and I returned to Guatemala in June 2016 to see friends and family but also to develop a plan to sell or rent a piece of property in Guatemala City that her mother had given us. Our idea was to use the funds to bring our children and grandchildren to Guatemala annually and maintain the relationship our family has to Ligia's home country and my adopted country. We started our visit in San Jerónimo, Baja Verapaz, where I'd met Ligia, forty-three years earlier, but where we'd never visited together.

As we drove to San Jerónimo, three hours from Guatemala City, we were amazed to see all the new buildings lining the road leading up to the town, which now had an arch at its entrance. We were sad to see that the stately ceiba tree had been cut down to expand the central park in front of the colonial church, which was built in 1537. We wandered around town and found the corner where we'd met all those years ago. At the time, there'd been a small store there, but it had since been converted back into a residence. I reminisced about the day I saw the strawberry blonde girl riding the white horse, whose name, I learned, was Guapo (which means "beautiful").

Our first visit was to the Hacienda, now known as the Trapiche museum. It had been the first sugarcane plantation in Central America, founded by Dominicans in 1601. Eventually, it would also produce cochineal (the insects dyes were made from), grapes, and liquor. The *trapiche*, or processing plant, included some impressive machinery which produced raw sugarcane. The process was driven by a waterwheel. Climbing up the hill from the processing area, we stopped in the three small museums that included artifacts from the people who had inhabited the area, including Afro Guatemalan slaves whom the priests had brought to cut the cane. The mixture of Spanish, indigenous, and black blood made for an interesting racial heritage, and led to much speculation on who was connected to the slave population (and had Afro Guatemalan blood). I got to know and appreciate San Jerónimo in a totally new way.

Different Latitudes

We stayed at the Hotel Hacienda Real El Trapiche, which Ligia's cousin Jorge owns, though his wife, Eva, actually runs it. It had a dozen rooms and was clean and not that far from the center of town. Plus, the food was excellent. Another cousin, Christabel, joined us. She and Ligia are both longtime teachers.

The next day, Victor Hugo Morales, whom I knew from my days at the Peace Corps experimental station, came across us in the middle of the main street. He told the story of how he had informed me, when I first arrived in San Jerónimo, that the proper way to greet the locals was, "*Buenos días, pisado,*" which translates to "Good morning, asshole."

Ligia and I, along with one of her two brothers, Roland, and his wife, Vera, went to the nearby community of Salamá for lunch, which would have been fine except that I picked up an intestinal infection. I had eaten the same things as everyone else, so it might have been a result of all the flies landing on our food. But when you have a schedule to keep, you pop the appropriate medication and head out. It's part of the journey, and I'd be back to normal in a few days.

Ligia and I contracted a tour group to take us up to Cobán, the capital of Alta Verapaz, a few hours from San Jerónimo. Our first stop was the Biotopo del Quetzal, a rain forest preserve and the home of the endangered quetzal—the national bird. It was drizzling—the locals call it *chipi-chipi*—as we climbed up the path. We were soon engulfed in a sea of green plants of every size and type, from ancient ferns to massively tall trees filled with orchids. We heard a female quetzal warbling and saw a multicolored toucan. The many streams and falls we passed over were a reminder of how crucial these rain forests are to the well-being of both plant and animal life.

On our climb down the mountain, we passed by a statue of the park's founder, Mario Dary Rivera, and Ligia mentioned that he'd been one of her professors at the University of San Carlos and that she'd worked on some research for him for this very preserve. After forty-plus years, I was still learning about all the things Ligia had accomplished.

We spent the next few nights at the four-star Park Hotel, just below Cobán, with its extensive gardens and small zoo, where you could find colorful macaws and screeching parrots. Then we headed out over a solid concrete road through San Juan Chamelco on our way to the lagoons of Semuc Champey. We passed through quaint villages like Sejoc and watched as the women and girls strolled along the road in their colorful *huipiles*. When we stopped in San Juan Chamelco for bottled water, I noticed three women and two children in *huipiles* buying bread from the bakery, El Mono (The Monkey). Directly to their left was a teenage boy, with a hip black T-shirt and a messenger bag, checking his email. It was like watching two different cultures side by side. Guatemalan women nowadays often have their own cell phones, though it wasn't long ago that phone communication was next to impossible due to the inadequate landlines.

It was another warm and moist day. This was the rainy season, which meant that everything was a dark green. I asked our guide why the roads were in such great shape. He said it was because of the market value of the crops, such as coffee, cacao, cardamom, and ginger. As we whipped over the road, I soaked in the spectacular variety of plants, including the corn, beans, and bananas that most farmers plant by their homes. The greenness and diversity extended as far as the eye could see.

After a few hours, we were met by a driver in a four-wheel-drive pickup to take us the last hour and a half to Semuc Champey. We traveled over bumpy dirt roads slippery with mud, and our resolve was tested during a torrential downpour. Fortunately, we were the only clients and had the front of the pickup to ourselves.

Once we arrived, we hiked up to the farthest lagoon. Semuc Champey is a 950-foot natural limestone bridge, under which passes the Cahabón River. Atop the bridge is a series of stepped turquoise pools, which we swam in—a great way to deal with the tropical heat and humidity. We went to the end of the bridge, from which we could see (and feel) the massive river under the pools. We stayed behind a rope fence, put in

place after two tourists got too close to the edge and fell into the churn-
ing waters that submerge under the earth and reappear downstream as
a massive tropical river. Some of the tourists' body parts were reportedly
found downstream a few days later. We stayed well clear of the edge.
Ligia didn't even want me to get close enough to take a good photo (but
of course I did). The natural caves and lagoons represent just some of
the innumerable natural wonders in Guatemala that Ligia and I plan to
return to see together.

We drove back from Cobán over the relatively dangerous road that
connects Guatemala City and Puerto Barrios on the Caribbean Sea. The
road is choked with large eighteen-wheelers, all trying to pass one another on curves, and a massive highway expansion project further complicated our trip back to Ligia's brother's home, where we were staying.
The day after we arrived, the Abdo/Ruiz part of Ligia's family (on her
mother's side) hosted our forty-third wedding anniversary celebration,
which more than thirty-five children, grandchildren, and cousins attended. Ligia's aunt Regi had passed on some eight years earlier, but
her home brought back fond memories of past parties when we hung
out with Ligia's cousins and their spouses with a Johnnie Walker on the
rocks, sharing stories and jokes until all hours.

One of the cousins, Emmy, prepared some scrumptious finger foods,
like fried yucca with cilantro (which I usually can't stand, but this dip
was exceptional). There was also *hilachas*, a special piece of stringy yet
tender meat cooked slowly, with small pieces of potatoes, onions, and
garlic, in a delicious tomato-based sauce, following Ligia's grandmother
Mimi's recipe. Emmy also made some tasty *chilaquilas*, corn tortillas with
cheese in the middle steeped in a tomato sauce. I got around to meeting
almost everyone but couldn't get used to the fact that the small babies
I'd known so many years ago now had beards and their own children.
The twelve-year-old son of one cousin was already the Central American
golf champion. I'm waiting for him to turn up in Scottsdale at a tournament down the line.

• • •

A ntigua, in the central highlands, is full of well-preserved Spanish Baroque–influenced architecture, as well as a wide variety of ruins of colonial churches. It served as the capital of the Kingdom of Guatemala and has been designated a UNESCO World Heritage site. No trip to Guatemala is complete without a visit to Antigua, and no visit to Antigua is complete without a lunch at the historic Posada de Don Rodrigo. We went there with our missionary friends Art and Lisa Camarena and Ligia's friend from Colegio Belga school days, Ana Beatrice. The hotel is designed after a monastery and always had a marimba group playing traditional music. Down the street is the iconic Santa Catalina Arch, which faces the yellow Merced Church with the Water Volcano (*Volcán de Agua*) looming in the background. The hotel restaurant has all the traditional food, including *chiles rellenos* (stuffed peppers) and enchiladas, which are toasted tortillas heaped high with cabbage, radishes, and beets, among other things, and topped with goat or Parmesan cheese. A folkloric dancing group was performing the *son* (pronounced "sown"), a popular dance which emerged in the nineteenth century and is danced differently by the Mayas as opposed to the westernized "Ladino." The actual steps reminded me of a waltz or a polka. I was dragged onto the dance floor and tried the dance with my hands behind my back until I made a fool of myself and told my Maya partner I needed to take some photos (which I did).

We always get together with Art and Lisa Camarena when visiting Guatemala. Ligia was their Spanish teacher in the 1990s, when they first followed their calling to become missionaries. Since Art's family was from Mexico, they assumed that would be their final destination, so they asked Ligia to teach them Mexican Spanish, but she refused. Guatemalans are very proud of their clear, well-spoken Spanish and don't appreciate all the compromises in Mexican Spanish, like "*el trucke*" (the truck), so she taught the Camarenas Guatemalan Spanish for several months and then stopped until Lisa called her and said, "We need to start our Spanish lessons again. Art had a vision last night, and the Lord is sending us to Guatemala!" We've supported Art and Lisa's ministry ever since.

During our lunch, Art mentioned that we were the only expats included in a video on the couple's new website. Even though hundreds of expats had volunteered with and supported them over the years, Art felt we were special since Ligia had taught them Guatemalan Spanish and I had connected them with one of the Guatemala City Rotary clubs. Through that connection, they had met former Guatemalan President Álvaro Arzú, who was a Rotarian.

I had also introduced them to Food for the Hungry's Hunger Corps, but Art decided against joining when the program asked him and Lisa to prepare for six months, which contradicted God's message to them to sell all their belongings and leave right away (which they did). I'd had no idea that we held this special position but have always tried to identify resources and networking opportunities for anyone wanting to go abroad and make a positive impact. The Camarenas represent that special group of extreme do-gooders I've had the pleasure to know over the years. Their ministry of promoting Christian values and combating corruption among the military, town governments, and businesses has impacted more lives than we could imagine, especially in a country that suffers so dramatically from excessive greed and graft.

• • •

The last leg of our trip was to visit our longtime friend from World Neighbors, Chati Cajas, who manages a hotel in San Lucas Tolimán, right off the spectacular Lake Atitlán. The lake is surrounded by twelve Maya villages, each named after an apostle, against the backdrop of spectacular volcanoes. Lake Atitlán and its best-known community, Panajachel, is a place where local and foreign tourists converge with local Maya groups. That magic culture, with its incredible artwork, colorful clothing, and array of traditional celebrations, invites constant commingling between the local rural Maya and tourists as well as wealthy Guatemalans.

Shortly after sitting down to lunch at the hotel's porch restaurant, which looks directly onto the lake, an old classmate of Ligia's joined us. Alex had reconnected with Ligia on Facebook and was reportedly going out with her best friend, Mamane (this was after her husband Carlos had died). Alex was a professor who had taught in Minneapolis for most of his professional life. He knew anthropologists like Richard N. Adams, one of my former professors from the University of Texas, and Ricardo Falla-Sánchez, who has documented violence against indigenous people.

Our ten-day visit went too quickly, but Ligia would return three months later, for a fiftieth-anniversary gathering of her schoolmates from the Colegio Belga, which I hadn't budgeted, but given all the grief Ligia had endured with me over the years, I figured it was the least I could do. Hopefully, these visits will be two of many more as we continue to marvel and enjoy this special country.

Different Latitudes

All my life I used to wonder what I would become when I grew up. Then, about seven years ago, I realized that I never was going to grow up—that growing is an ever ongoing process.

—M. Scott Peck, *Further Along the Road Less Traveled*

Writing this memoir has sparked images and incidents that had faded over the years. Some are stark and moving, while others are more subtle. I was able to reconnect with some of those whose paths I crossed over the years, and they strengthened this book with their own memories and stories. Most importantly, writing this book has put much of what I've done and whom I've met into perspective and has provided a new level of appreciation of those I have worked with and loved all these years. I continue to follow events in Guatemala, our second country, and am encouraged to see how many people from all over the world visit this fascinating place and enjoy its warm hospitality. At the same time, I'm constantly discouraged by the wide gap that still exists between the wealthy and those with limited resources. I was especially saddened by the recent news that more than 50,000 immigrants have escaped from Central America, most of them women and children fleeing the violence and poverty exacerbated by the growing power of the cartel that supplies illegal drugs here in the U.S.

As my generation—the so-called counterculture, antiwar, and pro-environment generation—slows down, I'm encouraged by the broader scope of experience and more global perspective of the younger generations. I've already pulled back and limited my professional activities in order to focus on teaching and training. I'm especially encouraged that my children speak several languages and are more politically progressive as I ever was.

My daughter, Nicolle, followed much of my career, starting with her experience in France with the Rotary Youth Exchange program and then professionally as she worked with volunteers and programs for such groups as the International Rescue Committee. She's even become a fundraiser and was still on the board of the Association of Fundraising Professionals after my term as chapter president ended. Nicky has been a strong advocate of human rights and has promoted an appreciation of refugees and the poor in the U.S. Most recently, she was interviewed in Spanish on Univision about the misperceptions and hate talk coming from many segments of the U.S. public against the hundreds of thousands of refugees fleeing the violence of ISIS and the brutality of the Assad regime. She talked about why the U.S. should continue its tradition of taking in those in need despite the perceived dangers.

My oldest, Michelle, is pursuing her career in languages by taking the federal simultaneous translator's test, as she has the gift of being able to think in two languages.

My son, John, continues to grow into his role as a judge and has been very supportive of our shared desire that his daughter, Evie, be multilingual and that she'd visit Guatemala with us to maintain a multigenerational connection with the Land of Eternal Spring.

Now Ligia and I can focus on helping our grandchildren become global citizens and appreciate their connections to Guatemala and Peru (our oldest daughter's husband is Peruvian). I can now pick and choose the international groups I focus my attention on and ensure that I impact those they serve. Consulting and writing allow me to work with a variety of groups, utilizing the skills and experience I've gained over the years while offering the flexibility to spend time with friends and do what I can to promote a new generation of globally minded people who will leave the world better off than it was when they entered. And Ligia—or Señora Walker, as she's known at Christian Prep, continues to teach Spanish and nurture children, sometimes several generations of the same family.

In the end, I'd have to agree with a young executive I led on a tour to Guatemala, when he remarked that, although I'd never strived for personal wealth, yachts, golf club memberships, or luxury cars, I did find treasures that most of the wealthiest and most powerful men in the world would never find.

Different Latitudes

The life of an individual is in many respects like a child's dissected map. If I could live a hundred years, keeping my intelligence to the last, I feel as if I could put the pieces together until they made a properly connected whole. As it is, I, like all others, find a certain number of connected fragments, and a larger number of disjointed pieces, which I might in time place in their natural connection. Many of these pieces seem fragmentary, but would in time show themselves as essential parts of the whole. What strikes me very forcibly is the arbitrary and as it were accidental way in which the lines of junction appear to run irregularly among the fragments. With every decade I find some new pieces coming into place. Blanks which have been left in former years find their complement among the undistributed fragments. If I could look back on the whole, as we look at the child's map when it is put together, I feel that I should have my whole life intelligently laid out before me . . .

— OLIVER WENDELL HOLMES, EPIGRAPH TO
GRAHAM GREENE'S *JOURNEY WITHOUT MAPS*

Mark, Ligia, our three children, six grandkids and a
nephew and his wife from Colorado, June 2016.

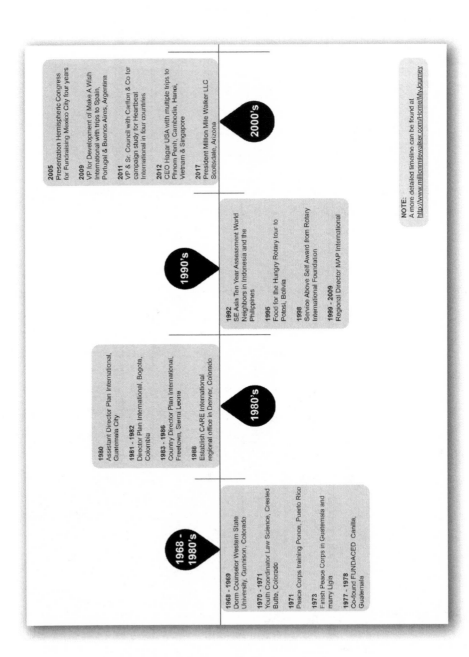

1968 - 1980's

1968 - 1969
Dorm Counselor Western State University, Gunnison, Colorado

1970 - 1971
Youth Coordinator Law Science, Crested Butte, Colorado

1971
Peace Corps training Ponce, Puerto Rico

1973
Finish Peace Corps in Guatemala and marry Ligia

1977 - 1978
Co-found FUNDACED Canilla, Guatemala

1980's

1980
Assistant Director Plan International, Guatemala City

1981 - 1982
Director Plan International, Bogota, Colombia

1983 - 1986
Country Director Plan International, Freetown, Sierra Leone

1988
Establish CARE International regional office in Denver, Colorado

1990's

1992
SE Asia Ten Year Assessment World Neighbors in Indonesia and the Philippines

1995
Food for the Hungry Rotary tour to Potosi, Bolivia

1998
Service Above Self Award from Rotary International Foundation

1999 - 2009
Regional Director MAP International

2000's

2005
Presentation Hemispheric Congress for Fundraising Mexico City four years

2009
VP for Development of Make A Wish International with trips to Spain, Portugal & Buenos Aires, Argentina

2011
VP & Sr. Council with Carlton & Co for campaign study for Heartbeat International in four countries

2012
CEO Hagar USA with multiple trips to Phnom Penh, Cambodia, Hanoi, Vietnam & Singapore

2017
President Million Mile Walker LLC Scottsdale, Arizona

NOTE:
A more detailed timeline can be found at http://www.millionmilewalker.com/Home/MyJourney

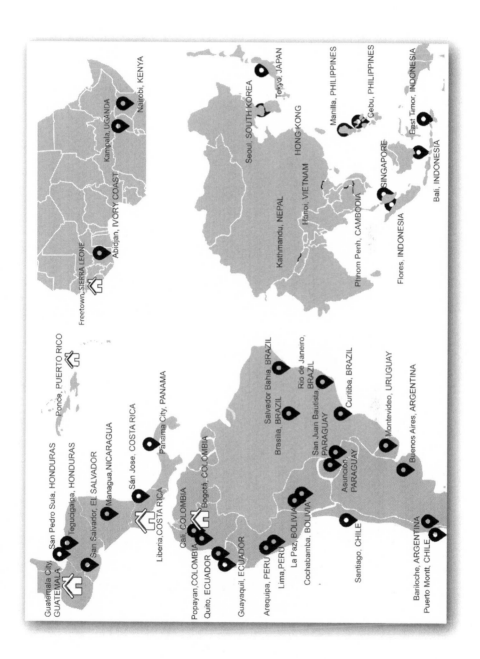

Acknowledgments

The people most essential to this book are its subjects: those I served and worked with, and the extreme do-gooders and philanthropists who took the time to share their wisdom, beliefs and insights.

Since the Peace Corps played such a key role in my professional development, and this book, three returned Peace Corps volunteers (RPCVs) with whom I worked in Guatemala provided important details and insights, not to mention constant encouragement: Paul Hickey, Alex Newton, and Dave Thompson.

Several RPCV authors, starting with anthropologist Dr. Bob Scully—with whom I worked for almost ten years at MAP International and who has written several books, including *The King History Forgot*—provided invaluable insights on all levels of the writing and publishing process. Ellen Urbani Hiltebrand, who wrote the memoir *When I Was Elena* when she was in Guatemala, was very helpful, as was my hometown author and friend Mike Stake (*Ripples in the Pond*), fellow fundraiser Mal Warwick (*The Business Solution to Poverty*), and Mark Wentling (*Africa's Embrace*). Chic Dambach, the former president and CEO of the National Peace Corps Association (NPCA) and the author of *Exhaust the Limits*, was helpful on so many levels. His book, like mine, starts with the Peace Corps and goes on to tell how his career (as a global peacebuilder) came out of that experience. Two notable Guatemala RPCVs were supportive: Glenn Blumhorst, the current NPCA president and CEO, and Ken Lehman, who was also a Peace Corps staffer and NPCA Advisory Councilmember. Filmmaker and RPCV Alana DeJoseph, who was working on *A Towering Task: A Peace Corps Documentary*, was always willing to reflect on the Peace Corps experience with me.

Alan Proctor, my friend and colleague from World Neighbors, provided the most detailed critiques in the initial stages. Alan is an author and poet who compiled and edited a memoir of his brother, *The Sweden File*. Other reviewers, who represented different types of expertise, provided invaluable input. They include Steve Albrecht, Bill Brackett, Earl and Suzanne de Berge, Cliff Nagel, Peter Nagel, John Scola and Rory Starks. Roland Bunch, an overseas director for World Neighbors and author of *Two Ears of Corn*, helped with the initial plans for the book and came up with the title, *Different Latitudes*. Several friends from Food for the Hungry—Kelly Hart, Ben Homan, Esther Niles, John Scola, and Rory Starks—provided insights and reminders of certain details.

My former boss Bill Brackett, the executive director of World Neighbors when I worked there, played a special role, as he supported my efforts as the new CEO of Hagar USA as well as providing guidance and helpful critiques of my book.

My high school buddy Dave Thyfault provided heaps of encouragement and inspiration. Dave is a successful real estate investor but had a less-than-stellar run as a student. And yet he was to go on to become the author of several how-to books, like *Stop Flushing Your Money Down the Drain*, and has since moved on to fiction, with a series of detective stories, starting with *Three Deadly Twins*. After his fifth book, I decided it was time to write one of my own.

As this was my first book, I needed all the technical support I could get. Esther Niles has been my faithful proofer, going back to when we worked together at Food for the Hungry. First Person Editing Services provided invaluable insights on how to improve the manuscript. Alexis Ofenloch, a family friend and a photographer from Ecuador, helped with the pictures and graphics.

The team of John Coyne and Marian Haley Beil of Peace Corps Worldwide was helpful. John was one of my first reviewers, and my most brutally honest one. He described my first draft as "once over lightly." It was a reality check on how much more I had to learn about writing—a challenge I tried to live up to. Marian guided me through all levels of the publishing process.

Others who have inspired or supported me over the years, making this book possible, include Andrea Beaulieu, Ray Buchanan, Roland Bunch, Chati Cajas, Dave Carlson, Ambassador Ed Corr, Jeff Cotter, J.P. Dahdah, Buck Deines, Ken Ekstrom, Larry Fisher, Dr. William Glade,

Bob Graham, John Harbison, Randy Hoag, Ron Huddleston, Dr. David and Heide Hungerford, Chuck and Sandy Laskey, Jim Lord, Darrow Miller, Alvaro Muñiz Michael Nyenhuis, Peter Okaalet, Merrill Oster, Sue Patterson, Roland and Vera Rodriguez, Ed and Pilar Ruddell, Rose Sandoval, John Scola, Dr. Hubert Winston Smith, Dr. Duane Vandenbusche, and Shaun Walsh.

My wife, Ligia, and our children, Michelle, Nicolle, and John, reviewed parts of the book and shared some of their own stories. I interviewed Ligia several times during the writing of the book on a number of questions I probably should have inquired about twenty years earlier. She was calm, considerate and insightful as always.

About the Author

Mark D. Walker was a Peace Corps Volunteer in Guatemala and spent fifteen years helping disadvantaged people in the developing world. He managed programs in Guatemala, Colombia, and Sierra Leone with Plan International.

Walker has written and made presentations in both English and Spanish on planned giving, major gifts and global philanthropy at such events as the Hemispheric Congress for Fundraising. He serves on the International Development Committee of the Association of Fundraising Professionals (AFP) and is the Past President of the Planned Giving Roundtable of Arizona. His honors include the "Service Above Self" award from Rotary International.

Other organizations Walker worked with include Food for the Hungry, MAP International, World Neighbors, Global Brigades, and the Make-A-Wish Foundation International. Walker was CEO of Hagar USA, a Christian based organization that supports survivors of human trafficking. He founded Million Mile Walker LLC. and is the Vice-President and Senior Counsel for Carlton & Company. His wife and three children were born in Guatemala.

Made in the USA
Lexington, KY
22 October 2017